Politics of Touch

Politics of Touch

Sense, Movement, Sovereignty

Erin Manning

University of Minnesota Press
Minneapolis
London

Published by the University of Minnesota Press
111 Third Avenue South, Suite 290
Minneapolis, MN 55401-2520
http://www.upress.umn.edu

Library of Congress Cataloging-in-Publication Data

Manning, Erin.
    Politics of touch : sense, movement, sovereignty / Erin Manning.
        p.   cm.
    Includes bibliographical references and index.
    ISBN-13: 978-0-8166-4844-3 (alk. paper)
    ISBN-10: 0-8166-4844-1 (alk. paper)
    ISBN-13: 978-0-8166-4845-0 (pb : alk. paper)
    ISBN-10: 0-8166-4845-X (pb : alk. paper)
    1. Behaviorism (Political science).   2. Touch—Political aspects.   3. Sex
role—Political aspects   4. Tango (Dance)—Social aspects.   I. Title.
    JA74.5.M357   2006
    320.01'9—dc22   2006016781

Printed in the United States of America on acid-free paper

The University of Minnesota is an equal-opportunity educator and employer.

12 11 10 09 08 07   10 9 8 7 6 5 4 3 2 1

with Brian

Contents

Acknowledgments

It used to be so simple. There were five senses and they created a picture of the world inside your head. But new ways of probing the brain are transforming this view of sensory perception. [T]he boundaries between them are being blurred. Maybe you don't need eyes to "see"—other senses may take over in ways that so far defy explanation. In fact the whole idea that our sensations depend on which sensory organ picks up the information is being challenged. Deep down, it is what we do that counts.

— *"Future Sense," New Scientist, 29 January 2005*

This book is about "what we do."

Politics of Touch is deeply indebted to Eric, Komala, Henry, and Stefan, whose love of tango sustains El Corte in Nijmegen, Holland. The tango lived and danced at El Corte is an inspiration both lyrical and political. In Montreal tango and beyond, I thank Mireille, Walter, Enrique, Richard, Ruth, Fernando, Toine, Ines, and so many other dancers with whom improvisation and creation go hand in hand.

Those who taught me to think hard about politics have a central place in the attempt to (re)articulate the political in *Politics of Touch*. I thank Michael Shapiro, Bill Connolly, Michael Dillon, Rob Walker, Jenny Edkins.

Interdisciplinary thinking finds a powerful voice in research-creation. Few writers capture that environment as well as Steven Shaviro, Brian Massumi, and Isabelle Stengers. My words would exist in a vacuum without yours.

Montreal is a magic place. I thank those artists—among them Luc Courchesne, Freda Guttman, Rafael Lozanno-Hemmer, Lynn Hughes, Richard Kerr, Chris Salter, Sha Xin Wei—who continue to make it a stimulating creative environment.

In 2004, I established the Sense Lab (www.thesenselab.com) at Concordia University with the idea that students, artists, and researchers could work together on projects related to the sensing body in movement. Thank you to those who have shared time, ideas, and enthusiasm. The Sense Lab would not be such a stimulating environment without the indomitable energies of Nadine Asswad, who is not only central to the conceptualization and orchestration of events but takes the research-creation approach to heart, bringing sincerity and generosity into the mix. Sincere thanks also to Tagny Duff, Nasrin Himada, Marie-Èvelyne Leclerc-Chevrier, Ronald Rose-Antoinette, Troy Rhoades, Alanna Thain, Céline Pereira.

There needn't be a gulf between thought, friendship, and family. I learned this with extraordinary warmth from Ben Jones and continue to live it with Margaret McCullough, Pascale Manning, Yves Manning, Eric Manning, Brian Massumi, Jesse Massumi, Mireille Painchaud, Ken Dean, Catherine Herrmann. This is where politics of touch begin.

Politics of touch exist in relation. Thank you, Brian, for your exquisite intensity, creativity, rigor. Thinking-with is an experience that has changed my life. This would have been another book without you.

I began this book with the generous assistance of a postdoctoral Social Sciences and Humanities Research Grant and finished it with the support of an ongoing grant from the Fonds québécois de recherche sur la société et la culture.

Introduction

Atypical Expressions and Political Inventions

Does a mother's touch alter her child's brain chemistry? According to Michael Meany, McGill University professor of medicine, "various stress-related illnesses, including depression, anxiety disorders, immune dysfunctions, drug abuse, obesity and heart disease, could hinge on early life experience" (*Montreal Gazette*, 2 October 2004). Early life experience, as Meany defines it, is intrinsically linked to touch. His research indicates, for instance, that baby rats with high-licking mothers have lower levels of stress hormones. This suggests that healthy children are directly proportional to touching mothers. Blood relations are not key: adoptive mothers can perform the same tasks with similar effects.

This article came to my attention late in the process of writing *Politics of Touch*. I foreground it now because it suggests that interesting new research on the senses is under way, and it allows me to make explicit the tools required to rearticulate the relation between bodies and senses. It also emphasizes my own progression as regards the project of *Politics of Touch*. When I began writing this book, finding work on the senses was such a challenge that I welcomed anything I could lay my hands on. Had I encountered the article three years previous, I would have been especially encouraged because the research demonstrates a qualitative change in bodies as a result of touch. At the time—in what I considered to be a disembodied political climate where political philosophy was completely disinterested in the senses—any research on the senses was welcome. Today—having located the senses in all kinds of peripheral environments and no longer expecting research on the senses to provide a straightforward re-articulation of the body-politic—I find the intriguing aspects of the study constrained by a research methodology that continues to situate the senses within a model of the body that is gendered and codified, a model reminiscent of the one *Politics of Touch* attempts to write against.

Let me foreground one aspect of Meany's work as a pertinent example of how research on the senses often continues to reconstitute the preconstituted Cartesian body even while it attempts to expose the body to new sensing configurations. Meany writes that "fathers cannot be included in the experiment because there are not enough research funds" (2004, A6), thus taking for granted gendered assumptions as regards the senses and the reason-senses, mind-body dualisms. Meany does not know what the father's role is in regard to the child's sensing body not only because research funds were not sufficient but because fathers have never been a research priority as regards the senses. Therefore, while Meany's research exhibits a qualitative opening in the reason-senses paradigm, he is finally incapable of recognizing the body outside the normative constraints of the very Cartesianism that has held the senses captive for at least three centuries: the father continues to be associated with reason and the mother with the senses. In addition, the senses remain organized within a motor-sensory system that retains the active-passive dichotomy between the one who touches and the one touched.

In *Politics of Touch*, I explore the ways in which research on the senses can extend beyond commonsense approaches to the senses and to the body. To write about the senses it is necessary to write against the grain of a mind-body, reason-senses model that continues to privilege staid readings of gender, biology, and politics. To write against the grain is to become sensitive, at all junctures, to how the body is defined, composed, and compartmentalized. This challenge becomes palpable when we return to Meany's work: despite the fact that his work explicitly attempts to rethink the sensory system and its biological effects, presuppositions as regards the (gendered) body undergird his arguments. It is in part because Meany does not question how touch works that his findings are not yet capable of extending beyond commonsense notions of touch. The challenge when working with the senses is to not presuppose that we already know what it means to sense.

That mothers can alter the experience of their young by touching them is not something I dispute. What I counter is the notion that the senses are controlled by one body and given to another or withheld. This attitude posits as its point of departure a stable body that exists in a pre-given space-time which contains an active giver and a passive receptor. *Politics of Touch* challenges this assumption, positioning the senses *relationally* as expressions of moving bodies. This presupposes a vastly altered concept of time and space. Whereas in the active-passive commonsense model, time and space are located as stable signifiers into which the body enters, within a relational model, space and time are qualitatively transformed by the movements of the body. The body does not move *into* space and time, it *creates* space and time: there is no space and time before movement.

Bodies on the Move

Politics of Touch seeks to do at least two things: (1) to expose the ways in which the senses—touch in particular, but always in implicit interaction with other senses—foreground a processual body; (2) to explore how thinking the *processual* body potentially influences the ways in which we articulate and live the political. The object of inquiry is therefore the body.

To speak about bodies is first and foremost to explore the ways in which bodies *move*. I locate touch as one way of thinking this body-in-movement. This is not to give touch preferential treatment: throughout, touch is to be understood synesthetically, operating along relational vectors always in dialogue with other senses (of which there are likely many more than five). To think touch synesthetically is to appreciate all of the ways in which movement qualitatively alters the body. As becomes apparent by the end of *Politics of Touch*, the senses prosthetically alter the dimensions of the body, inciting the body to move in excess of its-self toward the world. Sensing toward the world implicates the body in a worlding that re-organizes conceptions of space and time.

The body at work in *Politics of Touch* is a *sensing body in movement*. This is not a "new" body (though it always networks in new and diverging ways). It is a body that has always emerged through and alongside other bodies, be they political bodies, gendered bodies, raced bodies. What is "new" about the body foregrounded in *Politics of Touch* is not its shape or form but the *relational matrices* it makes possible.

In *Politics of Touch*, the exploration of touch is an interdisciplinary endeavor that depends on striking new relations between terms, subjects, and ideas. *Politics of Touch* begins with an exploration of how touch works.

Politics is defined in the first chapter as a composition foregrounding a
dynamic sensing body in movement. This body in movement is an improvised body—both at the level of its movements and its significations.

Argentine tango functions throughout *Politics of Touch* as a refrain (in
the Deleuzo-Guattarian sense).[1] Through the tango, I have attempted to
make the point that touch is not simply the laying of hands. Touch is the
act of reaching toward, of creating space-time through the worlding that
occurs when bodies move. Touch, seen this way, is not simply an addendum
to an already-stable body. Touch is that which forces us to think bodies
alongside notions such as repetition, prosthesis, extension. This is why
Deleuze and Guattari's concept of the Body without Organs (a concept that
forces us to rethink the boundaries of the body) takes central stage toward
the end of *Politics of Touch*.

In *Politics of Touch*, I attempt to engage the reader to stray from a commonsense reading of the senses. This, I hope, will allow the reader to imagine and express a politics that challenges the notion that the (political)
body is a stable locus of enunciation.

Invention

Politics should work by invention. *Politics of Touch* makes a pact to invent,
event-fully, what a body can do. Invention here takes the matter-form of
touch. Touch, alongside politics, invents by drawing the other into relation,
thereby qualitatively altering the limits of the emerging touched-touching
bodies. Touch is not graspable as a stable concept. The only thing we can
grasp, momentarily, are touch's inventions. Relational time-space, provisional
embodiments are inventions of touch: the body senses in layers, in textures,
in rhythms and juxtapositions that defy strict organization into a semiotic
system.

In the varied works over many centuries that explore the senses, the
body is regularly theorized in opposition to the mind, while the senses are
located strictly in the body. And yet there is a suspicion already within these
formative texts that the strict delineation of the sensing body in opposition
to the rational mind is less stable than it has been made out to be in the
canonical readings of these texts. Already in many of these works—including those of Descartes—the senses emerge as slippery concepts that complicate the pre-imposed discreteness of the body. The body, these texts seem to
say, is always in excess of our understanding. This is the point of departure
for *Politics of Touch*. What I propose to do is to contribute to a long tradi-

tion of dis-placing the body in relation to the senses.[2] I suggest that to think the body in relation to the senses is to: (1) encourage a thinking of the body in movement; (2) engage with the possibility that bodies are not limited to their organs; (3) shift the question of "what the body *is*" to "what can a body *do*." My engagement with touch is not an exploration of something I could strictly define as sensing per se but an encounter with the atypical expressions of a sensing body in movement.

Since the nineteenth century, few political theorists have concerned themselves with an exploration of the sensing mechanisms that drive the body and force it out of the grids of intelligibity that would like to capture it for service to the national body-politic and its measures of qualification. A link could be drawn between the normalization of state sovereignty and its adjacent body-politic, and the denial of the sensing body in movement. Without a commitment to the ways in which bodies move, bodies become stabilized within national imaginaries in preordained categories, such as citizen, refugee, man, woman, homed, homeless. Deliberately avoiding the entanglements inherent in articulating (and ordering) sensing bodies in movement, the state can claim that its body-politic is unified. The body can be described and its politics can be defined. Within state discourse, common sense is at stake, not the senses. To reclaim the sensing body in movement is therefore to think both alongside and against the nation-state.

Politics of Touch asks what a sensing body in movement can do through the prisms of tango, democracies-to-come, violence, security, friendship, gender, biology, sex. The politics of touch outlined here is a politics engaged in a pact to invent new bodies. The question posed is less "what is a sensing body in movement" than "how can I create a sensing body in movement?" The proposition is that touch—every act of reaching toward—enables the creation of worlds. This production is relational. I reach out to touch you in order to invent a relation that will, in turn, invent me. To touch is to engage in the potential of an individuation. Individuation is understood throughout as the capacity to become *beyond* identity. We individuate inventively. Relationally, we engage in individuations that require difference and repetition. Without difference that repeats, we foreclose the process, returning the body to territorialization, national body-politics, stable genders, political consensus.

To invent is political if we understand politics to be lured by the body's tendency to relate. Bodies respond to one another through metastable configurations between the microcellular, the multicellular, and the intercorporeal, creating new mutating configurations. Bodies are connected through intensities of composition that in turn produce new bodies.

Political Recompositions

An invention can only ever be a work in progress. A politics of touch acknowledges in advance the impossibility of creating a body per se. To identify a body as such would be to tame movement. To capture movement is to stop sensing. *Politics of Touch* works with the paradox that a sensing body in movement will always circumvent a project that attempts to characterize it in the name of touch, the senses, gender, race, politics. I accept this paradox and offer *Politics of Touch* not as a reading of what touch *is*, but as an exploration of what might happen if we are willing to direct our thinking toward movement, toward a relational stance that makes it impossible to pin down knowledge but asks us instead to invent.

In the chapters that follow, I have not attempted to develop a coherent politics (this would reinstate a linear space-time), but have instead sought to create lines of flight that invite us to rethink the ways in which movement alters many of those concepts we consider foundational. To think bodies in movement is to rethink the relation between space and time, between movement and stillness, between a politics of the nation-state and the Spinozean pact. It is to inquire into democracies-to-come and to wonder what politics might become were we capable of reinventing it. To think bodies in movement is to ask how knowledges/worlds are created, and whether these worlds are capable of expanding the "simple location"[3] of organic bodies. To explore touch in these ways is to be willing to engage with the body as excessive to the national body-politic, to express an interest in a body that is always more expansive than we have heretofore been able to imagine.

Politics of Touch begins with transculturation-in-movement, a concept that exposes the ways in which interweaving cultures depart from the often stultifying narratives of the nation-state. Transculturation comes to the fore in chapter 1 through the specter of Argentine tango, the legacy of a dance that invariably exceeds its parameters, be they cultural or national. Transculturation suggests that culture is always more than that which the nation identifies as its imagined community.

Transculturation proposes not only a cultural slippage but also a potential alteration in the relation of space to time. Through tango, transculturation encourages us to rethink the ways in which we touch and move together, and to explore how these movements instantiate new chronotopes. The foregrounding of space-time through the figure of the chronotope is a way of reminding ourselves that space and time (as defined by the nation-state or by a concept of culture that is embedded in national politics) cannot exist separately. Space and time are always space-time. Bodies in movement space time and time space rather than existing in an empty container of space marked by the passing of a linear time line.

The tango opens the way for an engagement with a cultural phenomenon that is at once fiercely nationalistic and startlingly inventive. To think tango both as a transcultural improvisation and as a national artifact is vital to the project of *Politics of Touch* because it reminds us that there is no clean slate onto which bodies are written and politics are made. Even while they potentially resist the boundaries of the state, transcultural phenomena often remain embedded within national imaginaries. Politics—like bodies— emerge out of frictions, accidents, disagreements, and interlockings that are both firmly institutionalized within pre-constituted space-times and that create emergent space-times. We must remember, however, that whether sanctioned by the nation or positioned transculturally in excess of the national body-politic, there is no body that exists before it moves. This means that bodies must always be stilled to be characterized. It is a back-gridding process. When stilled, politics—and bodies—can be stabilized in the name of a larger system (state sovereignty, the nation-state, the body-politic). But even then, these "stable" compositions must be ferociously maintained and contained, lest they begin to reach toward one another, engaging in compositions that remind us that bodies are always stranger (*unheimlich*) than they first appear.

Tango prepares the way for a thinking of the strange instability of bodies. This in turn lays the ground for a thinking of disagreement (Rancière), which emerges in the subsequent chapters. To think politics through disagreement is to resist a consensual model. To disagree (*mésentente*, in Rancière's words) is to foreground the process of coming to a decision. To "take" a decision (Derrida's concept) is what is at stake here. The process of decision-taking involves taking the risk that your decision might change the orientation of an event. Disagreement involves an openness toward this risk, a risk that places into question filial strategies that restrain politics to hierarchical models with which we are familiar (citizen/sovereign, refugee/citizen, homed/homeless). Disagreement in-forms politics. In-formation, a concept that comes from Simondon, allows us to conceive of information as a process. Disagreement and in-formation are relational concepts: both engage in the name of im-provisation with that which cannot yet be known.

Improvisation is the creative potential at the heart of any composition. Improvisation engenders new concepts. Although operative throughout, improvisation comes to the fore in chapter 4, where gender, engendering, endosymbiosis, and touch come together. Chapter 4 takes as its point of de-parture the notion that to engender is to conceive of matter and form not as inert and stable but as relationally metastable. I suggest that form and mat-ter regenerate through encounters with one another rather than occupying separate planes: the quality of matter is source of form, element of form. To borrow from Simondon, the transformation of matter-form involves metastable individuations. Metastable individuations foreground the fact that structures never precede individuations. An individuating structure partakes of transduction—the concept at the heart of chapter 4—which is any process (biological, physical, social, technical) in which in-formation or new taking-form occurs, enabling reiterations of the matter-form matrix. Transduction is individuation in progress: invention. If we think identity, we have returned to a stable body. A moving body—a sensing body—cannot be *identified*. It individuates always in excess of its previous identifications, remaining open to qualitative reiteration.

Politics of Touch rests on the originary assumption that there is no such thing as a body that is not relational. Bodies individuate in response to a reaching-toward and they reach toward as a response to their individuation. At its most political, to reach toward is to create a concept for unthinking the individual as a discrete entity. Sensing bodies in movement are not indi-vidual bodies; their individuations are always collective. They are worlding bodies that are one with the potential of movement. To become is to move toward something that is not yet. To exist in the not-yet is to individuate incorporeally or virtually. This shift toward the virtual does not preclude actualization, it suggests that to reach toward is to engage with what Deleuze calls the crystallization of time,[4] where the actual and the virtual coincide. Touch occurs at the intersections of the prism, creating a relation that is actual while flirting with the future anterior, the "will have come." The future anterior is dealt with in more detail in chapter 5, where I explore the ways in which democracy remains to-come.

The incorporeal is like a smudge that emanates from your body's poten-tial movement.[5] The smudge exfoliates in all directions, leaving traces of the potential of the animated body as it moves from here to there, from the now to the not-yet, from the after to the before to the will-have-come. The incorporeal is not the opposite of the corporeal. It is a stage of corporeality that reminds us that the corporeal is only ever *virtually* concrete. The body is always what it has not yet become. The body is in metamorphosis. This is the subject of chapter 3, which explores the ways in which the Bible narrates this metamorphosis in the name of touch. In a reading of violence and touch, chapter 3 foregrounds the metamorphosis of the exfoliating body, suggesting that a violence associated with a politics of touch may not concur with the biblical opposition between good and evil. To exfoliate implies shedding layers of skin. It also suggests a process of renewal and transition. To *become* a body is to alter all conceptions of what a body "is." Violence here becomes a way of exploring the consequences of invention.

Violence is potentially productive as well as destructive. To touch is always to attempt to touch the incorporeality of a body, to touch what *is* not yet. I do not touch the you that I think you are, I reach toward the one you will become. There is always singular becoming, but singular in the sense of a collective event, not in the sense of a coded number within a series.

Bodies without Organs (BwO) take central stage in chapter 6, where the consequences of exploring sensing bodies in movement become palpable: If bodies emerge in the act of reaching-toward, creating space-time through a "worlding" that can be violent, can we still conceive of the body as "organic"? Artaud's concept of the Body without Organs evokes the strangeness of a body-becoming that is always, in some sense, unreachable, both biologically and conceptually. *Politics of Touch* will not have been about a body we already know. Chapter 6 asks: If the body can no longer be defined as such, is it possible to secure this body? If the body is always in excess itself, what "body" is there for the state to secure? These questions mirror the concerns of chapter 1's dance between national identity and transcultural negotiations of difference: is there a body of the nation-state?

The BwO stands in for the becoming-body, the body that will-have-come. Bodies without Organs do not suggest that you have to divest yourself of your biology. To create a BwO means that you move toward the world in excess of your organs' organization. Politics of touch are politics concerned with bodies that are always qualitatively more-than their internal organizations. Bodies are not discrete entities facing one another in neutral space-time. Politics of touch imply reachings toward the world that create timed spaces and spaced times that themselves create bodies in relation. Bodies interrelate, extending form into matter and matter into form. BwO not only create relational networks with the world and with each other, these relations themselves become embodied. Bodies incorporate by becoming more than them-selves.

It is in this sense that bodies are machinic. Bodies cannot be measured solely by adding their parts (their organs), thus creating an ambulatory whole. Bodies engage symbiotically, incorporeally, virtually, always becoming more-than they already seem to be. They are as real as they are abstract, as virtual as they are actual. In the words of Deleuze and Guattari, they are abstract machines: they lack determinate form or actual content definition in any final way. BwO are central to a politics of touch because they reinforce the injunction to invent, operating always in the space-time of the "will have been," a future anterior that discloses the fact that we can never completely latch onto them. Bodies—all bodies—escape our grasp. They are not gras-pable partly because they exceed our expectations of them. Bodies are never quite there. They are not quite there because movement is characterized by its engagement with space-times that have not yet been charted, analpha-betic space-times as yet undisclosed, undiscovered. Bodies are strange ma-chines, machines because they produce extensions of themselves, because they generate systems both in and far from equilibrium, systems that resist strict organization.

An object is in equilibrium when the forces acting on it are such that there is no tendency for the object to move.[6] We know that bodies move. Therefore it is not conceivable that they are (always) in equilibrium. Bodies as machines are often far from equilibrium: changes in the surrounding environment cause changes in the system. Far-from-equilibrium systems are metastable, marked by an element of unpredictability, by a capacity for development, for individuation and mutation. Mutation refers as much to the way systems are organized, composed, and articulated as to divergences in those systems. Mutants are bodies by another name.

Mutants connote multiplicity. There is more than one way for a body to become. Multiplicity entails an undermining of the order of the system. Multiplicity is not 1+1. It is 1+ too many to count. The multiple does not simply refer to individuals *en masse*. The multiple is a rethinking of collec-tive individuation, an agglomeration of Bodies without Organs moving toward each others' incorporeality. Collective individuation is about more than community. To collectively individuate is to acknowledge the meta-stability of all machines as assemblages, to acknowledge that all communities are made up of more (kinds of) bodies than we can count.

Politics of Touch in every instance tries to resist a repositioning of the body as ontological. Sensing bodies in movement are ontogenetic. They are ontogenetic because they are always in genesis, in a state of potential becoming. An ontology of the body presupposes a concrete category of Being. Yet, bodies evolve in excess of their Being: they become. Becoming-bodies signal a certain antagonism within politics of the state. This does not imply that a becoming-body is unaccountable. A becoming-body is accountable to becoming more than its-self. But be careful: there is nothing utopic about becoming-bodies. Ontogenesis is a slippery category: it is that which is not yet. I cannot write the body in advance of its creation, of its movement. The body will remain in an antagonistic relation to its accountability.

Affect plays a central role in *Politics of Touch*. Affect is not emotion, though it does play on the idea of movement within the word *emotion*. Emotion is affect plus an awareness of that affect. Affect is the with-ness of the movement of the world. Affect is that which grips me first in the moment of relation, *firstness* in Charles Peirce's vocabulary.[7] Affect is an ontogenetic power of existence. Emotion is the back-gridding of affect.

When we back-grid, we have a tendency to move toward common sense. Aristotle defines touch as the common sense. He suggests that all senses are embodied through the single sense of touch. Yet touch is anything but common. Touch reaches toward that which is most uncommon: the will-have-been. Common sense as it is usually understood connotes a consensual politics that decides in advance what are the limits of political qualification. Common sense takes for granted a strict equivalence between bodies and the state. To be qualified politically within the nation-state system is to reside within the iterable bounds of citizenship. In this system, territory and identity are conflated, assuring strict narratives of national identity that frame the grids of qualification that permit us to speak authoritatively about the state as the organization of space and time. Yet, touch exceeds the state, calling forth that which cannot be securely organized. How, then, are we to consider touch and common sense together? See chapter 5.

Democracy is at stake throughout, though dealt with specifically in chapters 5 and 6. To think politics today is probably to grapple with democracy. Within *Politics of Touch*, democracy is foregrounded as democracy-to-come. Alongside Derrida, I suggest that democracy must be thought in the future anterior as that which remains (and will always remain) to be invented. A politics of touch is an exploration of a fleshy democracy. A fleshy democracy implies a political engagement that is as flexible and unpredictable as the machines it sustains and builds. This kind of democracy challenges discourses of security as they are maintained in the name of state sovereignty today. Sensing bodies in movement resist codings of state security by complicating the strict boundaries between inside and outside. What is the inside/outside of a skinscape that folds in and out of an exfoliating body? Where is the inside/outside of a collective individuation? If you cannot have a state without security, you cannot have a sensing body in movement and a state. Not without control mechanisms to hold a body in (its) place.

States and bodies coexist despite their great antipathy. Re-articulating politics implies rethinking governing structures. Bodies disarticulate states. States live in fear of bodies. This is the subject of chapters 2 and 6. Control mechanisms for bodies abound: gender qualifications (and disqualification), discrepancies between the rights of the homed and the homeless, racial inequalities, border patrols, war tactics, sexual stereotypes, election fiascos. Spinoza suggests the concept of the pact to think around the issue of states and bodies. Derrida suggests a politics of friendship. Pacts are about collective individuation, about affect and will. To create a pact is to *take* a decision within a multitude. A politics of friendship proposes the challenge of creating a relation that cannot be symbolized through a coding in a fraternal nationalism. To create a pact is to explore the limits of what a body can do. It is to take response-ability for an active engagement with structures that mutate. To live is to risk. To risk is to rethink liberty. Liberty must be thought outside the triumvirate: fraternity, liberty, equality. Liberty can become a risk-taking enterprise that foregrounds the potential within any reaching-toward. Liberty might be the freedom to touch, a politics of friendship with a sensing body in movement.

Central to *Politics of Touch* is the notion that to touch is not simply to put organs in contact with the world. Touch foregrounds the senses as machinic assemblages. I would like to think of the senses as prosthetic devices, always more and less than single and singular bodies. To think the senses prosthetically, I turn to the concept of originary technicity. Originary technicity suggests that a natural, originary body does not exist. Technology is not something that is simply added to the body from outside. Technology is a supplement, an aspect of the body that adds to it while it qualitatively alters that very body. "The dynamic of technicity will thus be the dynamic of the prosthetic—and thereby the human as non-proper supplementarity—in general" (Bennington 1996, 181). Originary technicity draws out the human, exposing humanity to its prosthetic attachments. Senses can be thought as prosthetic exfoliations of the body's technicity.

Technicity interlaces geographic, ecological, energetic, economic, and historical dimensions without being reducible to any of them. Technicity opens the way for a thinking of the consequences of ethology, a concept that emerges in chapter 6. Ethology is an ecological ethics, an ethics that takes into account the process of worlding. Worlding opens the way for a becoming-machinic of the world where I am no longer a passive receiver and you an active giver. Becoming-machinic is not something that happens *to* the world. Worlding is immanently machinic in the same way that my BwO is always more than its-self. "I" cannot conceive of moving. What moves is the technicity of the body: senses, extensions, matter/form. When I reach out to touch you, I extend the space I have created between me and you. This extension carries my sense perception (my almost-touch) and can therefore also be considered as prosthetic to my "organic" matter-form. Becoming-machinic is another way of expressing the immanence of Bodies without Organs incessantly creating themselves, for better or for worse.

Sensing bodies might be thought of as posthuman bodies. To be posthuman is not to be more or less human, nor is it to become a different kind of human. Posthumanity is simply another way of referring to the body's originary technicity and its prosthetic nature. Endosymbiotically, biology points toward the complexities of bodies in relation. Biologically, even, the body is always less than what it can and will become and more than what we can imagine or foresee. A body that is open to its processes of individuation is a posthuman body. Post: will-have been. To think of the posthuman body is to open oneself to a body-thinking that exceeds the realm of the national body-politic. It is to begin to engage creatively with what a body can do.

What a body can do depends on the expressions our reachings take. Expression is dynamic, altering the infinite combinations of matter-form, matter-content, form-content. An ethics of expression involves producing "atypical expressions" which constitute "a cutting edge of deterritorialization of language" (Deleuze and Guattari 1987, 99). To think agrammatically is to "bring out the tensile dimension of language by stretching its elements beyond the limit of their known forms and conventional functions" (Massumi 2002, xxii). Agrammatical thinking brings language to its futurity, to its event-ness, drawing it into the realm of the virtual. The sensing body in movement is an agrammatical invention.

1.

Negotiating Influence:
Touch and Tango

The twentieth century is, from one end to another, the century of tango. We cannot speak of the history of this century excluding tango, nor can we exclude jazz, its twin. Nor flamenco, its mysterious brother.

—*Horacio Ferrer*

Tangere: to touch (Latin)

As night falls, we meet in bars always difficult to locate. We change our shoes, we glance around the room to find a human connection, and we dance. These evenings that are often drawn out into the early morning are about an exchange of movement and touch, about a transnational negotiation of desire, of gender roles and communication. In New York, Berlin, Buenos Aires, Montreal, Honolulu, Brussels, Nijmegen, tango asserts its language of desire, its politics of touch.

Tango, a signifier of darkness and illegitimacy, of desire and counterculture, is more than a dance. As Horacio Ferrer writes, "before being an artistic expression, before tango came to light as such . . . tango was a certain attitude, a way of life adopted by those of diverse cultures" (1995, 11). In its popular representations, Argentine tango is described as a dance that evokes illicit sexual desire through an acrobatics that often looks choreographed. But Argentine tango is much more than this mythic evocation of a movement

of desire. Tango is everything from a dance of solitudes to a nomadic movement of cultural displacement to a fierce locator of national identity. It is a
dance of encounter and disencounter, a voyeuristic embrace of repressed
sensuality and a complex network of (mis)understood directions.

Like all social tangos, the tango I explore here is improvised. Indeed, it is
the improvised nature of tango that fascinates me and makes it possible for
me to advance tango as an example of a politics of touch. Since the movements of tango are always to come, it is impossible to speak of "a" tango, of
an ideal gesture or a "contained" politics. Rather, tango operates throughout as an invested attempt to explore relation in the context of a *potential*
politics-to-come.

Although tango could be introduced as the ultimate signifier of Argentine national identity, I do not approach tango from this vantage point,
preferring instead to locate tango as a transnational crossing of human and
political boundaries, as a politics of touch that displaces all notions of sedentary encounters with an other. For me, tango is a movement across time and
space, an errant politics[1] that calls out to the night-world to re-orchestrate
its systems of governance and exchange through bodies that exist not, first
and foremost, for the outside world, but for the inner exchange between
two silent partners, moving quietly, eyes half closed, toward dawn.

Tango as I encounter it is a peripheral engagement with the world that
introduces us to a different way of living with an other. It is a movement
that offers the possibility of improvising our encounters. It is a dance that
turns us toward an other to whom we might otherwise not speak. Tango
takes place on the edges of neighborhoods, at the magic time between dusk
and dawn, in the periphery of the social order. Its lyrics are about adventure,
heartbreak, the clandestine, the murmurs of desire and deception. Originally
a music composed by immigrants to Buenos Aires, tango is a dance that is
about a movement between here and there, about an exchange between two
bodies, about the pain of disconnection and the desire for communication.

A product of cultural exchange, tango has never ceased to transform
itself through contact with new cultures. As Ramon Pelinski writes, "nomadic
tango resides neither entirely on its own terrain, nor entirely on the terrain
of an other" (1995, 18). Yet, as Astor Piazzola comments, "in Argentina,
everything can change, except tango" (in Pelinski 1995, 27). Tango is a
contradiction in terms: even though tango is a transnational crossing of
cultures, for many, tango remains a stable signifier of Argentine national
identity. As a result of this paradox, many aficionados of tango resist all

transnational implications where tango is concerned, insisting instead that tango is the unique reference of the symbolic identity and territory of Argentine culture.

Despite these echoes toward a politics of Argentine national identity, I maintain that tango involves a transculturation, a state of becoming through alterity. Tango is a movement through politics that both reinforces the status quo of the politics of national identity and transgresses these very politics. This play between transgression and cohesion takes place in the weaving of tango's complex webs, webs entwined around tango's implicit desire to communicate, through the body, with an other. A dance that must be re-encountered with every new dancer, tango appeals to the senses. It does so through microperceptual movements initiated through improvisation and spontaneity that require an adequate response yet suggest, always, the possibility of subverting the expected.

Tango is the dance of the impromptu rethinking of the politics of communication. Tango is the dream of the known played out in the night of the unknown. It is the politics unwritten, yet the palimpsest on which everything political aspires already to have been written. It is the voice of the immigrant displaced through movement. It is the movement of the stranger, echoing in the distant resonance of a music that has many times crossed the world. Foregrounding this improvisational nature of a dance which requests the complete attention of an other, I shall draw a link between the transculturation of a movement of desire—tango—and the possibility of articulating a politics enunciated through such displacement. This I will call a politics of touch.

Toward the beginning of the twentieth century, tango was born as a music and a dance. Alienated from the Argentine middle class, tango expanded quite quickly in the underworld of Buenos Aires. The expansion of tango took place while Buenos Aires—a city in which more than 50 percent of the population was composed of immigrants—quickly grew from 187,000 to 1,576,000 inhabitants (Ferrer 1972, 146). Argentine society in Buenos Aires at that time was characterized by the presence of an overwhelming majority of solitary men uprooted and socially destabilized by conditions beyond their control. Many of these men frequented cafes and bordellos, first for the women, then for the tango (De Ipola 1985, 15).

Tango has never been a dance that could be contained. In the early twentieth century, tango travelled to Europe and Asia, and today Finnish tangos are second only to Argentine tangos in their production and dissemination.

In fact, between 1962 and 1965, tango was the most popular musical genre in Finland, and this not for a reproduction of a tango born in Argentina, but for the dissemination of a tango native to the aspirations and disappointments of a very particularly Finnish population. Finnish tangos, like their Argentine counterparts, are passionate, but the Finnish passion is not as polyvalent as its predecessor. Finnish tangos are slow and the dance is measured, described by some as a rigid interpretation and exposition of emotions and social protestation.

From Helsinki to Tokyo to Barcelona to Portland to Rome to Istanbul, tango continues to be danced, altered, exchanged and sent back, changed, to Buenos Aires. Tango expresses itself differently from one environment to another, from one couple to another: most often a heterosexual encounter in Argentina, tango in Holland increasingly blurs gender and sexual boundaries by challenging and altering the roles of the leaders and the followers. Hence, however adamantly ideologically withheld by those who seek to possess it, tango can be thought of as a music and a dance that lives through flexibility, mutation, evocation, pluralization, and transculturation.

Tango begins with a music, a rhythm, a melody. The movement of the dance is initiated by a lead, a direction, an opening to which the follower responds. Tango is an exchange that depends on the closeness of two bodies willing to engage with one-another. It is a pact for three minutes, a sensual encounter that guarantees nothing but a listening. And this listening must happen on both sides, for a lead is meaningless if it does not convey a response from a follower. As various tango aficionados have pointed out, the lead can never be more than an invitation, as a result of which the movement in response will remain improvised. This dialogue is rich and complex, closer to the heart, perhaps, than many exchanges between strangers and lovers.

"Politics," writes Agamben, "is the sphere of pure means, that is, of the absolute and complete gesturality of human beings" (2000, 59). I want to suggest that tango, a transcultural movement of desire, can be envisioned as a political gesture toward an other. Tango is an exile into the unknowable world of bodies. "The history of the tango is a story of encounters between those who should never have met or between those who, having met, will remain forever disencountered" (Savigliano 1995, xv). This political moment of (dis)encounter is initiated through an embrace that rarely lasts beyond the duration of the tango itself. This encounter, relentless and short-lived, proposes a violation of critical distances, inviting at once intimacy, tension, and conflict.

The tango embrace is the political gesture with which the mediality of tango is initiated. It is this embrace which invites the potential emergence of a medium, a milieu independent of pre-ordained constraints. This medium can feed an already troubled relationship between self and other, between woman and man, leader and follower. In this case, the embrace is a means to an end, signaling a familiar restoring of the genre. Or this embrace can challenge the concept of the milieu through a politics of touch that engages in the means, that is, in the potential of listening to the breath, the body, the distance and the closeness of another human being, a listening to what might be considered the very ethics-in-deconstruction of humanity.[2]

Agamben writes, "because being-in-language is not something that could be said in sentences, the gesture is essentially always a gesture of not being able to figure something out in language" (2000, 58). The gesture of turning to an other, of inventing a movement with another whom I do not know and cannot anticipate, is a gesture attentive to a resounding silence, in which I am exposed as a body in motion. In the case of tango, my language is what I reveal to you in the intimacy of the embrace, a language that introduces you to a movement that invites you to respond to a direction we initiate together.

Gestural Politics

The theorization of a politics of touch involves an appreciation of the manner in which human beings organize their lives in time and space. At its most concrete, this mode of living is symbolized through an attachment to the nation-state system wherein history and geography are confined to a comprehensive notion of time and space. Tango often crosses this chronotope, inviting and inciting me to re-formulate the distance between my-self and an other. Tango, operating here as the relationality of sensing bodies in movement, works as a trope through which I attempt to delineate a different way of facing an other, a different way of worlding the world.

For Aristotle, a good life involves social relations and institutions: man is a creature by nature adapted for life in a *polis*. The purpose of the state is to do what the individual man cannot: the state is put into place in order to extend beyond "mere" life. In this scenario, the state is synonymous with political partnership, a partnership established by nature to satisfy all the daily needs of the household (1961, 383). This partnership established by nature is considered "natural," which supports Aristotle's claim that "man is by nature an animal designed for living in states" (1961, 384). Aristotle argues that the state of which he speaks is a plurality that exists for the sake of the citizen prior both to the individual human being and to the household, for "the whole must be prior to the part": the state is a political organization of a like-minded plurality (1961, 384). Within this system, the citizen is not a citizen simply by virtue of inhabiting a certain place of residence, the citizen is he who has a share in the administration of justice in holding political office: "[t]he goodness of a reputable citizen is thought to consist of the right use of ruling and being ruled" (1961, 408).

If the state is essentially both natural and plural as Aristotle suggests, the important question is how this relation of the natural and the plural is theorized as a central component of his understanding of the state-system. Plurality is evoked here as a multitude of identifying practices that depart from a common ground: man. Man, for Aristotle, is natural (i.e., political) and therefore plural, whereas woman is not political, nor, by extension, plural. Plurality in the *polis* implies a system that supports the organization of a naturalization of the terms at stake (politics, gender, race) by like-minded men. This is not substantially different from state-systems today where a chorus of like-minded voices are united to pledge allegiance to the citizen-nation-state triad. Space and time are withheld within this system as markers for a stable geography (even in the international or "global" realm) and a consistent history. Plurality (in the name of most multiculturalisms) conforms to the dimensions of difference controlled and sustained within state sovereignty.

Politics of touch attempt to evoke a pluralism that radically departs from Aristotelian thought and celebrates a demystification of the naturalizations that allow ends to become means. Through a notion of politics that is produced as a means without an end, a potentiality rather than an actuality, we can begin to defy the constriction of time and space straitjacketed by the nation-state. Potentiality, as the insertion of difference in a moment of certainty, is one way of speaking of the divergence between normativity and the interruption of accepted norms. I read potentiality as that which exposes difference in systems that appear to be organized and unchanging. I do not seek to place actuality and potentiality in opposition, however. The passage from potentiality to actuality need not be ascertained as an elimination of potential. Rather, this passage can be theorized as potentiality itself, for potentiality resides within every interaction: potentiality is called forth every time language exceeds its syntax, every time an other exceeds my reach, every time I sense more than I comprehend.

A potential naming occurs not only in the spoken enunciation, but also in the textual moment of decision-taking, in the resounding silence of tango, during that moment that incites me to reach out to touch an other, not only with my words, but with my senses. Potentiality is at the heart of this reaching-toward. As Agamben writes: "If the 'thing itself' in language exists in the mode of potentiality, then it follows that language must originally have the form not of actual signification but of the mere capacity to signify" (1999, 18).

The potentiality that is at the base of my reaching out toward an other is not effaced in the passage to actuality. Quite the contrary: in my turn toward an other, I engage with the very potentiality of extending my-self, of challenging my-self to feel the presence (and absence) of that other. Aristotle, on the other hand, would argue that every gesture performed by a citizen (a man) is *pre-ordained* toward the potentiality of inaugurating a *polis,* or a plurality of like-minded individuals. Yet *gesture* (reaching-toward) as I am using it here implies something far more tenuous and ephemeral. As I reach toward, I reach not toward the "you" I ascertain but toward the "you" you will become in relation to our exchange. I reach out beyond the pre-constituted time and space of the Aristotelian *polis.* The Aristotelian notion of the *polis* seeks to stabilize the experience of encounter still so central to our understanding of the political, confining politics to a space-time that must be governed and contained. I would like to explore the possibility that a politics of touch as a discourse of potentiality-in-movement might function as the very antithesis of this evocation of the state-system.

To imagine a politics that exceeds a state-centered governmentality necessitates a vocabulary that resists and subverts the language of the state. Of course, language always carries the traces of coercion as much as those of difference. I am not suggesting, therefore, that I can invent a language that will not, always, in some sense, prefigure the system of state-sovereignty and its adjacent vocabularies. Nor am I thinking of language strictly in a textual sense. Tango—the infralanguage I use here—makes this palpable: tango is a cultural artefact that both conforms to the notion of state culture through its insistence of its evocation of performing "the" Argentine national identity and subverts this identification to the state through its transcultural movements of desire. Argentine tango thus reminds us that transgressions are porous, leaking both into and out of national receptacles. It is in this sense that tango can become a gesture toward a rethinking of a complex notion of the political, a political that will always be tempted to return to the coherence imposed and policed by state systems and their adjacent narratives of national identity.

Agamben suggests that gesture is "that dimension of language that is not exhausted in any communication of meaning and that, in this way, marks

the point at which language appears in its mere capacity to communicate"
(1999, 22). To foreground gesture

> is to consider a community inconceivable according to any representable
> condition of belonging: a "coming community," without identity, defined
> by nothing other than its existence in language as irreducible, absolute
> potentiality. (Agamben 1999, 23)

As a movement reaching toward, a gesture evokes an instance in which
nothing is absolutely maintained. A gesture explores the medium—be it
the movement, the touch, the word—as a means not of transforming potentiality into actuality, but as a way of eclipsing actuality by placing the
emphasis on the movement itself, on the exchange. As Agamben writes,
gesture "allows the emergence of the being-in-a-medium of human beings
and thus it opens the ethical dimension for them" (2000, 58).

A gesture interrupts language in the moments when language attempts
to convert itself to actuality. Challenging the notion that being-in-language
can be said as such, a gesture draws our attention to the challenges within
expression, leading us to the ephemeral realm of the unsayability of words
as completed thoughts. In this way, a gesture acts as a force that renders palpable language's instability, challenging language to become an infralanguge
of interrelation, where the felt is said even as the said is felt. Gesture reinforces the fact that communication is not linear, that language cannot be
concretely symbolized, that the words that "reach" an other cannot be completely comprehended. Certainly, language and/as gesture can organize a
certain version of a *polis,* but it does so more in the disorganization of like-
minded people than by encouraging conformity.[3]

Gesture as such has nothing to say. It is only relationally that gestures
create the possibility for exchange. Gestures negotiate both transgression
and understanding. I use a gesture to communicate something to you that I
don't feel I can adequately "say." What interests me about gesture is not its
strict positioning within a politics of touch versus a sovereign politics or in
a politics of language versus a politics of affect. I am concerned with the
manner in which gesture provides an alternate (and existing) vocabulary of
the political. I am interested in the ways in which gestures render *unheimlich*
the "messages" operating within the *polis.* I am fascinated by the ways gestures
provide alternate positionings of means and ends. For, even though gestures
can be rehearsed, falsified, mediated by a consensual thinking that privi-
leges certain exchanges over others, even though gestures can be devices of

and in language as well as prostheses to sensing bodies in movement, gestures continuously slip outside the grids of intelligibility of organized structures, potentially resisting containment, calling forth a vocabulary of the
political that *can* exceed sovereign methods.

Touching the Impenetrable

The surface of the body is a thinking, feeling surface. It is a gestural, linguistic, sensing skin that protects us while opening us toward and rendering
us vulnerable to an other. Our bodies are the bodies without organs of the
political, bodies formed and deformed by the division and sharing of communities, of communal and uncommon exchange. Our bodies are resistances—
to ourselves, to each other, resistances to knowledge, to language, to sensing, as well as to ignorance, to being touched, to being meaningful, to being
there. Touching, our bodies gesture toward each other and themselves, each
time challenging and perhaps deforming the body-politic, questioning the
boundaries of what it means to touch and be touched, to live together, to
live apart, to belong, to communicate, to exclude.

Turning to touch as a political gesture, I mean to bring the body to politics differently. Touch connects bodies, human bodies, bodies of thought,
intermittently. As a political gesture, touch is an utterance geared toward
an other to whom I have decided to expose myself, skin to skin. Touch is an
ethical discourse because I cannot touch you without being responsible for
doing the touching, I cannot touch you without being responsive. For touch
must always indicate its source, and its source can never be identified by an
individual: touch is singular-plural.

Touch reminds us that bodies are impenetrable. It is my surface that I
risk exposing when I reach toward you and place my hand against yours.
The impenetrability of your body is what initiates this political moment
wherein there can be no dream of an original sin, no drowning in a complete knowledge, no sense of an ultimate recognition. Touching resists these
tendencies, reminding us that all gestures are incomplete, that to reach
toward an other is never more (or less) than the act of reaching, for an
other cannot be discovered as such. It is only your impenetrability which is
penetrable. And this impenetrability is often beyond words, though not
beyond language. As I touch you, there is only the saying, the reaching.

What makes touch such an interesting concept is I cannot desist trying to
say what cannot be said about the body and my desire to touch it. I cannot

stop touching the speech of the body. Through the gesture of touch, a political moment is exposed, a moment of transition, a moment of incomprehensibility. Within this incomprehension, my body becomes the mode of articulation. My body is the medium through which touch can be negotiated, my body is the receptor for the politico-linguistic-affectual gesture that reminds me that my body is not one. Touch does not allow me to forget the contradiction of my body which is both "the dark reserve of sense, and the dark sign of this reserve" (Nancy 1994, 20).

Nancy writes: "*Sign of itself*, and *being-itself of the sign:* such is the double formula of the body in all states, in all its possibilities" (1994, 21). Wounded by the state, and a wound within the state, the body opens unto itself and unto an other. But the wound also closes itself, thick with scar tissue, anxious to touch and be touched, lulled into a commonsense revolution by a policing that holds an other (and its wound) at bay. At the same time, the wound itself lives within the body, resisting the closure of meaning, of sense. It is this resistance, this urge to touch an other, wound against wound, that potentially creates a community of resistance, a complex, disorderly, incommensurable community of those who cannot keep themselves from reaching out toward the world.

Offering my-self is always possible. It is a potentiality that can never be confirmed as a finite act, for there is no offering that is indelible, which takes place without remainder, without return. I offer my body and, in doing so, I open ourselves to receive. Within this relation, new bodies are engendered and shared, bodies of thought, bodies of knowledge. Sense, my sense of your difference, the sensation I experience when I touch your skin, this sense makes sense to me only insofar as it creates a body of work, a growing experience of what it means to receive the gift of touch. Touching you, I begin to write a corpus that defies the Aristotelian *polis*. This corpus tells a story, plural but not like-minded, of bodies reaching out toward one another, a story of the separation and sharing of bodies, of the transposition of the being-body, multiple, always in excess of its-self, excribed within a corpus I can never quite articulate.

Nancy writes:

> Touching one another with their mutual weights, bodies do not become undone, nor do they dissolve into other bodies, nor do they fuse with a spirit—this is what makes them, properly speaking, bodies. (1994, 28)

It is through touching you that my body is a body, for my body cannot be otherwise than singular and plural. At this limit between separation and sharing, this political limit that marks the edge of the sensing body in movement, where the very notion of community becomes incommunicable, touch becomes a political gesture. Touching is the thought of the medium without limit, the singularly un-absolute.

The absolute limit is instated by a politics that is sustained by the myth of the secure border. This limit concept that is at the heart of the state system is structured as an injunction to combine parts of a corpus into a whole. Yet there is no whole, no totality of the body: there is no such thing as *the* body. There are corpuses, many of them, reaching out, touching, being touched, corpuses that are recitations of multiplicities, of pluralities evoked by touching bodies. These corpuses are political potentialities, acts in the making, movements toward an other. Despite the incantations of the state, there is no completely docile body. There is only the policing of a corpus that writes the body as docile.

Te toucher, toi

Touch functions through a double genitive. I touch you twice, once in my gesture toward you and once in the experience of feeling your body, my skin against yours. You con-tact me. I cannot approach you tactilely without feeling that approach. I touch (you). From your body, I elicit a response, a response not necessarily felt or acknowledged through words, but through a return of the touching I initiate.

If embodiment is a precarious interplay, embodiment can also be conceived of as that which allows encounters to take place within a socio-historical (political) context, for a double-touching, an embodiment of touch, is a touching that can never take place unilaterally. Touch belongs first to an other: it comes to me from an other, already addressing itself to an other. Touch instantiates an interruption, it forces me to turn toward you, not necessarily face to face, but always skin to skin, hand to flesh, flesh to flesh. Touch is the prelude to a corpus that affects us. With touch, I enter (into communication with) you, with you I create the interval between me and you, I am moved by you and I move (with) you, but I do not become you. You are untouchable (inasmuch as there is a single "you"). What I touch is that untouchability. I negotiate that untouchability, that surface that cannot be penetrated, the unknown and (in)finite distance which separates me and you.

The surface is untouchable, yet demands to be touched. Without touch, the surface remains unarticulated, unaffected. It is the gesture toward you, the touch against your flesh, which makes me accountable to you. This gesture renders the exchange of subjectivities plural. This plurality is potentially political. The incommensurability of touch, the impenetrability of the surface, the impossibility of the *entre-deux*, passes through a chronotope—the space-time of the body, of the corpus, of the moment—resisting any idea of place as given, of time as organ-ization. Touch creates time and space, reminding us, through every gesture, that time and space articulate this very creation rather than pre-existing it.

The space-time of my body touching yours is a spacing, an *espacement*, before it is a space. It opens toward an opening, an interval, an incorporeal surface. To touch, in this context, implies modifying, changing, displacing, questioning, inciting a movement which is always a kinetic experience before it is a concrete articulation. Touching is a directionality toward a body which has-not-yet-become, not a body in stasis, but a body moved and moving. I touch what I cannot quite reach, I am touched by an other I cannot quite comprehend, I abstain from touching what I touch with an abstinence that holds within itself the desire to touch, to feel, to sense you.

Eventfully Tender

There is no touch in the singular. To touch is always to touch something, someone. I touch not by accident, but with a determination to feel you, to reach you, to be affected by you. Touch implies a transitive verb, it implies that I *can*, that I *will* reach toward you and allow the texture of your body to make an imprint on mine. Touch produces an event.

> We should therefore, without playing, ever, on the words, listen (entendre) and tender (tendre) tenderly these words. Tender and tender. . . . To tender is to offer, or give, what can be given without rendering, that is to say without exchange, or without waiting for an other to render—or to arrive *(sans attendre que l'autre vienne rendre—ou se rendre)*. (Derrida 2000, 111)

Touching you, I propose to you to receive, to touch. To touch is not to manipulate. I cannot force you to touch. I can coerce you, I can take your body against your will, but I cannot evoke purposefully, in you, the response to my reaching toward you. To touch is to tender, to be tender, to reach out tenderly.

Perhaps this tendering is always, in some sense, a violence: it does violence to my subjectivity, to the idea that I am One. But this need only be the case if we hold onto the concept of subjectivity. If we dare to think bodies as relational rather than as individual, the violence morphs and with it the imaginary of power-as-hierarchy that inhabits state bodies. Sensing bodies in movement produce power, violently, perhaps, but relationally, always. I cannot affect *you* violently: I affect *us*. To touch is to violently or gently encounter a surface, a contour. To touch is to feel the perceived limits of my contours, my surfaces, my body in relation to yours. To touch is to expand these contours, creating new perimeters. We share our surface in the moment of touch, we interrupt our-selves.

> "Touching the goal" [scoring] is to risk missing it. But an origin is not a goal. The End, like the Principle, is a form of an other. To touch an origin [to begin], is not to miss it: it is to properly expose ourselves to it.... We touch ourselves inasmuch as we exist. To touch (ourselves) is what renders us "us" and there is no other secret to discover or to hide behind the touch itself, behind the "with" of co-existence. (Nancy 1996, 32–33)

To touch is to share. This sharing takes place as a trace, a detour, an erring. When I touch you I do not contain the experience within a preconceived narrative. To touch is to open us to a story we have not yet heard, to an unworked work,[4] a narrative without a beginning and an end. To touch impenetrably evokes this undecidability of/in time and space, a dilemma of the *entre-deux* that necessitates both a coming-towards and a coming-between. I cannot envelop the space of our sharing. If I cross this space without regard for this sharing, I engage in a violent accosting that becomes a blow. To touch is to conceive of a simultaneity that requires the courage to face the in-between. When I touch you I reach toward that which I cannot yet define, a worlding of our own creation. This is a finite effort, an effort firmly lodged within a creation of our space-time, within a willed present. I am in con-tact with you. "Touch signifies 'being in the world' for a finite being" (Derrida 2000, 161). There is no world without you.

Worlding Touch

If there is no world without you, it is because reaching toward you initiates the creation of both my becoming-body and my becoming-world. My becoming-world occurs at the intersection of our touch. The political gesture that is our touch occurs in the *entre-deux* which makes inter-relation with you both possible and insurmountable. Faced with each other, we experience a being-with that must remain, always, a being-without, a simultaneous moment of feeling the direction of your body, and knowing that this touch, though directed at me, will serve to mark the separation, the schism between us. This is politics: the moment when I re-cognize that to touch an other is to touch the impenetrable.

A gesture toward an other—a politics of touch—is never static. Like touch, politics is that which orients me toward an other in a movement, in a directionality. A politics that is a politics of touch evokes a displacement—where, often, the terrain from which I diverge seems much more familiar, more comprehensible, more certain—a displacement that produces affinities, attractions, mirages, magnetisms and divergences, ruptures, fissures, and dissociations. Rancière suggests that politics is a term synonymous with democracy when politics refers to an "evanescent moment when tensions arising from a human being-in-common produces instances of disruption, generating sources of political action" (Panagia 2001, 1). Politics of touch is the practice of asserting a position which disrupts the logic of *arche*. Speech that is political must involve an argument that is neither pre-established nor regurgitated. A politics of touch must not be conceived as a politics of community: with touch the center cannot be formulated, let alone reached.

A politics of touch is based on the logic of disagreement, of misunderstanding *(mésentente)*. Language in circulation, gestures in movement: this is a politics of touch. Politics of touch are not the exercise of hierarchical power, but an opening toward a production of power that incites us to act. Too often we conflate politics and a repressive understanding of power, as a result of which we have a tendency to assume power as an heir to the sovereign, thereby confining politics to the state. Politics should not be defined on the basis of a pre-existing subject. Politics must always be thought in relation.

Rancière writes:

> If there is something "proper" to politics, it consists entirely in this relationship which is not a relationship between subjects, but one between two contradictory terms through which a subject is defined. Politics disappears the moment you undo this knot of a subject and a relation. (2001, 2)

Politics is dissensus, where dissensus is not the confrontation between interests or opinions but the manifestation of a creative engagement. Dissensus is the productive element that allows our worlding to occur: when I reach out to touch you, my gesture will not reinstate a forgotten commonality. Together, we negotiate influence. Dissensus rejects any pre-constituted communicative subjectivity. At the heart of dissensus is the realization that I am not yet. Consensus, on an other hand, is the assumption not only that I exist, but that I can convince you to recognize yourself in my image. Consensus is the end of politics of touch, the silencing of disagreement, the impossibility of difference. It is, as Rancière notes, "simply the return of the 'normal' state of things which is that of politics' non-existence" (2001, 14).

A politics of touch implies a spiraling politics in-creation, an eternal return of the unknowable. A politics of touch is the affirmation that we must make space and time for politics, where this space and time can exceed the current state (of affairs). Politics of touch are tactical discursive tactics of the unknowable.

> More than a style, more than a manner, of fingers or hands, we find here a movement of the body, a syntax that calculates without calculating, of the whole body, "in flesh and blood," to encounter things, to be in the world, and to touch it without touching it. (Derrida 2000, 248)

The body, the political corpus, is flesh, limited, wounded, challenged and challenging. The body senses, dissents and consents. To touch is to engage in a con-sentment that is confronted by the specter of incommunicability, of disagreement. The terrible challenge inherent in a politics of touch is that is excribes presence, denying me the possibility of presenting myself to you as always already whole. Touch traces the trace, the incorporeal, effacing you as presence, inviting you to be a political corpus in process, a Body without Organs, a becoming-world.

"Because to touch . . . is to allow myself to be touched by touch . . . by the 'flesh' that I touch and that becomes touching as well as touched" (Derrida 2000, 312). A politics of touch touches touch. This touch remains incalculable: touch evokes dissymmetry, reminding me that politics, like all worldings, must remain uncertain, uncountable. Yet, as Nancy writes, "we must not give 'touch' credit too easily, and we must especially not believe that we could touch the sense of what it means to touch" (1992, 13). To touch is to excribe touch, as a verb, as a terminology, to deflect and question its insertion in a vocabulary that would seek to stabilize politics and/as the body once more. To touch is to acknowledge that I must also be touched by you in order to touch you. "In the 'touching you(r)self' (se toucher toi) the 'self' is as indispensable as the 'you'" (Derrida 2000, 326).

Tango is evoked through a politics of touch that resides in the intent listening to(ward) an other. This attention to a gesture carried within the movements of the body is a listening that carves space in time with our sensing bodies in movement. In the best cases, there is not one dance to be

Two dancers, Montreal, Canada. Photograph by the author.

danced, but a myriad of possibilities generated by two bodies, often foreign to one another, touching one another. I lead, you follow, yet even as I lead, I follow your response, intrigued by the manner in which we interpret one another, surprised at the intentness with which our bodies respond to each other.

When we tango, I invent space-time with you, a you that is always singular-plural. The room dances. Sometimes I hesitate and cannot move, troubled by my fear of not reaching you, confused in my intermittent discovery that the body I share with you can be heard through my skin. Always a reference to the exile of its displaced roots, tango is burdened by the sadness of the ephemerality of the encounter with an other who must remain other. Yet, tango can also be the deeply satisfying acknowledgment by an other that I have been heard, if only for a moment.

Tango speaks a complex language, especially when it exceeds a passive engagement with an other. In these instances, tango produces an encounter with an other that challenges ordinary politics of belonging. Reaching toward you, we create a world encapsulated in an improvised encounter that must always resist the notion of a fundamental accomplishment. The politics of touch experienced in and through tango are always, in some sense, inaccessible politics. Tango is a dance that eludes me even as I move toward you, touching you with my desire to communicate, to inter-relate. Born of disillusionment and disorientation, the music and dance of migration and immigration, of love and loss, tango lends its name to all forms of exile and post-national attachments. There are no origins to this dance that must always return to new begettings, to different and surprising encounters. "If tango has a history," writes Pierre Monette, "it is all it has: this is why we constantly return to it. This music of the deterritorialized has no other geography than that of errancy" (1995, 332).

Tango as a political gesture is the exhibition of the between: between my interpretation and your creation, between my lead and your response. Tango allows the mediality of experience to shine through, exposing the ethical dimension in the relation, celebrating the sphere of that which cannot be known. Of course, not all tango appreciates this challenge. Politics is never simple or straightforward. At its most common, tango replays the drudgery of the defined roles of self and other, relishing the segregation of sameness. But even then, tango demands a response, a response that can never be accurately predicted.

Tango will remain the dance of the milieu—the in-between. Incapable, like the immigrant, of tracing its roots, tango will never finds its rightful place, dancing instead at the borders of existence in the interloping worlds between here and there. It is not the dance of cities or countries, but the dance of the ghetto, of the space that cannot be accurately named or defined. Tango's uncanniness resides in the velocity of the movements that traverse its experience of listening to an other, an other who enters and remains in-between, an other I touch, who touches me.

2.

Happy Together:
Moving toward Multiplicity

Wong Kar Wai's *Happy Together* begins with a silent red screen. Passports are stamped with an entry into a different space, not Hong Kong but Buenos Aires. We are introduced to the refrain of the film: "Let's start over." This is May 1995, and two men, Lai-Yu Fai and Po-Wing, are making their way toward a place of improvisation—the world of tango—to challenge the possibilities of reinvention. Shifting from color to black and white, this first scene of the film is narrated by Lai-Yu Fai's voice-over: "Ho Po-Wing always says, 'Let's start over,' and it gets to me every time. We have been together for a while and broken up often. But when he says start over, I find myself back with him. We left Hong Kong to start over. We hit the road and reached Argentina."

Happy Together is a film about love, friendship, about two bodies seeking sensation, about translation and strangeness, about touching bodies moving toward multiplicity.[1] It is a film about gay men, about tango, about the impossibility of staying in one place, at one time. More than anything, it is a film that warns us not to accept the myth of the body's static encampments in time and space. This is a film where the bodies move, where they fight and make love, where they dance and suffer, where they encounter one another not *in* time and space, but *across* time and space. This is a film about the multiplicity not only of origins, but of beginnings and endings, the multiplicity of identity, of displacement, of encounter. This multiplicity—what I will later

19

call a certain politics of friendship—enables a re-reading through *Happy Together* of the manner in which bodies challenge the very idea of movement, of touch, of sensation.

When the body is figured simply as discursive, it is held in a place where it can signify but not sense: sense is not something than can easily be captured linguistically. As Brian Massumi writes, "Sensation is utterly redundant to [signifying gestures'] description. Or worse, it is destructive to it, because it appeals to an unmediated experience" (2002a, 2). Too often, when we speak of sensation, we stop the movement of the body. This happens because we have delineated the body as a signifying subject in language. In and of itself, this is not a problem. The issue is, however, that when we position the body to signify only discursively, we often stop its movement, placing it on a grid from whence we render it intelligible. But sensation cannot be stopped, and this is the reason it is difficult to render sensation within a linguistic signifying system. To sense, we must cut through time and space, moving, challenging both semantic and geographical boundaries. Sensation is not a coding of bodies. When we sense we are not producing a map that will lead us back to an "origin."

In *Happy Together*, Wong Kar Wai produces an uneasy map of bodies sensing across time and space. In the work that follows, I explore the potential of sensation to produce what I will call a politics of friendship, a politics of touch that reaches toward an other in a movement of desire. Wong Kar Wai's film enables this dialogue between sensation and friendship, between movement and multiplicity, by refuting all easy engagements with the issues it frames: migration, sexuality, movement, tourism, belonging, home. There will be no easy return, in Wong Kar Wai's *Happy Together*, to an original myth of homosexuality, an original begetting of Asian beginnings crossing into the mythologized passions of the tango. What we will locate instead are multiplicities that challenge these very categories by exposing the body not as a point on the grid of experience, but as an experience, a sensation, that *creates* the chronotopes through which it navigates.

Happy Together is haunted, from the outset, with the impossibility of reaching the Iguazu Falls, the ideal tourist journey. In the first scenes of the film, we watch as Po-Wing and Lai-Yu Fai lose their way, unable to make it to this tourist destination. There will be no idyllic reaching of the falls for these two Asian tourists who recognize already, in their buying of a lamp that mimics the movement of the Iguazu Falls, that the falls exist only as pre-packaged gadgets in stores catering to tourists. Always already recognizant—despite the fact that they as yet have no vocabulary for this gathering of time and space—of the challenges of attempting to "enter" time and space rather than creating it, Lai-Yu Fai and Po-Wing hesitantly accept for the moment that the closest they will get to this idyllic rendering of Argentinean nature romance will be through the supremely tacky lamp they buy on their way. In this lamp where the falls are reproduced, they see pictured their dream of new beginnings infinitely produced for the pleasure and consumption of the tourist trade. In this lamp, they see not bodies in movement but a replicated instance of static repetition, a dream of renewed beginnings of perfect symmetry.

"Here we had no idea where to go," says Lai-Yu Fai in a voice-over, the image in black and white. "Then Po-Wing bought a lamp. I really liked it. We wanted to find this waterfall and finally we learned it is at Iguazu. We wanted to go home after it, but we lost our way." Losing one's way becomes the metaphor of *Happy Together*, and with it comes the stark realization that "starting over" provokes a loss of footing, the impossibility of finally locating the body in a pre-ordained time and space.[2] There will be no "going home" for Lai-Yu Fai and Po-Wing because, already, home has become the ever-falling Iguazu that remains unreachable. What is within reach is a multiplicity of sensations that will lead Po-Wing and Lai-Yu Fai both together and apart, that will challenge the bonds of their friendship and their love, and relocate both Hong Kong and Argentina within the maps constructed by their desiring bodies moving in and across time and space. "We never did find out where we were that day," continues Lai-Yu Fai in voice-over. "He always said days with me were boring, that we should end it, that one day we might start over."

"Starting over" for Lai-Yu Fai and Po-Wing is a complex entwinement of the limits of friendship and love, of distance and desire, of treachery and betrayal, since "starting over" does imply locating the place of the beginning. If we seek beginnings, we will always find ourselves—as Lai-Yu Fai and Po-Wing do—at the tremulous intersection between friendship and fraternity, between identity and nationalism, between stagnant homosexualized bodies seeking the ultimate experience of "together-ness." This is the challenge expressed in the film, a challenge wherein the body both yearns for and resists a straitjacket of belonging (in terms of gender, sex, nation) that would monopolize this life either as deviant or unique. This is not a film "about" homosexuality and its relation to the specificities of "home." It is a film that questions the very premise that to speak of homosexuality would be any different than speaking of any other desire across time and space. It is a film that cries out for a different way of thinking love, be it in the name of home, of encounter, of experience.

There is nothing unique in this relation between Po-Wing and Fai of friendship and love and yet it is absolutely singular. It is a relation like all others and a relation that plays itself out in the specific creative dimensions available to these two homosexuals from Hong Kong living in Buenos Aires, a relation that seeks its bearings in the space-time between two moving bodies who desire to move in rhythm with a world that challenges this very idea of motion. This is a contradictory desire that produces a friendship at once homesick for an impossible fraternity (of home, love, friendship) yet aware, ultimately, that fraternity can be nothing but the erasure of the multiplicity which both men seek, in their very different ways. Via this contradiction, a politics of friendship is evoked in *Happy Together,* a politics of sensation that is not arrived to but toward, which each character hesitantly moves while trying to re-locate himself in a space-time that calls for continued movement and re-positioning.

"Why would the friend be *like* a brother?" asks Derrida. "Let us dream of a friendship which goes beyond this proximity of the congeneric double, beyond parenthood..." (1997, viii). Friendship that might be worthy of the name, that is, a politics of friendship, would be a movement of desire that cannot be symbolized through a coding in a fraternal nationalism. It would be a friendship of and toward sensation, a friendship toward the multiple movements of an other. Not a friendship toward establishing identities of coupling, identities of nationhood and belonging, but a friendship that is always starting over, with all the complexities of a process that can never quite begin nor end. This is not a straightforward friendship, not an easy friendship, not a friendship of ease. It is a friendship that carries as its impossible memento the lit image of unreachable waterfalls of touristy romance, the impossibility of definitively locating one's-self, either here or there.

A politics of friendship is an unfolding of the space of the crossing, of the gaps between the positions of the grid. Such a politics senses an other, touches an other, rather than simply locating (and imprisoning) an other within its grids of intelligibility. This is not an encounter first mediated by linguistic significance: there is no "signification" which precedes sensation. This is a sensed encounter, an encounter experienced through the body, where it is the body that calls forth the politics and not vice versa. "When a body is in motion," writes Massumi, "it does not coincide with itself. It co-incides with its own transition: its own variation.... In motion, a body is an immediate, unfolding relation to its own nonpresent potential to vary" (2002a, 4). Bodies in movement always reach toward one another, hence the dream of "starting over." Touch is always a process we must begin anew.

One of the richnesses of Wong Kar Wai's *Happy Together* is the lack of simplification in relating this friendship and love affair between the two men, both of whom find themselves caught between the need to re-create themselves and the temptation to believe in the lamp's story of make-believe. While Fai intellectualizes the process, ultimately accepting the "return" home as his way of facing the inevitable loss of the "ideal," Po-Wing does not succumb either to his dream of the ideal nor to his incessant desire to "start over." This is not a story of simple beginnings and endings, but a story of multiplicitous yearnings toward love in and across both time and space. It is a story about the incommensurability of Buenos Aires and Hong Kong, of the inevitability of difference in friendship and in love, of the unevenness of translation in and between cultures, of the redundant desire to start things anew. It is a film about silences, about the inability to put suffering into words, and about the surprises of friendship with those we might meet along the way never to see them again upon our return to the places we thought of as our beginnings.

Happy Together is not a democratic film, if we understand democracy as a fraternization between those of similar strands of identity. There is no ultimate commonality, either in the representation of Buenos Aires, nor in that of Hong Kong. In both places, the decentering of commonality takes precedence, whether in the image of Asian boys playing European football in the streets of Buenos Aires or in the upside-down images of Hong Kong. The world has fallen on its head, and with it a politics of fraternization we have come to understand as "the democratic." What is at stake here is something different, an operation that seeks not to recognize the "friendship/democracy" (the fraternity) at hand, but the creation, the production of the possibility of friendship under another name. This politics of friendship is an act rather than a state, it is a movement toward multiplicity that loves before being loved. As Derrida writes, "One must start with the friend-who-loved, not with the friend-who-is-loved, if one is to think friendship" (1997, 9).

This moving-toward friendship is not an abstract concept. It is in and of the body, it is a movement toward sensing an other, a movement where I reach out to touch you, acknowledging the implicit violence in my act of crossing time and space, an act that can never be present in position, but only in passing, an engagement of our bodies in their indeterminacy. This does not always imply a touching (indeed, touch would be more present in "love" than in most "friendships") but it does involve the *possibility* of touching an other in the here and now. Such a reaching-toward can only be considered a politics (in the proper sense of politics, that is, politics as an encounter with the unknowable) when it is carried out in an indeterminacy that is inseparable from the bodies in motion. I can only touch you in friendship when I allow my body to create a space-time for that friendship by moving indeterminately toward you. In friendship, my body is in passage. With your body, I accept the paradox of the body's incorporeal dimension: I acknowledge our bodies as sensations of movement, as touch, as the "points of indistinction between violence and the law" (Agamben 1998, 32). "Real, material, but incorporeal. Inseparable, coincident, but disjunct" (Massumi 2002a, 5).

This continuity of movement subverts any idea of a stable body, be it a body-politic or a fraternity, be it a national or a sexual identity. This continuity of movement produces, rather, a multiplication of space-times created in and by the bodies in movement, enabling a desire to keep reaching toward not *measure*, divided in the crossing, but toward a *rhythmic* multiplication of space-times. Any positionality in this process is not a stopping but a quality of the movement: the body never stops (desiring). The body moves toward desire as the friend reaches toward an other, this with the knowledge that I am always reaching toward the horizons of my death, of the death of our friendship. The friendship must always start anew, otherwise it is not a friendship but an imprisonment of the self as self-same. In a politics of friendship I cannot distinguish between self and other, I cannot position myself as the self-same: within this politics there is no other movement than the complexly reciprocal movement toward one-another, a movement that leads us in multiple directions, not always to an other toward whom I thought I was reaching. Friendship is political, in these instances, because it is multidirectional, because it does not decide in advance whom and how to touch.

Such friendship gives itself in its withdrawal, in the time it takes to touch. Touch involves a return, a return not to the self-same but to the body as it has shifted through the process of making time and space with an other. This is a politics of modification, a politics carried out through an other as much as with an other, a space-fullness that carries within itself the ineluctable inconsistencies inherent in the composition of timed spaces and spaced times. Friendship challenges linear displacements, offering itself not as a movement from here to there, but as a decision-*taking* process that reflects on everything that remains—and will always remain—to be decided. Friendship—a politics of friendship—inhabits the chronotope of the not-yet-decided through which bodies create them-selves. A politics of friendship is not a certain state, but a quality in and of movement, a "suspended indecision, the undecidable *qua* the time of reflection" (Derrida 1997, 15). Such a politics is a singular endeavor not to collapse an other into the same, but to bring forth the becoming-political of any reaching toward, the becoming-political as sensation, as decision, as choice. This is a politics in process where the question of democracy (of identity, citizenship, subjectivity) is re-posed not in a static manner, but in movement.

The qualities of the political in and through friendship are *ontogenetic*, that is, equal to emergence. They are not qualities derived in mediation, secondary to other primary qualities. Friendship, in this political sense, becomes the signifying field of all other political categories, be they those of gender, race, or sexual orientation, of identity, of multiplicity and territoriality. Here, as Massumi suggests, "passage precedes construction" (2002a, 8). Only afterwards does construction back-form its reality. Gridlocking occurs, but it is a positioning on the grid that continues to displace itself, a potential moving-off the grid, a process of grid-remaking that *can* interrupt the process of feeding back into static time and space. Ontogenesis here refers to the capacity to emerge, to invite a moving-off the grid that challenges stagnant organizations of signifying bodies. A politics that is ontogenetic is a politics that disturbs ontology, a politics that incites us to remember that ontology is always a process of re-placing the body on the grid. A politics of touch, if we consider that friendship always invites a certain touch, can be conceived as a process of de-forming the gridlock capacities of fraternization. By re-connecting (and dis-placing) the points of the grid, and by understanding motion not as something that occurs between two points but as that which creates those very points, we can begin to challenge static notions of identity and belonging.

In Buenos Aires, Fai takes a job as a doorman at a tango bar. While he works on the outskirts of the tango, Po-Wing plays on the inside, partaking of the multiple and contradictory strands of desire inside the tango bar. The tango, in *Happy Together*, is a local space of contradiction, at once a tourist trap (for busloads of Asians) and a local nightclub. It is a place to dance, to love, to fight, to desire, to be friends, a place at once startlingly heterosexual and calmly homosexual after hours. The tango bar featured in *Happy Together*—El Sur—is the nemesis of the Iguazu Falls as much as their reflection: tango functions both as the signifier of exoticism and of a transcultural movement of desire. Through an engagement with tango, *Happy Together* negotiates the complex webs of transnationalism. Tango is at once pictured as the exotic dance that travels so successfully from Buenos Aires to Asia and back, and as the dance that will always remain resolutely Argentinean. This paradox of tango—with Fai waiting outside and Po-Wing participating inside—is rendered in all of its complexity, leaving us not with a simple image of tango's Argentine-ness but with the recognition that we must continually be aware that our improvisations will invariably lead us to spaces we cannot yet envisage.

Tango always symbolizes a certain exoticization of an other, brought to bear through external imperial interventions. Even tango's early history— the fact that it was widely accepted in Argentina only after its adoption in Paris—calls forth this sense of its early imperialization. Yet, tango as an *improvised* encounter challenges this model of colonization/imperialism. Tango in *Happy Together* dances at these two extremes as a provocative example of the unclassifiable challenges of improvisation and the concurrent orchestration of cultural discourses under the mantle of the nation-state. *Happy Together* provides an unusually rich reading of this paradox, exposing the fact that gridlocking tango never actually succeeds, but it does leave some of us symbolically outside its mechanisms of exoticized unpredictability: not everyone can dance tango. This is apparent in a tango scene, where Po-Wing attempts to teach Fai to follow. Po-Wing tries to simplify the complex endeavor of creating a dance together by showing Fai the steps rather than leading them, thus deforming the improvised character of tango. This is no longer tango, but a mimicking of its displacements, a stabilizing of the improvisation, a "following" that is known in advance. There will be an improvised tango by Fai and Po-Wing, but it will only be danced much later, when it has become clear that there is no other possibility for the body to make con-tact with an other than through sensation. My body is not in movement when I still think I can predict my steps.

Tango Movements

The tango as it is portrayed in *Happy Together* is one of the most multi-faceted portrayals available on film today, interesting not only because of the complexity of its identification with the dance, but also because it challenges the roles of the leader and the follower, of the national and the transnational, of the homed and the unhomed. This (despite the rendering of an exoticized tango for consumption) is always-already inscribed in the (hi)story of the tango, a dance that has, from its beginnings, spanned the globe, gaining importance not as a dance located in Buenos Aires, but as a dance that travels.

Certainly, one might argue that Buenos Aires is one of its main points of origin, but tango itself resists so stridently the game of origins that even this is debatable.

Tango as we know it found its debut in the streets and bordellos of Buenos Aires, conceived largely by immigrants searching for a vocabulary to express their place-lessness in their new country. A music and dance born of many influences, including rhythms of Africa, Europe, and America, its music from Spain, Africa, the Caribbean, Italy, France, and Germany, it is a verb that means "to touch." No matter how we define the tango and its "origins,"[3] touch never strays from the importance of tango as an improvised encounter with an other as other. Nothing prepares us for this touch, no place, no time, no identity, no sexuality. Interestingly, this touch has remained relatively untouched by the rampant exoticization of tango's movements of desire. For touch as an improvised reaching-toward—a politics of touch—is not easily exoticized, especially if we consider exoticization to be a hierarchical classifying of an other. Touch cannot be subsumed to a single event: touch demands a re-accounting that would defy every such organizing within the grid-forming practices of sovereign signifying intelligibilities.

Through tango, we have a gripping story of the seductions of imperialism. In order for the dance to be appropriated, it had to become less the dance of touch, and more the choreographed dance of exotic associations with difference (difference understood here as the stable dichotomous presentation of the self-same). A focus on touch and its unpredictable reachings-toward would have been difficult to appropriate and exoticize without endangering the position of the usurper. Hence, what is generally emphasized in the story of tango is the eroticization of two bodies moving together rather than the improvisational touch necessary to this movement. The story of tango thus becomes halted within images more like that of Fai being taught his "follower's" steps, than the final image of *Happy Together* where Po-Wing dances with the man in the tango bar, continuously exchanging the roles of leader and follower.

What imperialism requires for its dissemination of power and control is not a politics of touch but a replication of the displacements which would de-politicize this very touch. Tango therefore becomes legendary not as a movement that is political but as one that is thoroughly depoliticized—the exoticized encounter with desire for consummation by busloads of tourists.[4]

In 1913, Lugones writes: "Tango is not a national dance, nor is the prostitution that conceives it" (in Savigliano 1995, 140). To appreciate tango as a transnational movement of desire, it is necessary to acknowledge its disputed beginnings, its contested origins, and its complicated presents. There have always been contestations where tango is concerned, be it the indignation of the Argentinean elite as a betrayed dignified class, or later the immigrants' disillusionment when the same upper class re-appropriates the tango as its own once it has been usurped by Paris. The story of tango is fraught with such appropriations, with stilted beginnings and truth-seeking nationalisms, with legitimate and illegitimate births and deaths. There is no "true" tango, be it that which is danced in Buenos Aires, or that which is danced in Finland, Nijmegen, Montreal, Berlin. Tango is an improvised movement—at its best and most challenging, a politics of touch—carrying within its sensory mechanisms the potential instantiation of a politics that might be called a politics of friendship. Tango is a challenge to fraternization as the maxim for democracy even while it is the dream of a nationally unified identity. Tango is all of these contradictory movements of desire.

The paradox at the heart of tango's practices of appropriation and dissemination is expressed in *El Diario*, an Argentinean newspaper, in the early part of the twentieth century: "If tango—already a *poor* representation . . . of the national being—was going to stand for Argentina, the Europeans could at least respect the authentic Argentinean practice" (in Savigliano 1995, 140). What we see in this story fraught with "inconsistencies" is a strategy in movement rather than a stable discourse. Interestingly, what is always cast aside in the appropriation of tango for consumption in an exoticized state (whether by Europeans, by Americans, by Asians or by the Argentines themselves) is the body. What is not considered is the body *as* the instability within this signifying system, the body in and as movement, the *bodies* touching, listening, engaging, responding. These multiple bodies are cast aside because they complicate the discourse of tango, because they cannot easily be located on either the grid of colonialism or imperialism, on the grids of intelligibility of nationalism or exoticization. Bodies, when they appear within the discourses of tango mobility, are cast not as conditions of emergence of tango but as re-conditionings of the emerged, where touch is conceptualized (if thought of at all) as a static process that can be calculated and disseminated within a stratified chronotope. Ironically, despite tango's exoticization as the true image of sensuality (and even sexuality), there is nothing erotic in this desire-less rendition of pre-fabricated tango.

Brian Massumi writes: "Conditions of emergence are one with becoming" (2002a, 10). The body is the condition of emergence of space, it is the "retroduction" (Massumi 2002a) of space-time in the crossings of bodies touching. It is the sensation in and of the space-times we create that remain intervals between our (un)touching bodies. Bodies here are productions, movements, initiating and re-troducing space-time. This is not space measured: "[m]easurement stops the movement in thought ... yielding space understood as a grid of determinate positions" (Massumi 2002a, 10). Space-time re-troduced could be thought as a becoming-body of touch, an engagement with processes already in motion. Body and object are no longer distinct, they ally in process, traversing space-time, re-creating themselves and/as space-time as/in movement. This is tango: an *event* in a politics of touch.

As a politics of touch, tango undermines all theories of coherence, rendering it inexplicable why certain areas of the world become tangoed and others less so. Tango moves, and through its displacements bodies are instantiated. Bodies are in motion, traversing each other, touching each other, listening or not listening to one-another. This is not an idyllic circumstance, it is a learned desire to be aware, awake, attentive to an other as an-other. It is a desire in movement, a desire to know the spaces our bodies create together, a desire to feel the touch, to share the space of touch, to inaugurate a politics of touch that must always start over. It is, largely, a badly paid proposition, an endless moving-in-circles, a walk-that-goes-nowhere, an encounter with the night when "those who do serious work" sleep, a silent moment of reciprocity with someone I will perhaps never meet again. It is therefore not its "usefulness" (in any economic sense of the term) that brings politics to tango, it is its touch, a touch that cannot be categorized, classified, organized, defined as anything but the moment-in-passing when I listen(ed) to you.

This touch is, in Massumi's words, a "miraculation." It is a sensation that "presents a directly disjunctive coinciding" doubled, always, by an other's sensation (2002a, 13). This movement with and toward an other is a doubling that does not assume my singularity but incorporates it to create an other body. Touch cannot take over my singularity (because my singularity is always more-than-one): this protects touch from assimilation or exoticization. In reciprocity — in movement — singularities proliferate. The multiplication of sensation that occurs in this movement of relation refutes strict measure: bodies are always more than one. Bodies fall apart as they fall together, in the interval. "Resonation [is] not on the walls [but] in the emptiness between them" (Massumi 2002a, 14). Bodies in touch resonate, caressing the fullnesses in-between, creating not distance or closeness but movement toward, always toward. This complex dynamic is an event that "remains in continuity with itself across it multiplication" (Massumi 2002a, 14).

Tango reverberates and echoes in the lives of two young Chinese men from Hong Kong who remain apprehensive but cannot resist the friendship and the love that grows and gets crushed between their two impatient bodies. "Seeing Ho Po-Wing again," says Lai-Yu Fai in voice-over, "I didn't want to 'start over' but return to Hong Kong." Staged as a situation of either-or, *Happy Together* places the friendship and love affair between Po-Wing and Lai-Yu Fai as an impediment to a return to the homeland. And indeed it is, if we consider the "homeland" as a place one could return to, unscathed, with the "home" always nostalgically unaltered. Buenos Aires here operates not as the "other" homeland, or even an other home, but as the constant reminder that "home" cannot be reached in any definitive sense. Worlds are intermixed, as in tango, lacking any definite points of departure we might want to call origins. Our bodies move, and in so doing, we create temporary places we can call home, but there can be no ultimate return that does not do violence to the multiplicities created in and through our bodies-in-motion. This is not a question of decision-making, but a question of emergence, for until we recognize that all homes are of our own making, we cannot decide to return there. We must recognize the emergent qualities of our bodies in motion to understand the ways in which we manufacture the homes of our dreams and our nightmares.

Lai-Yu Fai and Po-Wing seem tied, for the moment, to Buenos Aires. Not because of a desire to play out their romance on foreign soil, but in order to learn that there is no soil that is not, in an important sense, foreign: the soil we understand as "foreign" is also our creation, its foreignness an ally to the idyllic dreams of unity and self-constructed similarity/difference. Lai-Yu Fai and Po-Wing are startled to have to face this paradox between the homed and the unhomed, desperately anxious in the face of the realization that now nowhere will be "home" in the proper sense (as a unique place of belonging, a national identity, a closed space). "I wanted to go back but I didn't have any money," screams Fai. "You regret?" asks Po-Wing. "You fucking bet I do! I had no regrets until I met you, now my regrets could kill me. Why the fuck did you call me?" "I just wanted to be with you," responds Po-Wing. "Fuck!" screams Fai as he leaves, not even glancing back to Po-Wing who is lying in a fetal position, crying on the bed. This is a scene violent not only in its confrontation between the two men, but also in its realization that there is nowhere to turn now but to the choice of friendship, of incommensurability, of survival. There is no return to a place of origins.

Yet Fai and Po-Wing keep returning to one another. Not simply because they love each other, but because they still believe that their friendship and love can offer them a sense of refuge in a world that no longer promises beginnings and endings. A world characterized by movement, an engagement with ourselves and each other that is a politics of touch, this is not a world easy to navigate. It demands a constant awareness, a reciprocity in action and thought, a movement that can become terribly exhausting. It is easier to stop, to buy the lamp, to build walls to keep each other out, to speak of nations and national identity, to speak of difference as though it could be categorized, organized, located in its sameness. The world of move-ment (what other world is there?) is a dangerous world of incommensurable bodies-in-motion, of sensualities and sensings, of difficult friendships-in-process, of miraculation.

The inexplicable, the resonant, the emergent is what is at stake, and very little in the grids of intelligibility of our state-systems prepares us for this loss of ground. Yet, despite our best intentions to steer clear of the unknowable, we experience it, we live it, touching, dancing, reaching out toward an-other. This is the living contradiction of our temporary world-ings: we sense, we feel, and yet we grid-lock sense in the name of politics. Pol-itics defines itself in this grid-lock where potential—as politics-to-come—is long forgotten. For potential—according to the restraints of sovereign policymaking—is not economical, useful, securing. Indeed, potential is none of these things in and of themselves. Potential is violently relational, in-tensely productive, it is incipient action. Politics of touch are such politics of potential. A politics of touch, a politics of friendship, a movement toward an other, these are emergent political moments that call forth a plethora of sensations that guide the moment without casting it in stone. They are political precisely because they cannot be counted and redeemed as a politi-cal agenda that gives only certain stable bodies a voice. By continuing to confuse the stable with the political, by continuing to think potential only in the strictest of economic terms (where the individual always precedes the relation), by treating the body as simply an instance of the state-orchestrated body-politic, we continue to stabilize (and silence) the body of the political and to exoticize the instantiations of our touchings.

This is where tango comes in, not as a dance in which we must partake in order to recognize the workings of a politics of touch (that would be an exoticization of this rearticulation of the political), but as an example of one of the potential counter-movements of politics today. There are other examples, certainly, including the transgressions of time and space initiated by friends, lovers, and strangers every day. Tango is but a rich enunciation of what might be sought after by those who seek to transgress boundaries of self and other, immigrant and national, homed and homeless, by those who would like to resist the political stagnancy of state politics and inaugurate a politics that might begin to acknowledge (and sense) our bodies differently. Tango is often exoticized (both by those regarding from the outside and those dancing) precisely because it threatens the organizing of social and political locales that depend on national and state limits of identity and territory. This is why within nation-state vocabularies of identity and territory, tango will continue to be located as the Argentinean dance of national identity, as the stable rendition of passion and loss experienced by immigrants to Buenos Aires in the early twentieth century and embodied today by many Argentines, in particular the porteños of Buenos Aires.

But there are other stories, and these continuously leak out from under the nationalized mantle of tango, infringing on the tangos danced elsewhere (where the "elsewhere" also includes Buenos Aires), impinging on representations of national identity through dance, challenging bodies in movement with improvisations that exceed representations of national identity and cultural territoriality. These tangos challenge race, class, and gender/sexual distinctions without being tied down to an imaginary of national identity. These tangos acts as reminders that national identity is never more than a dream, personified by a lamp of the Iguazu Falls. Despite their pretenses to the contrary, discourses of identity and territory are not easy to maintain. Even our best intentions cannot silence the multiplicities within identity practices. This is apparent in tango, that double-edged sword that both places Buenos Aires on the map of the world and traces all of the lines of flight enabled and instantiated by its politics of touch. Tango is not satisfied by territoriality, just as touch is never a moment that can be encaged within a spatio-temporality. Tango depends on movement, on recordings that cross nations and continents, on improvisations that never make their way home, wherever that is.

Tango Friendships

The next time Lai-Yu Fai and Po-Wing meet, it is in a state of physical need. Po-Wing arrives at Fai's apartment bloody from a fight. Fai takes him to the hospital and then brings him home where he takes care of him. During this period of their relationship ("Some things I never told Ho Po-Wing," relates Fai in a later voice-over, "I didn't want him to recover too fast. Those were our happiest times together"), Po-Wing depends on Lai-Yu Fai in a different sense, and I believe it is this hierarchy of care that most puts into jeopardy their love and friendship. For, as Fai later admits, he relished this period of Po-Wing's dependence, and where there is dependence there are hierarchical nets of power that lead in the direction of a state-governed understanding of politics rather than towards a politics of friendship. There is no touch in this kind of care, not if care becomes entirely dependent on need. Care, a certain *Mitsorge* in the Heideggerian sense, must remain reciprocal, even in periods of greatest need, if desire and friendship are to be created. But, as these scenes in the film poignantly demonstrate, it is tempting, always, to engage in a relationship of dependence, particularly in an era in which the vocabularies of reciprocity with which we are most familiar are based on parameters of hierarchical positioning. We are given the tools, in a society of fraternity, to understand friendship within the terms of charity, not as a multiplicitous movement of desire that invents new bonds.

Po-Wing's state of dependence marks the end of the sexual relationship between the two men. Lai-Yu Fai makes a point of marking the separation clearly by setting up twin beds. Every time Po-Wing attempts to transgress this new territorial rule, Lai-Yu Fai condemns him, warning him that he will kick him out of the apartment if he misbehaves. Rules become homebound, spoken in Platonic vocabularies of belonging. Emotions are organized, calculated, specified, their locations gathered into perimeters that defy rampant and unpredictable desire. Po-Wing's familiar phrase, "Lai-Yu Fai, we could start over," uttered once more in the hospital, no longer carries with it the potential of the unknowable for Lai-Yu Fai. He no longer gives in to Po-Wing's unpredictability, preferring the imposed cadence of being his benefactor. Now, when Po-Wing utters the words, Fai doesn't even answer. In silence, the camera moves from the end of one bare hallway to the next, capturing them in black and white, at the end of one corridor, sitting side by side, facing nothing and no-one.

Po-Wing's infirmity leads to his imprisonment within Fai's domain. We watch as Fai prepares Po-Wing's bed, Po-Wing's head captured on the screen from behind the bed's cast-iron bars. Fai washes him. "Did you get to see the falls?" Po-Wing asks Fai. "No. Did you?" "I was waiting to go with you," Po-Wing responds. "We'll go when I'm better." "We'll see," answers Fai. This exchange signals a change occurring within Lai-Yu Fai, who is not yet able to give up Po-Wing, but already understands that the nostalgic dream of the falls is an impossibility in the world they have created. Ultimately, the hierarchical caretaking will lead them to the same place of nostalgic impossibility as the dream of the falls, but for the moment Fai only seems to understand the one impossibility and not the other. Both caretaking and touristic image-seeking are pursuits based in a discourse of the state, but for now only the more obvious of the two is apparent to Lai-Yu Fai.

The scenes that follow are all colored with the same paradox of the imprint of national vocabularies of belonging on a world that resists being fashioned strictly along territorial lines. Fai seeks an ultimate sense of belonging, which he can only achieve by imprisoning Po-Wing within his web of caretaking. Toward this end, he increases Po-Wing's dependence on him by stealing his passport and refusing to let him leave the apartment. Po-Wing, with his bandaged hands, somehow represents for Fai the lost home—as much the image of a lost love as of a lost nation: impossible, ungraspable, bandaged. Paradoxically, even as he is caged into Fai's bondage-house of deceit, it is Po-Wing, despite his faults (his lack of continuity in the friendship and love affair, his promiscuity), who finally teaches Fai the lesson that the home will remain ungraspable as a stable entity. He teaches Fai tango. However, this is not something Fai can learn, not yet. Lai-Yu Fai must retain the upper hand, but at an incredible loss, the loss of a friend and a lover, as well as the ultimate loss of the dream of home, though that doesn't sink in until much later.

Friendship that gives and takes time, friendship that survives the living present, is a movement of desire that depends on the unknowability of an other. What Fai tries to steal from Po-Wing is his freedom, but even in taking his passport, all Lai-Yu Fai actually manages to take from Po-Wing is his friendship. For freedom is not so transparent as to exist solely in appearances of dependency such as those of citizenship and infirmity. Freedom may be the opening toward friendship. Friendship is not about home, about identity, about ethnic similarity or cultural appurtenance. Friendship is that which retains unknowable potential because it remains other, unknown, of the present yet-to-come. The impossible schism between democracy (as it is lived within the state-system) and friendship thus becomes apparent: democracy cannot live up to its name without constraining friendship to fraternity. How can a politics of friendship and democracy be reconciled?[5] Derrida writes of this paradox: it is "tragically irreconcilable and forever wounding. The wound itself opens with the necessity of having to *count* one's friends, to count an other, in the economy of one's own, there where every other is altogether other. . . . But where every other is *equally* altogether other" (1997, 22).

If we understand the political as that which operates in the space of indistinction between friendship and democracy, in the interim space-time between alterity and counting, between the counted and the uncountable, we locate both friendship and democracy-to-come as a certain politics of touch. When friendship becomes a question of touch, a question of a politics of touch, we can situate friendship as that which must function in the "to-come," in the "perhaps," in Lai-Yu Fai's "we'll see" or in Po-Wing's "let's start over." But the perhaps is not all there is to friendship, nor is the perhaps, as such, enough for politics. What is also necessary is touch, a movement of desire toward an other, a re-engagement with sensing bodies in movement. This is why Fai's "we'll see" and Po-Wing's "let's start over" lead neither to a continued desire nor to a politics of friendship. It is not enough to want to return to the same. We must be willing to return to the not-yet-invented. Touch in its unpredictability and reciprocity—a rigorous politics of the unknowable—is necessary. Otherwise, both the "let's start over" and the "we'll see" are statements of elision, of lack of courage in speaking honestly about a future that is not to come, as is the case between Po-Wing and Lai-Yu Fai. What Wong Kar Wai signals via these transitory statements is the paradox of the perhaps, that is, the many processes of negotiation that occur in a world in which multiplicities invade the straightforwardness of closeted "identities." Po-Wing and Fai explore and challenge the bounds of friendship, love, and ultimately, politics. Their failure, in the case of their love affair, is their lack of con-tact, the impossibility of touch as creation.

With regard to friendship, Derrida writes: "The possibilization of the impossible possible must remain at one and the same time as undecidable—and therefore as decisive—as the future itself" (1997, 29). Friendship must be thought as an eruption in time and space, a rupture in movement, rather than a point on a grid. It is an interruption because it leads bodies in motion in new and unexpected directions, in a suspension that calls forth an other. Friendship is a movement of desire that threatens to make us lose our balance. It is a movement that eludes consistency while redefining this very concept. Friendship is a relation of permanence that defies the permanent, a presence that must remain an absence, an existence that grows bifurcated like a rhizome erupting at the frontiers of chance and necessity. Friendship is a politics of touch not because it incites us to touch, but because friendship knows no other way of *taking place* than in con-tact, in a placing of oneself into the space-time of an other, a reaching for an other's place, a touching of that place initiated in the process of reaching-out.

Friendship, as Derrida suggests, is a certain "telepoesis," a poetic reaching toward, that which speaks to and at a distance, a poetics of distance at one remove. Friendship is "an absolute acceleration in the spanning of space" (Derrida 1997, 32). Friendship is the miraculation of time and space. Friendship, at its most political, is the rethinking, the resensing of body, subjectivity, and social change in terms of movement, force, and violence. Friendship is sensing the body beyond the law ("where meaning carries a sentence," Massumi 2002a, 66), allowing the body to sense across the space that links my body to another. Friendship is locating singularity as that which positions itself within a topography of the always-already in a politics of emergence. Friendship is touch, if touch is conceived as the modification of timed-spaces and spaced-times. Friendship, the in-between (the space between friends) is not an effect of the always-already positioned but a creation of a reciprocal space of encounter where we reach out to gather space and curve time. In a politics of friendship, there is no reference to a pre-emergent singularity or subjectivity. Each singularity is created in and through friendship, each singularity is an embodied political instance of a becoming-touch.

The space of friendship, the in-between space of a politics-in-the-making of touch, has its own logical consistency. This space is not a post-original space, a filiative chronotope. It is, rather, a "being *of* the middle—the being of a relation" (Massumi 2002a, 70). This emergent space is not pre-constituted nor given in advance. It is the mode of sensation where potential is present in the perceiving body. It is the moment of reception of that which has been and continues to be in relation. This in-betweenness is the unknowable of that toward which I reach. This is a composite moment, a sensory experience where heterogeneity inhabits the multiplicitous spaces of the body and modifies that body. In fact, the in-betweenness *is* the body in the same sense as it *is* space, for the body knows nothing but its own movement, a positionality that can only ever be in relation to time and to space. In this sense, the body is the "event-dimension" of potential (Massumi 2002a, 76), the transportative dimension of the interrelation of body and world.

Multiple Movements of Desire

Desire cannot be captured, domesticated, housed, mortgaged, or nationalized. Desire does not belong to the state or to state-sanctioned practices. Desire, like touch, is a point of indistinction, an intransigent momentary reaching toward that is in excess of both violence and the law, even while it potentially reconstitutes them. "Desire is desire for the absolutely other" (Levinas 1969, 34). Desire is movement, it is the body in movement. How can there be movement without desire, when every desire implies a moving toward and any movement implies a desire to move? Desire is the potential toward positionality, if positionality is conceived as temporary, for desire never becomes encapsulated in a gridlock without losing its emergence. There is no desire that survives the grid. Desire is the unreachable in the effort to reach toward. Desire is the movement of intransigence necessary to the continuation of any movement, of all movements, and hence of all politics and all touch. A politics of touch is at once a politics of movement and a politics of desire. A politics of friendship, in turn, is a politics of touching desire in movement. Love, perhaps, is the extreme form of this kind of politics.

To think about the body is to think about desire in movement. Sensation is the embodiment of this desire. Desire exceeds the "meaning" of the body because it is continually in movement, in process toward the exploration of yet another desire. Desire is insatiable. Desire is the becoming of friendship, the field of potential for a sensory meeting between two bodies. Desire is their field of immanence.[6] Desire is not linear, but a constant re-organization of emergent chronotopes of time and space. As Massumi writes, "It is only by leaving history to reenter the immanence of the field of potential that change can occur" (2002a, 77). Change occurs within this immanence, this "perhaps" that is disconsolately dizzying and excruciatingly exciting. And it is this "perhaps" that continues to pull Po-Wing toward Fai despite the apparent closure of Fai's all-knowing "we'll see." This "perhaps" is configured, in Wong Kar Wei's *Happy Together*, as the tango.

If Fai's caretaking was an attempt to domesticate Po-Wing, it goes terribly wrong. This is apparent is Po-Wing's ultimate escape to the night world as well as in Po-Wing's response to Fai when Fai himself gets sick. Po-Wing does not want to be the caregiver. Certainly desire can survive and even flourish in a caring relationship, but when caregiving forgets reciprocity to instill a hierarchy of power, desire is left by the wayside: desire wants nothing to do with hierarchies of consumption and dependence. Hence, we are increasingly faced with a relationship between Fai and Po-Wing in which the asymmetry of desire and caretaking never quite allows them to come together. As Wong Kar Wai demonstrates, desire is slippery and is perhaps most challenged in situations of need and loss of footing. When Po-Wing is sick he seeks care through desire, and when Fai is sick, he seeks desire through care. A stinging example of this dynamic takes place when Fai lies shivering and sick in bed and Po-Wing complains that he hasn't eaten in two days and asks Fai to prepare some food. "Are you cold-blooded or what, asking a sick man to cook for you!" exclaims Fai as he gets up to serve Po-Wing.

So many mistakes and misunderstandings occur in *Happy Together,* not least of which is Fai's acceptance of the victimized position as cook and servant of Po-Wing. But desire is not silenced so easily, even now: it is in one of the following scenes that tango makes an entrance between the two men. This first and last tango—an ambiance that will return later in the film—seems to be a final attempt to evoke their bodies through an unpredictable movement of desire. Unfortunately, too much has been destroyed in this friendship to be able to salvage their love affair, though feelings of closeness seem to remain until the end. Tango's emergence is therefore true to its form: an emergence of the possibility of touch without return. As it is wont to do, tango makes no promises, especially not the promise of desire. Tango is about touch, which is about movement, which is about desire, but this is not a promise of possession or culmination: it remains a desire to move. Bodies in movement speak to one another as only bodies can, in and across space, promising nothing but this movement, this listening to a moment in space-time. It is essential to recall this when thinking of a politics of touch in order not to fall into the trap of attempting to domesticate either movement or desire through touch. Touch is temporary, it is an event, an invitation, and a response. Tango is but one instance of that reaching-toward.

The beginning of the tango scene has Po-Wing leading Lei-Yu Fai into a back step, neither one of them really listening to each other. In frustration, Po-Wing tells Fai to practice his "steps" alone (a sure sign that it is neither tango nor touch they are practicing at the moment). In the following scene, we cut to the sounds of Piazzola and the dock area of Buenos Aires and then return to the kitchen where Po-Wing and Fai hold each other, dancing something between an embrace and a tango, kissing. This sensual moment between the two men, something we have not experienced since the first scene of the film, frames, momentarily, the touch that has been missing since Po-Wing's hands were bandaged and Fai refused to touch him. This scene is a recalling at once of the desire of touch in love, in friendship, and our disconsolate ability to be in proximity without contact, without movement, without desire, without touch. This scene recalls the difference between friendship and fraternity.

Might we conceive of friendship as an improvised tango? What would a friendship be like that delineated clearly between the speaker and the listener? What would a friendship be that wanted to possess movement, stopping it in its tracks? Is a telepoesis not a calling forth of poetry at a distance, a withdrawing that produces an event, a coming-together in the reaching-

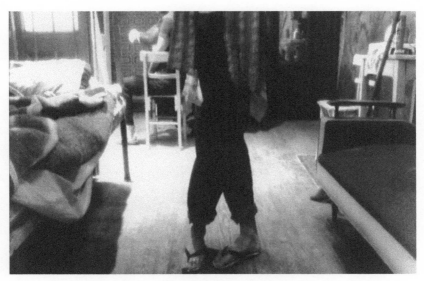

Fai crossing in *Happy Together* (Wong Kar Wai). Courtesy of Kino International; used with permission.

toward, a politics of touch sensed as a friendship which is not-yet? We must remember that telepoesis always calls forth the silences between words, between gestures, between steps, between friends. There is no friendship in the myth of full presence, as there is no touch without withdrawal, no tango without pauses. Politics, all politics must be patient with the absences, the intervals, the holes in the story. Reciprocity here is not the reciprocity of the same but a coming-together of difference, not a fusion but a con-fusion. For there is nothing more con-fusing than desire, nothing more uncertain than the "perhaps" that is to come.

Faced with this "perhaps," Po-Wing and Lai-Yu Fai eventually go their separate ways. Before their final leave-taking, we observe Fai on the phone in endless conversations with Po-Wing who we assume is waiting for him at home or in bars. We watch as Fai slowly pulls away from Po-Wing, looking at maps of Iguazu with a solo journey to the falls in mind, a journey he still thinks will eventually lead him "home." Home still figures in Lai-Yu Fai's vocabulary, even if it has become somewhat unmoored by his recent experiences in Buenos Aires. This desire for "home" is also present in Po-Wing's narrative, though we have no sense of home being somewhere in particular for him. He does want his passport back, but we do not know if it is for a

Fai and Po-Wing dancing in *Happy Together*. Courtesy of Kino International; used with permission.

return to Hong Kong or merely for the illusion that he once "belonged" somewhere. A relationship that has been framed by a tacky lamp is coming to an end.

Friendship is never far from enmity, according to Carl Schmitt. For Schmitt, the enemy is the figure at the heart of the political: losing the enemy would imply a loss of the political itself. In order to conjure the political, the enemy must be invented: "The specific political distinction, to which political actions and notions can be reduced, is the distinction *between* friend and enemy" (Schmitt 1996, 26). Friendship understood in these terms foregrounds opposition rather than emphasizing the figure of the one-more that qualifies the politics of friendship we have been discussing so far. Questioning this need for the enemy within a political understanding of friendship, Derrida asks: "Is there another thought of calculation and of number, another way of apprehending the universality of the singular which, without dooming politics to the incalculable, would still justify the old name of democracy?" (1997, 104). The question of the count, of the one more, is an essential question if we are to arrive at a reading and a writing of democracy that does not return to Schmitt's dichotomy, if we are to understand politics as that which is no longer necessarily constitutive of terms such as nation, state or citizen. For it is apparent that for Schmitt the question of friend and enemy cannot be thought separately from the state, and more particularly, the state of exception.

What I am seeking here is a friendship that cancels out a certain genealogy that depends on filiation, on fraternity, on national belonging: "to think and live a politics, a friendship, a justice which *begin* by breaking with their naturalness or their homogeneity, with their alleged place of origin" (Derrida 1997, 105). As Derrida suggests, "no deconstruction without democracy, no democracy without deconstruction" (1997, 105). Wong Kar Wai's *Happy Together* could be perceived as this kind of engagement, as a deconstruction of the idea of democracy achieved through the complication of the matters at its core: love, friendship, sexuality, touch, nation. The difficult challenge the film embraces is the very open-endedness necessary to think a democracy-to-come that would also be a friendship-to-come. Wong Kar Wai expresses these contradictions through a narrative of desire that ultimately "fails," if failure is understood here as the undoing of the dreams of the past. There is no happy ending for Lai-Yu Fai and Po-Wing. Yet something else is achieved in this processual space-time of becoming, and this is a certain openness to the challenges of friendship and bodies-in-motion.

This is expressed through the growing friendship between Fai and Chang initiated toward the end of the film. Chang brings a special quality to Fai, not touch, but hearing. The two men meet in the Chinese restaurant where they work. This new job of Lai-Yu Fai's is a rebellion against his position as an outsider in the tango bar. At least here, in the Chinese restaurant, we might surmise, he is amongst "his own kind." But there really is no such thing in Wong Kar Wai's films, and so what we encounter in this new place is not familiarity but simply another kind of difference. Chang observes Fai and takes over the voice-over of the film. The mood of the film is somber: in the previous scene we witnessed Fai lying on a barge on the river with shots of La Boca and the sad and complex music of Piazzola's "Zero Hour." The water in this scene is shot as though it were an endless highway, strangely reminiscent of the long stretch toward the not-yet-reached Iguazu Falls.

In the following scene, Fai is sick and Chang takes care of him, taking him home and putting him to bed. Too worn out to make an effort toward this new friendship, Fai listlessly accepts Chang's help. Over time, however, they do become closer, though Fai continues to find it difficult to confide in Chang. It is only at the end of the film that he finally takes the initiative to pursue this friendship, and by then, Chang is nowhere to be found. This is the challenge of the "perhaps," that moment of indeterminacy of the yet-to-come. If friendship (and here we could substitute the political) is a certain suspension in time and space, it is only in this portion of the film that we begin to take count of this suspension, a suspension arrived at through a focus on hearing. "I had an eye problem when I was little," Chang tells Fai. "But I never lost the habit of listening. You know, I think ears are more important than eyes. You can see better with your ears. You can pretend to be happy, but your voice can't lie." "Touch with your ears," Chang seems to be saying to Fai, for whom any contact at all has become too painful.

A friendship of hearing? Could we conceive of hearing as that which might lead us (if we listen carefully) to a notion of friendship that would circumvent the concept of hearth, of presence, of resemblance, affinity, analogy? Perhaps. An "aneconomic" friendship, to use Derrida's term (1997, 155). "I hear you!" we might joyously exclaim. "I am listening, finally." There is something to this, particularly if we return to tango as an analogy. Touching is always also a listening, a moving away from the economic (oikos) toward a condition of emergence that calls forth an improvisation of body, of movement, of sexuality, of friendship, of the political. Is the listening of which Chang speaks not an opening toward an other, an appealing to an other that calls an other in his or her retreat? I touch you to listen, I listen to you touch, I am in con-tact with you. I cannot touch you without listening to your response, without responding in turn. No touch (haphe, in Greek) without con-tact.

The final moment of contact between Chang and Lai-Yu Fai is poignant, expressed through the sense of hearing. Chang explains to Fai that he is on his way to Ushuaia, a place known as "the end of the world." There, the legend goes, people are invited to dump all their emotional problems. Since Chang does not like photographs, he asks Fai to leave a few words on his tape recorder as a memento, words he will then leave in Ushuaia. "Anything from your heart," Chang tells Fai as he moves away to dance. "Even say something sad. I'll carry it to the end of the world." "I'm not sad," Fai responds. "Something cheerful, then." For a long time, Fai holds the recorder to his mouth, sitting alone in the corner. Then he begins to cry, to sob, to throw up. He cannot speak, he cannot make contact. Chang leaves with the empty message. Lai-Yu Fai returns to hug him. "How is it we've become so close?" Lai-Yu Fai asks himself in a voice-over. "For a moment all I can hear is my own heart beating. Does he hear it too?" Through listening (even to his own silence, to his own heart beating), Fai has been touched, he has made con-tact.

Po-Wing and another man dancing in *Happy Together*. Courtesy of Kino International; used with permission.

Chang and Lei-Yu Fai's friendship is *unheimlich* (strange, uncanny, home-less) in a way Fai and Po-Wing's never was. Chang and Fai do not speak of "home." Instead they allow their friendship to lead them to "the end of the world." Within this *unheimlich* quality of unknowability, we sense a politics of touch not unlike the tango we experience, in the last scene of the film, danced by Po-Wing and another man in El Sur, a tango during which it is no longer visible who is leading and who is following. "The body of the friend," writes Derrida, "his body proper, could always become the body of an other. . . . outside all place or placeless, without family or familiarity, out-side of self . . . strange, but also 'a stranger to'" (1997, 177–78). The friend-ship emerging between Chang and Fai, an *unheimlich* friendship experi-enced only in the last moments of their "togetherness," is like the last tango danced in *Happy Together*. It is a friendship-to-come, an uncanny and strange friendship that does not bind them as individuals but instead allows them to sense one another, to listen, to hear, to touch, to make con-tact.

Theirs is a friendship of potential. It is a modification of space-time, a shifting between and through two bodies, a movement that evokes the in-betweenness that are bodies-in-motion. This latent friendship echoes later in the film when Lai-Yu Fai returns to Hong Kong via Taipei. Despite his separation from Chang, it feels as though their friendship has flourished.

What we begin to perceive, in this last section of the film, is the manner in which the body can become what Massumi calls a "sensible concept" through a politics of friendship. If perceptions are, as Massumi argues, always possible actions, what we experience in the final scenes of the film is the possible action of a friendship, a friendship as a possibility-to-come. And since there is no ideal beginning or end to a politics of friendship, we are faced with a vision of the "perhaps," framed, as it so often is, in Wong Kar Wai's haunting cinematography, through discordant and hesitant shots where self and other remain asymmetrical to themselves and to one-another. The camera refuses to name, to classify, to hold down. Instead, singularity is maintained, envisioned through a camera that remains curious, tentative, engaging.

Massumi suggests that "sensation is the registering of the multiplicity of potential connections in the singularity of a connection already under way. It is the direct experience of a more to the less of every perception.... [I]t is a limit of experience immanent to every step along the continuum" (2002a, 93). Sensation is multiplicitous, multi-identificatory, multifaceted. There is never linearity in sensation: we have all experienced the way a sound can lead to a smell, to a memory of a touch, to a taste. The senses combine, layered, infused into one into another. Sensation, this movement of reaching-toward, lies at the basis of a politics of friendship that would no longer be a dichotomous practice functioning as a democratic moment of filiation, but a composite event, an emergence that leaves our senses peaked. "Sensation is the point of co-conversion through which the variations of perception and thought play-out. It is the singular point where what unfolds is also unfolding" (Massumi 2002a, 94).

Left without Chang in Buenos Aires, Po-Wing no longer actively in his life, Lai-Yu Fai wanders the streets in search of human contact, finding himself, ultimately, in a gay bathhouse. Here, where the quiet partitioned spaces evince their loneliness, Fai realizes that he is no different from other lonely men: "I never liked hanging around in toilets," he says in a voice-over. "I thought it was dirty. I thought I was different. Turns out that lonely people are all the same." Po-Wing hovers in the shot. Isolation is embodied in this scene alongside (absent) desire and the craving for contact. Desire propels the body. Without desire, movement slows down and the body becomes heavy, limp, increasingly unreachable. Politics becomes masked behind need as initiative wanes. Touch becomes unthinkable. To touch, an initiative is necessary, and it is this initiative, so essential to love, to friendship, to politics, that Fai finds so impossible to envisage as he makes his way through the bathhouse. Even the blowjob he gives another man in the movie theater seems to be devoid of contact. Fai is hurt, sad, lost, and alone. It is this terrible alone-ness that incites him, once again, to reach for the specter of "home."

In response to his loneliness, Fai places a call to his father in Hong Kong, but the call does not go well. It seems his father has nothing to say. Fai is even further away from "home" than he thought. Lai-Yu Fai finally decides to assume his responsibility in his conflictual lure toward "home" and begins to write. This is a moment of initiative, a moment of con-tact that permits Fai to face the nostalgia he associates with "home." Yet, it quickly becomes apparent that he is not ready to allow "home" to become a transitive space rather than an intransigent locus of belonging. "Today is my day off," he says in the voice-over. "I want to send Father a Christmas card but it turns into a long letter. At home I didn't talk to him, now I want to tell him many things. I hope he'll give me a chance to start over." This time it is Fai who wants to start over. He doesn't seem to see the irony. In a following scene, when Po-Wing asks him over the phone to return his pass-port, Lai-Yu Fai responds in a voice-over: "I don't mind returning it. But I won't face him. I know what he'll say if I see him." Later, unable to sleep, Lai-Yu Fai imagines Hong Kong upside down.

Sensation turns our world upside down.

> Sensation is an extremity of perception. It is the immanent limit at which perception is eclipsed by a sheerness of experience, as yet unextended into analytically ordered, predictably reproducible, possible action. Sensation is a state in which action, perception, and thought are so intensely, performa-tively mixed that their in-mixing falls out of itself. Sensation is fallout from perception. (Massumi 2002a, 97–98)

Sensation's excessiveness is what Fai experiences in these lonely moments of upside-downness. These are moments when he perhaps realizes that Hong Kong will continue to be upside down, depending on the position from which one perceives it. There is no ultimate directionality, no ultimate positional-ity. There are simply moments, chaotic moments of sensation and choice, moments when we sense our political present through touch, through bodies in motion, through friendship, through writing. These are moments, as Massumi writes, in which "the world concretely appears" (2002a, 98), where we realize that *we* world our crossing of paths, the imbrication of rhyzomatic sensations, the texturing of writings. Sensation is an event. It creates spaces for experience as well as gaps, holes, emptinesses and losses. "Meaning" is not guaranteed.

A Last Tango

Finally, Lai-Yu Fai is on his way to Iguazu Falls, Piazzola playing in the background. The road is flat, uneventful. The shot frames Fai driving, shifting then to Po-Wing, in the very different setting of El Sur, dancing. The scene cuts to the kitchen tango between Po-Wing and Lai-Yu Fai, the images moving restlessly between the past and the present. In Buenos Aires, night falls as Po-Wing passes out on the cobblestones in front of the tango bar. Silence. It is midnight. We cut to Fai cleaning out the apartment, to longer night silences, to Fai losing himself in the lamp of the falls, crying, Piazzola playing once again in the background. "I finally reach Iguazu," says Lai-Yu Fai in the voice-over. "Suddenly, I think of Po-Wing. I feel very sad. I believe there should be two of us standing here." The falls are majestic, alive, caught by the lens of the camera in shades of blue, the camera itself wet from the mist and the drops of water in the air. This is a long, slow shot. Time is no longer of the essence. The bodies have shifted, creating a new time and space, a spaced-time, a timed-space.

Friendship is also loss, the multiplicity of singularities and the singularity of multiplicities, the impossibility of a future without a present. There is never a sole friend. Friendship cannot be calculated. This is politics, a politics of friendship: in politics, calculation cannot happen in advance. A politics of friendship is akin to what Derrida terms "destinerrancy," a movement without destination, a politics without end. A politics of friendship is about disagreement, about misunderstanding, about the necessity to listen in order to be heard in order to listen again. A politics of friendship is alive through the touch of an-other, embodying the insatiability of my need to reach out toward you, to touch your singularity, my difference, to make con-tact with you. "The crucial experience of the *perhaps*," writes Derrida, "imposed by the undecidable—that is to say, the condition of decision—is not a moment to be exceeded, forgotten or suppressed. It continues to constitute the decision as such . . ." (1997, 219). Response-ability carries within itself an ethics of contact, of response, a necessity to cross the space-time between me and you, even perhaps to do violence to space and time in order to be certain that movement is what is at stake. Without movement, there is no capacity to respond, to touch, to be a friend. How can I be responsive if I do not reach out toward you?

"Sensation," writes Massumi, "the substance of the body, is not the presence of the flesh in its envelope, but the presence in the flesh of an outside force of futurity" (2002a, 115). My body opens toward yours. Even without contact, there is no closure of the body, just a holding-in, a slowing down of the movement. In movement, I sense you, I alter the space that I cross between us, that you cross to reach me, I allow you to touch me, to make con-tact. "The body is opening itself to qualitative change, a modification of its very definition, by reopening its *relation* to things" (Massumi 2002a, 116). Sensation is the potential to invent, to invent the in-betweenness out of which my body, your body, moves, senses, and multiplies. Sensation reconnects the body, not to its-self, but to relation. Desire is one of the main ingredients of this re-cognition. I sense to desire, even if I do not necessarily desire to sense. I touch contact. Movement is not indexed to position, our positionality is our movement, our politics is our friendship, our touch is our politics.

Chang arrives at Ushuaia, at the lighthouse that is the end of his journey:

> July 1997. I finally arrive at the end of the world. I left Taipei because I hated home. I always have to serve at the stall. Actually, serving at the stall isn't so bad. I made a fool of myself. I feel very happy. I promised Fai to leave his sadness here. I don't know what he said that night. Maybe the recorder broke down. Nothing is on the tape. Only a couple of strange noises like someone sobbing.

The camera frames Chang, alone, on top of the world, the blue sky radiant behind and above him. Later, Chang searches for Fai in Buenos Aires, to no avail: "The night before I leave for Taipei, I come back to Buenos Aires. I want to say goodbye to Fai. Nobody knows where he is. I thought I'd hear his voice here. Maybe the music's too loud. I can't hear anything." Chang still tries to hear Fai, he believes contact is possible. And he's right: the next shot shows Fai in Taipei, searching for Chang.

Friendship is not a telos. Desire prevails as the moment of uncertainty whose gap in space and time we cherish, whose politics we acclaim as the point of departure, of disagreement, of sensation, of hope. "If man has friends," writes Derrida, "if he desires friends, it is because man thinks and thinks an other" (1997, 224). Friendship is human, it is of the world, it worlds. Friendship is political, it is a reminder that all thought, all sense, all touch, all language is for and toward an other. As Derrida writes, "there is thinking being—if, at least, thought must be thought of an other—only in friendship. . . . I think, therefore I am an other; I think, therefore I need an other (in order to think)" (1997, 224). Friendship is a movement of sensation, a politics of touch that challenges me to (mis)count myself as other. Friendship is a condition of emergence, it is where my senses lead me, it is the fold of experience out of which a certain politics is born. Friendship is a space of experience, "a topological hyperspace of transformation" (Massumi 2002, 184). Not a phenomenology, and certainly not a return "home."

Perhaps this is why Chang and Fai do not meet in Taipei. Their friendship—a friendship-to-come—is not about home, nor is it about "returning." "I don't know when I'll see Chang again," says Fai in the voice-over once he has arrived in Taipei on his way to Hong Kong. "What I know is, if I want to, I know where I can find him." Friendship turns the world upside down, subverting identities, transgressing nationalities. This is being "happy together." There is no "home" in this image, no certainty or predictability. It is not about Buenos Aires or about Hong Kong, it is about the movements in the space-times in-between. Is there a thought of democracy here? "It would therefore be a matter of thinking an alterity without hierarchical difference at the root of democracy," writes Derrida (1997, 232). Can being "happy together" in the sense Wong Kar Wai gives the notion be thought of as a certain agonistic democratic experience of difference? Can bodies in motion meet "democratically"? "This democracy," writes Derrida, "would free a certain interpretation of *equality* by removing it from the phallogocentric schema of *fraternity*" (1997, 232). A democracy without symmetry, an infinite alterity, a movement that invents divergent positionalities that converge, that make contact, that disperse?

Friendship is not given. If we accept this, can we not accept that neither is democracy a given? Can we not listen to one another disagree, instead of imposing consensus and thus silencing all others, even ourselves? A consensual democracy is nothing other than an act of exclusion. This is why the condition of possibility of democracy is at the same time the condition of impossibility of its full realization (Mouffe 1995, 36). "Democracy remains to come" writes Derrida. Democracy, like friendship, like the political, like touch, belongs to the chronotope of the "perhaps," in the present-to-come. There is no future for democracy, not if democracy is to be political, that is, reinvented, re-contacted, re-sensed. "Even when there is democracy," writes Derrida, "it never exists, it is never present, it remains the theme of a non-presentable concept" (1997, 306). A politics of touch exceeds democracy as it continues to be implemented, reminding us that democracy can never precede the movements of the body. Through movement we feel, we sense, and it is now, in con-tact with our reaching-toward, that we begin to listen, to engage, to concede, to disagree. This is democracy-to-come, a politics of sensing bodies in movement.

3.

Erring toward Experience: Violence and Touch

Might we conceive of touch as the original sin? In Genesis 3:3 (all citations from King James Version), God says to Adam and Eve: "But of the fruit of the tree which is in the midst of the garden . . . Ye shall not eat neither shall ye touch it, lest ye die." To eat the apple, to be seduced by the snake, these are the obvious sins, the sins that condemn humanity forevermore to exist in a fallen state. But what of touch? Why is touch—the moment of decision—forgotten, cast aside, ignored? Is it not touch, this decision, this responsibility toward fallenness, that in fact condemns Adam and Eve to face the world outside the garden of Eden?

To make a decision is a political event.[1] It is a moment of response-ability, a tempered instance of reaching-out, a touching of that which I do not yet know, a touching of an other in a reciprocal engagement with the unknowable. In the garden of Eden, the apple signifies all that is unknown. To touch, and then to eat the apple, is to make the decision to opt for the life of the earth over the life of the heavens. The touching of the apple is the violent entry into the political, if we conceive of the political as the moment of decision that engages us toward the world and therefore toward an other. Reaching out and touching the apple—opting for the finite instead of the infinite—is a violent decision because it implies a fall, a loss of ground, an unevenness between what can be imagined and what is beyond the scope of my experience. A certain violence takes place the moment I realize I must make a decision. A certain violence is omnipresent in the realization of the potential rupture between the endless vista of conformity heaven represents and the chaos of the world. The violent moment of decision in the touching of the apple is the moment when I realize that I have "fallen," that there is no longer a separation between self and other, between Adam and Eve and the rest of humanity. As Hent de Vries and Samuel Weber write, "violence" could no longer be considered simply to "befall" its victims from without, but rather would be related to what is generally presupposed to be its other: the "inviolate" self (1997, 2).

The Bible frames touch as both that which contaminates, "Or if a soul touch any unclean thing, whether it be a carcase of an unclean beast, or a carcase of unclean cattle, or the carcase of unclean creeping things, and if it be hidden from him; he also shall be unclean, and guilty" (Lev. 5:2), and that which heals, "And withersoever he entered, into villages, or cities, or country, they laid the sick in the streets and besought him that they might touch if it were but the border of his garment and as many as touched him were made whole" (Mark 6:56). In either case, touch represents a certain violence of transformation. Violence, here, is the suggestion not of a transcendental category, but of a rupture within humanity as humanity understands itself, a rupture that induces at once guilt and healing. For some, it appears, touch is the ultimate gift, for others, the certain demise into the filth of humanity.

Can I touch without violence? Can I think of transformation without being jolted by the violence of change? Can I even consider the reciprocal relationship that exists when I reach out to touch you (when I become other through touch) without being aware of the violence induced by my recognition of myself as other? As de Vries writes, "What would it mean to think of violence as an inescapable horizon or inherent potentiality of any act, or of any refraining from action?" (1997, 18). Is violence not intimately engaged in the historicization of the body, of Being as such? "Discourse," suggests de Vries, "whether infinite or not, whether ethical or not, demands some negotiation with its other—namely, violence—if it is to minimize the risk of allowing the worst violence to come to pass" (1997, 24). Must the discursive body, the body in movement that reaches out to touch, always also be a violent body, and if so, can we recognize violence not only as the harbinger of guilt but also of experience? For the apple is about experience, even if this experience is that of the "baseness" of humanity.

Could we suggest, then, that reaching out to touch an other is a moment of acknowledgment, a moment of recognition of the will not toward God but toward the earth? Might we conceive of touch as a reaching out toward the everyday, toward the textuality and the movement of our bodies, of our lives, of our diverse experiences on the earth? Touch is not, it seems to me, a bordered practice: we know our bodies to exist always outside of their skins, beyond our-selves, in excess of our three-dimensionality. It is not the body's spirituality that I am trying to evoke here, but the body's surplus, its sensations, its smells, its visions, its joys, its pain. We are these excessive bodies. Yet our history in the West is, at least according to Christianity, one of great repentance about this excessiveness. To atone, we must refrain, return the apple to the garden, withdraw the touch that seduces us, inciting us to continue to reach toward experience and debasement, desire and madness.

Touch is the articulation that continues to hold us, virtually, to the garden. In reaching out to you, I entice you to become a medium of expression. I ask you to participate. I invite you to experience. As my sensation translates itself to you, you immediately convey to me a response to this touch. This multidimensional movement of desire is violent, for it presupposes a certain demand, a decision, an instance of response-ability. This response charges your body with the potential seduction of wanting to re-embody itself with and alongside mine. There is no need for the creation of space-time in the garden of Eden. "Refrain!" screams God. For in each of these con-tacts, a new body is born, an articulation is taken into consideration, a bite of experience is consumed, and the risk of a loss of footing is guaranteed.

Touching—this articulation toward an other—therefore occurs in a general economy of violence. Derrida writes,

[T]here is no phrase which is indeterminate, that is, which does not pass through the violence of the concept. Violence appears with articulation. And the latter is opened by the ... circulation of Being. The very elocution of non-violent metaphysics is its first disavowal. (1978, 147–48)

This does not mean that it is violent in and of itself. What it means is that the risk of reaching out to touch you is an engagement in an ethicopolitical decision. This process of decision-"taking"[2] is always in negotiation with an economy of violence because it implies an articulation that is a rendering-other of myself. As Derrida writes, "Each little gesture of an other towards me obligates me to respond by sacrificing an other of an other, his or her... other gesture" (1995, 68). This response-ability toward an other is a demand of an other to return the gesture, for there is no such thing as touch without consequence. Touch induces a repetition, a response that is unique, since it is a reaching toward the unknowable. Touch is a reaching out toward the discursive silences and noises of the body, to the temptations of life on earth.

Now that the link between touch and violence is becoming more apparent, it is necessary to draw a map for violence and the political. It will then become possible to orchestrate a symphonic rendering of the link between touch and the political, a link which I believe will be useful in the rethinking of what it means to touch an other. Here, the political implies a relationship (in disagreement) with an other that calls for an important measure of difference and can assist in the creation of time and space. I would like to imagine creation of time and space in accordance with the notion that the body exceeds its own boundaries, making it impossible for us to draw a sensual body as a stable entity within time and space. Time and space here become excessive even to themselves, an echo of the multidimensionality of sensation, of difference, of overlapping reciprocities. I would like to suggest, also, that the violence that erupts through the many ruptures and transformations involved in the sensing, touching body can be conceived of as different from and more productive than the violence the state imposes onto the "stable" bodies of its citizens.

Within the vocabulary of nationalism and the nation-state, violence reigns as the constant signifier of (in)security. To evoke a discourse of security, the threat of violence must persist. Manichean thought attempts to resolve the issue of violence by associating violence with the other who is generally understood, within the vocabulary of the nation-state, as the adversary. The positing of the other as adversary results in a tendency to construe violence as the intrusion of the other who must remain outside the bounds of my territory (usually the nation-state). Violence is thus articulated as the violation of the self-same by an external intruder. If we consider the body as congruent with the national body-politic, we might be led to believe that any intrusion into the body would be a violence in and of itself (even the touch of a virus, for example). Yet it seems to me that this vocabulary short-changes the body. Is the body not in excess of this easy distinction between inside and outside? If so, might we not be suspicious of a political body that acts as such a stern guarantor of the limits of inclusion and exclusion?

Within the vocabulary of the nation-state, violence is not simply framed as the exclusive character of the other, but is even more powerfully conceived of as a means through which the self is constituted and maintained. Touch challenges this dichotomy, creating not a self and an other, but a third space, a reciprocal body-space that challenges the limits of both self and self as other. Touch refuses a simplified condensation of the encounter between you and me, refuses to speak only about the point of departure and the point of return. Touch grapples with the impossibility of fusion in the movement of desire that is directed toward you and, reciprocally, toward myself. The violence is not in the moment of apprehension (if touch is reciprocal, I cannot touch you "violently," that is, without your con-sent[3]), but in the decision to reach toward. The violence exists in the reaching out toward that which will remain unknowable. State violence, on the other hand, seems to rely on the pretense that the unknowable could simply be the unknown and therefore potentially conquerable through comprehension and domination.

God's warning regarding touch is a directive to resist the temptation of the unknowable. For there is a difference, in the Bible, between the injunction made through God not to touch given to the populace, which is always phrased in the conditional, "Then said Haggai, if one that is unclean by a dead body touch any of these, shall it be unclean. And the priests answered and said, It shall be unclean" (Hag. 2:13), and the act of touching perpetrated always by Jesus, which is phrased in the active tenses of the past, present, and future, "And the whole multitude sought to touch him: for there went virtue out of him, and healed them all" (Luke 6:19). It appears that the only one who is allowed to challenge the unknowable is the savior himself, the one who has been sent to heal us from the unknowable, the one who solves the mysteries of humanity through his miracles.

Might we then conceive of the touch of God himself, or the almost-touch we encounter on the ceiling of the Sistine Chapel, as the temptation to relay to God the unknowability of life on earth? In this scene between God and Adam, we recall the gesture of God's index finger reaching towards Adam's finger without ever quite touching it. Did Michelangelo, whose work evokes touch brought to life through sculpture, know something about touch and its virile potentiality that most biblical scholars and art historians continue to ignore? Was Michelangelo, with his image of the almost-touch, perhaps trying to relay to us the impossible violence of that first touch, a touch that causes the fall from grace, a touch which, had God reached Adam's finger, might have given God a real glimpse of humanity? For God cannot touch in this manner, that is, not if touch is a reciprocal act, since God, as he is conceptualized in the Bible, is the absolute other through whom every notion of alterity is transformed into the self-same and with whom reciprocity does not even come into play. God knows better than to touch: "God hath said, Ye shall not eat of it, neither shall ye touch it, lest ye die" (Gen. 3:3). For God, reciprocity is embodied in the very condition of touch: it is reciprocity above all that Adam must avoid if he is to resist humanity.

Marjorie O'Rourke Boyle writes:

> Aristotle erred in asserting that humans had hands because they were intel-
> ligent; Anaxagoras was, perhaps, more correct in stating that humans were
> intelligent because they had hands. (1998, xiii)

An interesting aspect of Michelangelo's image of Adam and God with fingers almost touching is that it is difficult to tell who is reaching toward whom. In this regard, the fresco symbolizes touch in its most transparent reciprocity. I cannot touch you without you touching me in return. I cannot feel your skin without you feeling me. This, it seems to me, is imprinted on the ceiling of the Sistine Chapel: Hands are dangerous, for in reaching toward an other, they can undermine the hierarchical opposition between self and other, reducing this exchange to a moment of sharing that potentially exceeds the two individuals, the two bodies in motion. These are transactional bodies, bodies engaged in the decision to touch or not to touch an other. Through touch, bodies are created. Is that why, in this particular case, the fingers do not touch? One interpretation would be that God does not decide to reach far enough toward Adam to actually touch him. Yet they are both reaching, meeting almost half-way, which might lead us to believe that there is something more at stake in the moment of unreachability between the Self-Same and the unknowable.

In the consensus of interpretation, what we witness in Michelangelo's scene of creation is God infusing life into Adam, finger to finger. Traditional interpretation does not privilege this moment as one of near touch, for, in much of this literature, touch is conceived of as the sense that pertains not to the soul, but to matter, hence a sensation that would have no place in the realm of God. In addition, as we have seen in the Bible, hands are not instruments of deification (except when used by Jesus) but of degradation and hence not generally associated with God himself. This tradition is carried through in Aristotle's work, in which touch is theorized as the sense of the earthly, a sense foreign to God's otherworldliness. Indeed, as art historians have pointed out, if God chose to bestow his touch upon humanity, it was much more common for God to touch the male figure's head, shoulder, or chest rather than his finger or hand. And if, by chance, touch were associated with God through the figure of the hand, it is not the index finger that traditionally would take precedence, but the thumb, for the thumb denoted the sovereignty of the creator, designated since Hippocratic medicine "the great finger."

What are God and Adam's index fingers reaching toward, if not the touch of an other? Perhaps one of the things taking place on this remarkable ceiling is the realization of the earthly impossibility of touching God. Perhaps there is, in this exchange between fingers that do not meet, a suspicion of the violence necessary for their meeting, the violence that would challenge the sovereign God to actually touch the chaotic masses who themselves have taken the risk to reach toward the unknowable and who are continually transformed through this contact with the body-in-metamorphosis. Is it possible that these index fingers reaching toward one another connote a larger and more explicit act of reaching-toward, symbolized through the hand? Indeed, in Renaissance art the hand was often conceived of as a metonym for the human body. In fact, the thumb (*pollex*, derived from the verb *polleo*) continues to be connected to the notion of political rule, symbolizing strength, power, and potency.

Something is on the verge of being created on Michelangelo's ceiling. Seductively, erotically, majestically, bodies are reaching toward one another, producing the potential violence of con-tact. What is this violence of the almost-touch? Could we concur with Nietzsche's suspicion that violence is not embodied by an other but is, rather, the medium that enables conceptualization itself?

Arrestation and the provocation—the reaching out toward and the touching of an other—exist in an economy of violence. Violence never befalls innocence. This is perhaps the point. The traditional biblical text would like to associate Adam and Eve to an innocence that is sullied by the experience gained through the act of touching, and then ingesting, the apple. But this claim of innocence is itself a violence, for there is no text that is not always already written and therefore implicated in the violence of transformation. Adam's "innocence" before God's extended finger is a discursive innocence idealized to prevent us from acknowledging that to enforce a dichotomy between touch and innocence would be paramount to suggesting that our bodies exist as separate entities from our senses. There is no body without touch, as medical officials are quick to point out: a child left untouched is often a child left to die. Why this pretense, then, that Adam's state before the Fall is one of "untouchability" in the face of God? And why, once again, God's finger extended toward Adam's in Michelangelo's fresco?

Perhaps because Michelangelo, the artist who sought more than many others to arouse the human imagination to the sense of touch, displaying in his many sculptures the tactile sensuality essential in modeling the human body—could not conceive of a relationship between God and Adam that didn't begin with touch. Perhaps because it is time to consider the violence—the eruption of adjacent space-times—created by that touch that has been neglected, the touch necessary for a broader understanding of the manner in which we interrelate and invent the politics by which we live and die.

For Derrida, violence is equivalent to the operation of the trace (1974, 101). The violence referred to here is not the violence that differentiates good and evil, the violence of the loss of innocence and the Fall. Violence understood in Derridean terms is not something that supervenes upon innocence to surprise it. Derrida asks: "Is there an experience, and, above all, a language, scientific or not, that one can call alien at once to writing and to violence?" (1974, 127). The supposition here is that any act between self and other will be textualized, made into a writing, and this making, this very writing, is a violent act. Can one say the same for sensual experiences? Can I suggest that touch, as a movement of desire toward an other, is also a violent writing of the relationship between self and other? Touch inaugurates a violence since it compels us to write the relationship between self and other differently. Does this not imply that any attempt to touch the political is to engage violently with the discourse of politics? I believe that when I reach out to touch you, when you and I create a space-time for our bodies to react reciprocally, we make the decision to acknowledge a certain kind of violence. This violence which I encounter in my desire to touch you is not necessarily a violence toward you or toward the spaced time we create through our touch. This violence is symbolized through the entry into the realm of unknowability. "There is no ethics without the presence of an other, but also, and consequently, without absence, dissimulation, detour, difference, writing. A violent opening" (Derrida 1974, 139).[4]

Critiques of violence are not without violence. My exploration of a politics of touch is a potentially violent encounter with the unknowable. This is not a (potential) violence I want to condemn. If we think of a violence that moves in more than one direction—a violence quite different from that sustained within the hierarchical system of sovereignty and security ordained by the nation-state—violence need not necessarily be considered a threat to difference. Rather, violence can work as a reminder of that very difference that prevents me from being subsumed into the self-same. Violence can be a manner of writing a body that defies the imposition of stability, that challenges space and time through its sensuality. The body, seen as a potential site of a violence of touch can be conceived of as an exfoliation in the sense José Gil gives the term. The body exfoliates by always already unfolding into the spaces it occupies (1998, ix). This is a state of violence insomuch as it is an infralanguage that speaks through and across the body, creating multiplicities and discontinuities both in my living, sensing body, and in yours, when I reach out toward you.

The exfoliant body that reaches across time and space embodies a violence in its resistance to conform to corporeal expressivity, to the signs and codes that are immediately understood as the space and time a body should occupy within the (national) body-politic. When I touch you, what I cannot know is what infra(sensual)language our reciprocal touch will create. Nor can I predict how my touching you will provoke spaced times and timed spaces. Of course, I can never predict the body "itself" either (since there is no such thing as the body always already whole), hence the state's continual imposition of the "national body-politic" to establish a normative vocabulary of the body to which we agree to conform. Without a stable body there can be no body-politic, and without a body-politic, bodies will not conform, proclaims the state. What touch achieves in opposition to this state-centered dynamic of the body-politic is the potentiality to apprehend bodies not as containers of preordained individual significations, but as orbs continually readjusting themselves to the infralanguages and movements of desire through which they interact.

When I touch you, I confuse the codes of our encounter by altering the space-time between you and me. I also alter something else, a quality difficult to delineate. Touch is first and foremost a sensation, a manner of incorporating the world, of embodying the actuality (and virtuality) of an other. Whether I touch my body or yours, I am reaching out toward you beyond a language of comprehension. I cannot predict the effect on my skin, since I cannot know your reaction to my touch and vice versa. This is what makes touch so difficult to embody comprehensively, what makes touch ungraspable and indefinable in and of itself. There is no touch that does not reach out. And there are no sign-systems that can completely guarantee that the space I cross to touch you will remain the same after that crossing. Touch is the embodiment of a sense that acquiesces to the unchartable qualities of a body in motion.

Gil suggests that of all languages, it is only articulated language that fully realizes the code of translation: "Because it is a metalanguage, it can handle all the codes, create metaphors, move from one domain to an other; assemble them and pull them apart" (1998, 5). Body "language" does not operate as a metalanguage, however: "the body does not speak, it makes speech" (1998, 5). Sensing, the body responds to various strata and textures of articulation and gesture, incorporating and excreting the myriad incongruities of any encounter, be it sensual and/or textual, with an other. It is therefore a fallacy to consider the body linguistically without acknowledging the complex layering of the senses, for the body is, first and foremost, a sensual apparatus of movement toward the world, a sensing body-in-motion that worlds. This is not to undermine the importance of a textual language of gesture, or of a "grammar" of the body, but rather to underscore the importance of conceiving the body *as* movement.

If the body cannot be reduced to a language, how can we speak of the body? How can we articulate touch as a mechanism in and of the body? How can we locate the importance of the concept of touch for the political? And, ultimately, how can we disentangle the body from the straitjacket of the nationally and state-sanctioned body-politic? Perhaps we can begin by suggesting that space is "modeled" by the body itself (Gil 1998, 17). If space is no longer something the body "inhabits," where space is conceived of as a pre-made container for the body, we can begin to think of the body as a mechanism for reaching out across and instantiating time and space. As Gil writes,

> bodily movements impress in space the traces of essential corporeal form, and create configurations there (in the relation between things) for which the matrices and lineaments are made up from the morphogenetic forms and possibilities of the body. (1998, 17)

It is not a question of thinking of the body that touches (as two separate movements) but of the body as touch. If my body *is* touch, and both touch and movement signal a displacement toward an other, I can begin to conceive of my body as that which produces the spaces for its movements of desire. My body spatializes space insofar as my body remains alive to touch. The space inhabited by my body becomes the space of my body. When I touch you, I not only incite you to a reciprocity, I create space with you.

The space that is the body is not a stable, continuous space. It is a space hardened by lack of contact, awakened by the surprise of touch, a space alive with the incompleteness of its spacing (*espacement*). The body is a space and touch is its articulation. Touch articulates the body, giving it a language through which it can begin to feel the world. The skin is a limit for touch, yet this limit is as finite and as infinite as the multiplicity of skins that make up the world. Touch embodies difference: through touch I ascertain the difference between bodies and surfaces. This *espacement* that marks the difference between spaces introduces my body to a becoming-space of time and a becoming-time of space. This becoming is the constitution of a subjectivity that is in movement, a subjectification that is formed within the tactile hollows of difference.

According to Gil, "Exfoliation is the essential way a body 'turns onto' things, onto objective space, onto living things" (1998, 21). Touch might be considered one method of exfoliating the body, since touch crosses space via the body, creating a becoming-body while establishing diverse relations with all that surrounds our bodies. The desire to cross space—to touch an other—is a desire in movement as well as a movement of desire. This investment of desire resignifies the space that separates me from you, awakening my body to the different sensations your body evokes in me. Together, we manifest new sensations as touch expands to an infinity of combinations of skin upon skin, body toward body. This connection of touch that traverses time and space establishes a relation that in turn affects the form and space of all bodies including the "body-politic," inviting the body as embodiment of a diverging chronotope to become other to that of the nation-state's solitary spaces of confinement.

This negotiation of space is a political event. Its politics are in contradiction with a linear and bounded conception of space-time proposed by state sovereignty. A politics of touch does not adhere to the notion of a strict interiority and exteriority. Rather, it expands the chronotope of the body through a qualitative expansion of exfoliations and surfaces. The decoding process is no longer one made in a vertical relationship between the sovereign and the citizen, or the national and the refugee. There is no decoding process as such. There are experiences, events, that operate in and through the spacings of the body: a listening, a seeing, a tasting, a smelling of the senses of the body through touch, a providential integration of one surface into another only to realize that these singularities cannot be meshed but must instead stand alone, side by side, in the third space they create together. What emerges through touch is not a decoding but a qualitative translation of time and space as regards the body, a transformation of space into spaced-time, timed-space. As Gil writes, the decoding-body gathers up, brings together, unites, dislocates, spreads, and separates thanks to the spatial forms that contain in themselves (because they bring about) the properties of unification and division. (1998, 24)

Means without an End

The body as a sensory modality engages with an other through a touch that exudes potential violence in its desire to transform the space between self and other. What differentiates this from the national body-politic's organization of the body is the fact that touch as a reaching-toward is a means without an end. There is no final destination where touch is concerned. In fact, there is no self or other as such. The body is the intermediary through which I create, with you, the shared space of our touch, our subjectivity-in-process. Touch as a reaching toward is a gesture of *espacement,* an instance of the inexorable violence of difference, of the unknowable. Touch is a movement toward an other through which I re-cognize myself differently, spacing time as I time space.

My gesture toward you is a momentary one. There is no touch that can last beyond the first moment of contact. To touch longer, I must touch again: as my focus shifts elsewhere, my skin soon forgets to acknowledge yours. To touch me you must return the touch to and from yourself in an ongoing process of exchange. Because it is temporary and immediate, the gesture is never more than momentary. This is a political moment in the most ethical sense, for it demands a continual re-articulation rather than a subsuming into the same. If I attempt to subsume you through touch, I will not reach you. Instead, I will inflict the worst kind of violence upon your body: your body will act only as the recipient of my directionality. Your body will become prey. If, instead, I acknowledge the ephemerality of the gesture, I risk an opening toward "the sphere of *ethos* of the most proper sphere of that which is human" (Agamben 2000, 57).

The moment of touch as reaching-toward is a rare moment when the political and the ethical exist side by side. It is rare not only because it happens seldom, but also because it is haphazard, momentary, ephemeral. It is an ethico-politics in deconstruction that briefly resists security, stability, classification. This ethico-politics, violent as it may be (since it is always the result of "taking" a decision), releases us momentarily from the border-making dynamic of the state apparatus that, if it were to contend with touch as a means of codifying the body-politic, would make an attempt to imprison this newly created third space within its grids of intelligibility. It is this ethico-politics that I am attempting to put my finger on, an ethico-politics that is, by necessity, always slightly out of reach.

Touch, as an ethico-political moment, breaks with the false alternative between ends and means that paralyzes both the ethical and the political within the matrix of regimes of state-imposed territoriality. The mediality of touch is nothing more than a process made visible, a process geared toward the creation and dissemination of my body through the reciprocity of your body, not as an entity as such but as a potentiality. Because touch makes the means of reaching out visible, it can be envisioned as a counterpart to a political moment of encounter, a moment in which there is an emergence of the being-in-mediality of humanity. This moment is ethical not because of the intentions of the one who reaches toward, but because the reaching does not assume anything beyond the intermediacy of a response, that is, beyond the creation of a third space. Even if I pull back and do not quite reach you, I have already altered the space that modulates our bodies-in-relation. The gesture that is touch, whether it reaches you or not, becomes the communication of a communicability. This gesture does not speak in sentences, it speaks the body, reminding us that our skins are always in movement through time and space, shedding themselves, shedding our-selves.

The encoding of information through the body's sense organs is achieved through a relation between body and the environment. Sensory perceptions depend on the world meeting the body as the body becomes world. The senses translate the body not as the individual but as the relational exchange between worlds and bodies. As Gil writes, "[t]he exfoliations of the space of the body, as abstract forms, integrate the information coming from a perceivable body and make possible its translation into a different object belonging to a different sensual sphere" (1998, 25). The exfoliations of touch on the variegated surfaces of the body as space-time result in the disappearance of the One and the appearance of a singular difference in motion that forever deconstructs itself. Exfoliating, the body dissolves into space, becomes space, re-emerges as space.

This is the metamorphosis of the body of which José Gil speaks, a "condition of the activity of code translation: each exfoliation is the metamorphosis of all an other forms in a spatial *one*" (1998, 38). One is the space of relation: there is no unified body. There are skins, receptive surfaces, gestural movements, desires toward an other. The body is active potential, not tautology.

Aristotle observes throughout his writings that the most common primary perception is touch. Touch, Aristotle suggests, is necessary to the other

senses. The medium that corresponds to touch, according to Aristotle, is the
flesh, and the element of touch is the earth. Aristotle somewhat complicates
this understanding of touch by suggesting that the organ of touch "must be
inside us" (1961, 11, 423b). The invisibility of the organ that represents
touch leads Aristotle to ask himself whether touch is one sense or several.
For Aristotle, touch is the first sense, the one most necessary for the maintenance of life: "The well-developed sense of touch is the condition of man's
intelligence" (1961, 9). Touch for Aristotle is the sense one cannot live without, the sense that human beings have just for the sake of being, whereas
other senses, Aristotle suggests, "we have for the sake of *well-being*" (1961, 13).
Touch for Aristotle is the "common sense," not something above, higher
than the separate senses, but their common nature.

Touch as the "common sense" draws us back to the political realm of the
state's *res publica* and its consensus-based practices of inclusion and exclusion. It recalls also the uncanny shift between con-sent and consensus, as it
is usually defined. "Common sense" in the Aristotelian sense is closer to
con-sent in its etymology of with-sense. Yet, both these terms are usurped
within politics to symbolize a gathering of the like-minded. Common sense,
like consensus, is often associated with a politics that makes assumptions
about its constituents' knowledge base, a certain affiliation within a pre-
defined political group. Common sense is too often the dream of consensus
that propels the imaginary of the nation and its adjacent narratives of identity and territory. "For the common good" is the practice and the promise of
consensus-based politics. Jürgen Habermas's public sphere and Charles Taylor's politics of recognition come to mind here.

The internal vocation of state politics is the unification of aims and the
organization of these aspirations into a unique spatiotemporal whole. State
politics does not happily suffer tears in its social fabric: politics must be
common, and where commonality cannot be located, a line must be drawn
to create a fissure between the inside and the outside, between the known
and the unknown, the self and the other. This unification of forces for the
"common good" condones domination in the name of a re-balancing of
social relations. Each body must be put in its place. The placing of the body
is necessary in order for the distribution of power to adequately inscribe the
social order within its own grids of intelligibility. The body becomes intelligible insofar as it becomes common. Intelligibility as commonality is the primary political articulation within the language of the nation-state.

Yet there always escapes from the body-politic's grids of intelligibility a
disarticulated remains. These remains contest the sovereignty of the nation-

state from within, even when resistance is not enacted with this purpose in mind.[5] A politics of touch is one of the mediums through which the body resists the state. Touch as reaching-toward foregrounds the unknowability at the heart of all bodies of knowledge, reminding us that we cannot know the body as the state claims we do, for no body is ever thoroughly articulated. Every body moves differently, in-difference to the state.

Touching an other in a reciprocal gesture of unknowability underscores the incompleteness of the state, which invariably remains incapable of fully subsuming the body into its realm. Touch emphasizes the discrepancy between the violence of the body as multiplicity and the violence of the body as identity. What we know about the state is that it cannot operate without violence: State power cannot exist unless it holds the ultimate and exclusive right to force. And this violence reproduces itself in the name of security as long as the state has not identified and rendered docile all the bodies in its midst (and along its borders). The violence of touch is, on the other hand, not about policing. It is productive. When the state takes over the body, it attempts to create a bond of reciprocity that is solely hierarchical. When the body leaves the (imaginary of the) state, the body begins to create other bodies, other worlds. Violence is operational in both these instances. Yet, when the body departs from a sovereign, territorialized, bounded space to a worlding, a chronotope emerges that cannot be cleanly delineated but through which a juxtaposition and a convergence take place that multiply space-time through textual layerings, creating new bodies-in-movement. Space grows with the body and shrinks with the state.

Certainly violence remains deadly, but in this case the violence is not held exclusively by the state. Now the violence can be envisioned as a network of forces that produces effects of power and knowledge with which the body can work. Whereas within the system of state sovereignty infractions remain crimes against the state, the body that challenges the confines of state sovereignty shares in the potential for violence and therefore conceives of violence not as a moment of an external "be-falling" but as a moment of response-ability. This is an important shift, for when violence is the exclusive right of the state, everyone becomes guilty of being guilty, whereas when violence is a shared enterprise between bodies through the complex modality of touch, violence becomes the measure of a response in the taking of a decision which involves a response-ability not only toward an other but also toward myself.

The state needs the body. If we dislodge the body from the state (a conceptual predicament always already in progress since the body is continually in the process of metamorphosis), the network of forces that sustain the image of the state immediately languishes. It becomes apparent that the body never belonged to the state: the body always exceeded its containers. This does not mean that there is not a representation of the body active within nation-state politics today. For the concept of the nation to be operative, bodies are essential.

Conceivably, the nation-state could be called the body-state. This is why the state's body-politic is so focused on drawing an image of the body that must remain dependent on the imaginary of the nation-state. If we remove the body from the state, the conflation of identity and territory cannot be sustained. If we imagine the body not as a container that returns to the state for sustenance, but that challenges the state's pre-determined enclosures of belonging and insecurity through its unpredictable states of metamorphosis, we are left with a state-less body and a body-less state. This state-less body touches across space and time, not reaching toward striated grids of intelligibility but toward new networks of power/knowledge. This body is alive in its infralanguage, not in its silent recitations of the state's incantations of sovereignty.

Violence

Hent de Vries asks:

> Should one think of violence as a transcendental category—the very introduction of a "category" or "concept" of violence being the first act or declaration of war—or should one restrict this term to the interruptions that mark the contingent historical and political or psychological and symbolic instances of all empirical conflict? (1997, 14)

Walter Benjamin makes a distinction between two kinds of violence: law-making violence and law-preserving violence (1978, 277). The founding violence is the one that institutes and positions law, the preserving violence is the one that maintains, confirms, and insures the permanence and enforceability of the law. This suggests a complication for the state: the state must conceal its own founding violence in order to violently preserve its laws. Violence is inbred into the concept, the formation and the dissemination of state practice.

Foundational violence is the companion to preservational violence. In relation to law, individual violence is prohibited and condemned, not because it poses a threat to the individual as such, but because it profoundly threatens the very juridical order that sustains the state. "Law," writes Derrida, "has an interest in the monopoly of violence" (1992, 33). This monopoly protects not legal ends, but law itself. Violence threatens from within, operating at the heart of state-sanctioned law-making practices. To think violence as that which does not emerge from the law's exterior is to understand the implicit violence in state formations: "The foundation of all States occurs in a situation that we can call revolutionary. It inaugurates a new law, it always does so in violence" (Derrida 1992, 35).

Yet even within the state model, the body remains an agent of juxtaposition and transformation, for the body can never be completely incorporated within the semantics of the nation-state and its body-politic. Situated practices alter the body as the body alters these very practices. Allen Feldman writes: "The cultural construction of the political subject is tied to the cultural construction of history. This intersection results in political agency as an embodied force" (1991, 2). Political agency here is achieved not as a given but on the basis of a practice that alters the body: political agency is conceived of as an effect of situated practices. This view of political agency is supported by Nietzsche's concept of work, where agency is understood not as the state of the political body itself, but as the product of that body's work. It is important to hold to this supplemental relation of the passive and the active body in order not to fall prey to the mythologizing renditions of a body-in-process that focus not on the movements themselves but on the mythos of a stable, coherent body:

> there is a need to interrogate the mythicizing reception of violence in order to trace the path by which ideological readings of violence engender the subject of the act and the extrinsic site of legitimation in a single movement. (Feldman 1991, 3)

What is often left unwritten in renditions of the body (-politic) is the notion of antagonism on which the body rests. This antagonism is a mechanism of the reproduction and transformation of subjectivity that produces both effect and affect, troubling the political rationalities sustained within the imaginary of the nation-state. Within this matrix of antagonism versus victimization, political enactment stands out as the intersection between local histories mapped onto the template of the body and bodily spaces that challenge the very writing of history (on the body). The multiple subject positions factored by political agency within the vocabulary of state-sovereignty are versions not of a metamorphosing body, but faces of the state. The body is thus rendered redundant. But the body always appeals this redundancy, for the senses that give movement to the body are never still enough to allow the body to fully become stabilized within a state-centered chronotope. The unified subject shifts between transactional and transnational spaces as well as from linguistic discursivity to somatic dissonance:

> If social space and body space continually predicate each other and if both are subjected to an ongoing reconstruction by violence, the notion of a stable relationship of agency to nomothetic social frames, such as class, ethnicity, or political ideology, becomes problematic. (Feldman 1991, 4)

Operating amid the body of the national body-politic and the metamorphosing body (one always an extension of an other, even within the imaginary of state-sovereignty) is the notion of violence. Within the state, the body becomes the mechanism through which violence plays itself out—not *with* the body but *to* the body. The body becomes a container, a mediator, or an apparatus for violence. As both a Janus-faced mechanism of state practice and an outlaw of the state, violence reflects and accelerates the organization of state society, calling forth both its successes and its potential demise. For what violence always holds as its secret is its very indeterminacy, that is, the indeterminacy of its productivity, its force, of its knowledge and power. Violence always exceeds its-self. In this sense, violence is always witness to the incompleteness of its own project. Violence is the constant reminder of the body's potential for metamorphosis, of its movements of desire and its multiplicitous sensations. Violence is both perpetrator and conduit.

This is not to suggest that violence cannot inflict terrible pain upon the body. I do not underestimate the horrors of violence perpetrated in the name of the state or even in the name of touch.[6] I simply want to point out that violence also exceeds the state, despite the fact that the state claims ownership of its measures of "security." A certain violence is often instrumental in undoing the state, in rendering the state body-less and therefore without the conduit for the production of measures of security that work against the body. This would not be a revolution against the state, but a state-less revolution, a revolution that exposes the state for what it is and risks a certain violence in the name of a decision to approach the skin of an other for no other reason than to reach toward touch, to become political, ethically.

The question of political qualification—who can be a political subject?—is simplified to: who will risk the touch of an other? This is a risk: the skin of an other will always lead me back to my own skin, a trajectory that may inspire nausea[7] or even horror.[8] Sensations are not governed easily; they reach deeply into and around the body, creating space and altering the trajectories we thought we could delineate cleanly, legitimately, between sensing bodies in movement. Sensations are prey to homesickness and to motion sickness.

The social fracture that ensues in response to a politics of touch is a floating dispersion of the center. Sites of disavowal and disownership, of belonging and abandonment appear in the most unexpected places. Space is rewritten, re-sensed, only to be altered again. Within this shifting network of movements of desire, political agency is transformed into a political subjectivity-in-process, which takes decisions and makes demands. These demands exceed the grids of intelligibility that would otherwise contain them. Their violence is breath-taking. It is here that the political body re-emerges: "It comes into view as a mise-en-scène with its own genealogy of domination and resistance" (Feldman 1991, 6). This body is touched by the world even as it reaches out toward it. It is a politicized body that realizes that there is no story of movement that does not do a certain violence to the space it traverses. Violence can be horrendous. But the body is political only when it can both receive and disseminate violence, touch, alterity. "The body, altered by violence, re-enacts other altered bodies dispersed in time and space; it also re-enacts political discourse and even the movement of history itself" (Feldman 1991, 7).

Violence is a mode of transcription, both textual and sensory. Reaching out, I do violence to my interiority. Touching you, I do violence to my-self. Receiving, I cut across time and space violently. Violence circulates from one surface to another, from one space to another, from one body to another, from one space-time to another. History is rewritten through violence, not always as the history of the state-sanctioned practices operating in the name of (in)security, but also as the textures of the body in time and space, a body that is not simply mine, which can never simply be mine, but must also be yours, your skin, your touch. "Struggles," writes Feldman, "will occur over competing transcriptions of the same body and of different bodies. This contest over adversarial transcripts fractures the body as an 'organic,' 'natural' object and thus accelerates the body's subjectivation" (1991, 7). The body cannot operate on "its" own. There is no body (other than the fabulated body of the state) that can operate separately from the chronotopes it creates and crosses. There can be no separation from the body's marking of an other and the body itself. History is the body. Spacing (*espacement*) is the body. The body is not political, it is the political instant of space being created in time now.

Feldman writes:

> The spatial inscription of practices and power involves physical flows, meta-
> bolic transactions and transfers—exchanges which connect, separate, dis-
> tance, and hierarchize one space in relation to another. The command of
> space further entails the setting aside of places of imaginary representation,
> eulogized, purifying, or defiling spaces that mobilize spectacles of historical
> transformation. (1991, 9)

This, according to Feldman, "involves the setting up of novel codifying
apparatuses such as the reorganization of the senses, mental maps, topo-
graphic origin myths, norms of spatial competence, and rites of spatial performance" (1991, 9). Space-time is what is at stake here, not *of* the body,
but *as* the body. It is now that we witness the productive capacities of
touch, even if we consider touch linked to a certain violence. Touch crosses
space and/as the body, calling forth not only a reciprocity but attesting to
space-time as that which does not exist *between* bodies, but which is formed
through the movements of these very bodies. Space-time, understood this
way, is the very possibility of a sensory re-articulation of the political: space
is no longer reserved for the vocabulary of the nation-state, which cannot
understand chronotopes otherwise than as pre-existent striated operations
of identity and territory that feed its stultifying imaginary. The state apparatus striates space-time in a refusal to acknowledge the continual creation
and transformation of the sensing, moving bodies in its midst. Were it to
do otherwise, the state would risk losing its perceived hegemony over its
body-politic.

According to Nietzsche, there is no difference between the body as a
political structure and the political structure as the body (1968, 492). The
body is the fractured product of the differential effects of intersecting
antagonistic forces. As Deleuze writes, informed by Nietzsche's comments
on the body: "Whether chemical, biological, social or political . . . any two
forces being unequal constitute a body as soon as they enter into a relation"
(1977, 80–81). The body assumes not one form but as many forms as there
are powers orienting it. "The intersection of forces (political practices) cohere
into an economy of the body. The body is a cumulative effect of exchanges
between agonistic forces" (Feldman 1991, 177). The body is not simply that
which conforms to the state's grids of intelligibility onto which its politics of
interiority and exteriority are transcribed. The body is a point of transaction,
of transculture, of disagreement.

The state does not react calmly to such treason. The state continually
reproduces its limits by transcribing alterity into a system of self-same bodies

that perpetuate the task of policing the border between inside and outside in order to be certain that we do not reach over that border to touch another who is not our-selves. The body is incited to remain that which is attached to the state, lest its detachment result in political disqualification. Within the national imaginary, the body functions as the recuperation of the integrity of the state, an integrity that is only "achieved" through violence. But the body finds ways to escape the grid of sovereignty. This occurs despite our-selves, since we cannot stop our-selves from reaching out to touch an other. We touch an other to see if our vision serves us right. We touch to feel if we, if you, exist. We touch, always, beyond the boundary of self and other.

Erring

The violence of a politics of touch can be conceived as a certain erring toward an other. Derrida writes: "Like pure violence, pure nonviolence is a contradictory concept."

> A Being without violence would be a Being which would occur outside the existent: nothing; nonhistory; nonoccurence; nonphenomenality. A speech produced without the least violence would determine nothing, would say nothing, would offer nothing to an other; it would not be history, and it would show nothing; in every sense of the word, and first of all the Greek sense, it would be speech without a phrase. (1978, 146–47)

A critique of violence embodied through a politics of touch engages in the interstices of violence where violence does not seek to uphold law but to creatively propel contradictory readings of juxtaposition and relation. Critiques of violence will remain violent, with the goal of producing a concept of violence that escapes the strict dichotomy between law-making and law-preserving violence.[9] I denounce violence while negotiating the violence of the denunciation. The question is: Can I do so without mobilizing a violence of my own that projects a new kind of founding violence?

Derrida asks: "Can [critiques of violence] do justice without doing justice to this justice?" (1978, 147). The violence of the concept is what it at stake here. A politics of touch is violent in its very articulation. It is violent because it tears the fabric of state politics in order to ask about the relation between touch and violence. It is violent because it raises questions about how erring toward experience must lead toward the unknowable. Touch is not impervious to an economy of violence. Entering an economy of violence is to engage the relation between touch and untouchability, between touch as reaching and touch as an erring that never quite succeeds in finalizing its

approach toward an other. Touch is a threat even while it creates an opening. Touch threatens as it marks the inevitability of its untouchability: I
touch you as the one who will always, in some sense, remain untouchable.
Your untouchability exists in an economy of violence from which I cannot
safely emerge as long as we are in relation. Yet, in relation, we also create
worlds through which we redefine violence.

Touch errs. Being in relation is about the experience of erring, which is
at the heart of any desire to reach toward. It would be fallacious to argue
that the body is always constant in its directionality. A politics of touch
must be errant.[10] Social consensus is precarious precisely because it rests on
an injunction not to err.[11] Consensus, as the mechanism for a prescribed
democracy ordained within the state system, is the ultimate form of uni-
directionality. It embodies a different violence than that of erring toward an
other. State violence takes count only of the goal, and not of the process.
Consensus ignores the fragility of an erring movement: it pretends that its
displacements are always known in advance. The violence of consensus is
most hazardous, since it believes it cannot err.[12]

In a model of consensual politics, the citizen cannot have an unstable
body, for that body would challenge the organization of the body-politic.
Any unstable body is always eventually disqualified from state politics.
The other, the outside, the homeless, the refugee or the stranger, the sexual
"deviant," none of these bodies "exists" within the realm of social consensus. How could they? These are bodies that err from the grids of intelligibility of state politics, these are bodies that resist the national imaginary, bodies
without citizenship, without passports, without legitimacy. They are, as
Rancière writes, the uncounted, the uncountable. The ultimate violence of
the state is precisely this: to allege that it does not err. In its desperate attempts to maintain the coherence of its grids of intelligibility, the state's
body-politic attempts to erase all forms of power/knowledge that might alert
us to the porosity of its consensual apparatus. The body, every body, and
most certainly the "nonexistent" body at the borders of the state, threatens
the state's strict dichotomy between inside and outside. These deviant bodies
emphasize the porosity of their mobile, sensing fleshiness. Violence (of the
state, against the state) makes the performance of this encounter visible,
registering differences in kind.

Reaching out beyond the limit blurs the boundary between law-preserving
and law-instituting violence. Law has an interest in a monopoly of violence.
The violence it unleashes threatens to lead to its demise and must therefore
be kept well concealed within the nation's practices of securing: every sys-

tem of law and order is predicated and maintained by a violence that could dissolve it. The state asserts that to be safe (free of violence), we must consent to state governmental practices. "Violence exists at the core of Constitutional power to the State (in the name of the People) to practice violence over the people, while the office of the judge includes a fully sanctioned and absolved 'homicidal quality'" (Gourgouris 1996, 132). As Robert Cover suggests, state violence is not explicitly stated in these cases because violence is written into the very idea of government (in Gourgouris 1996, 132).

Yet, in many ways, the sensing body is anathema to the national body-politic, to its politics of consensus, to its violent politics of exclusion. "I am the continuous, necessary overcoming of myself," writes Nietzsche, "... nothing but struggle and becoming and purpose and contradiction of purposes" (1969, 3:271). We are our body, and we are the spaces we create and embody as we reach-toward. We are the embodiment of homesickness that attests to the fact that ultimate stability (consensus) is impossible. To live, we touch, or conversely, to stop touching is to die, to deprive ourselves of a body. Tactility is fraught with an ambiguity we cannot resolve. This ambiguity, this complex worlding, is perhaps the most difficult thing to sustain over time. This is the founding paradox of the national body-politic.

Divine Violence

The parting words of Benjamin's *Critique of Violence* lead us back to God's Word: "Divine Violence, which is the sign and seal but never the means of sacred execution, may be called sovereign violence" (1978, 300). God has spoken: to touch is to be violently expelled from the garden. The violence of the Fall, the violence of sovereignty, is transposed into the word. John writes: "In the beginning was the Word, and the Word was with God, and the Word was God" (John 1:1).

The Gospels are propelled by the word of God. God speaks, and his language will be the language of creation beyond and despite and because of the Fall; his will be the language of an exclusionary garden that negates the creative potential of experience. His words will trace within their wake the primacy of reason.[13] Yet touch and/as untouchability are still at stake, as we see in Mark 16, despite what seems initially to be a departure from the concerns of the originary garden. I am referring here to the *noli me tangere* (do not touch me) episode, a strange encounter with the senses that is my entry point to a second reading of the encounter between touch and untouchability in the Bible. This reading of the untouchable will lead me to the

Titian, *Noli me tangere*. Courtesy of the National Gallery, United Kingdom;
used with permission.

work of William Blake, where another rendition of the Fall will seek to
undermine any leftover dichotomy between good and evil, between reason
and the senses, exposing the supplementary relation between touch and
untouchability.

In the *noli me tangere* scene, Mary Magdalene faces Jesus. As she reaches
out to touch him, Jesus says: "Touch me not; for I am not yet ascended to
my Father: but go to my brethren, and say unto them, I ascend unto my

Correggio, *Noli me tangere*. Courtesy of the Prado Museum, Madrid; used with permission.

father, and your Father; and to my God, and your God" (John 20:17). As the news of Jesus's resuscitation begins to spread, Thomas remains unbelieving and beseeches Jesus to allow him to touch despite the injunction not to touch. Jesus responds: "Reach hither thy finger, and behold my hands; and reach hither thy hand, and thrust it into my side: and be not faithless, but believing" (John 20:27). In this scene, we witness once more the biblical relation between touch, presence, absence, faith, and untouchability.

Interdiction of contact is the first injunction. When he appears to her, Mary reaches toward Jesus. Asked not to touch, she does not lay her hands on his body. Thomas, who refuses to believe, demands to be allowed to touch Jesus. After laying his hands on Jesus' body, he calls Jesus his savior. At first glance, it would seem that Jesus is touchable only for Thomas, that a certain relation is established between Jesus and Thomas, rather than between Mary and Jesus. It seems to me that something more is at stake. If we think of touch as a reaching-toward that moves in the direction of experience rather than toward a pursuit of knowledge (a means to an end) might it not be Mary—as befits her role as the bearer of touch in the Bible—who in fact engages touchingly toward Jesus? If this is the case, would Thomas— as befits his role as the doubting disciple—not be seen engaging in the act most distant from a politics of touch, that is, in an act of discerning the "truth" through a laying of hands? The injunction *not to touch* in the *noli me tangere* scene is perhaps about delimiting the political and ethical difference between reaching-toward and the amassing of pre-definable knowledge.

"Do not touch me" signals a potential danger. It is an admonition that touches at the core. "Do not touch me" announces an immediate relationship between touch and untouchability, signaling not necessarily that "I am untouchable" but emphasizing the imperative that for touch to alter political and ethical vistas, knowledge must be arrived at through experience rather than "truth." "Do not touch me" touches not on a "fact" of untouchability, but on the impossibility of a final reaching toward that would "know" through touch. "Do not touch me" evokes the infinite separation between your finality and my finality. You cannot touch me unless you register that I will remain untouchable. To touch the untouchable (to hold my untouchability captive) would be to subsume me into your narrative of presence. What Jesus says to Mary is: I am here, untouchable, virtually reachable.

Touch, untouchability, is evoked as the foundational absence that lurks in each potential relation. An impenetrable distance remains between me and you, a distance exposed by my desire to reach toward you, to engage in a politics of touch. Incommensurable, this politics signals your difference not from me per se, but from any narrative that would attempt to bridge the impossible distance between our bodies. This is the originary distance of relation. Relation exceeds self and other, expressing the desire not to seek a commonality in the particularities that differentiate us but to engage the difference as the untouchability that will forever draw me outside my "self." Untouchable, I realize that I have no self, that I exist in relation, that I am in relation to my own untouchability. My body is not One.

Over and over in the Bible, Jesus is touched and his touch heals. This touch is a laying of hands,[14] an ingestion of an other not unlike the swallowing of his body in the form of the host. Only once does Jesus ask not to be touched: when he returns to his grace and Mary reaches toward him. This moment of touch/untouchability takes place when Mary is faced with a different (incarnated) body. Jesus' resurrection alters the status of touch. He seems to say: "Do not touch me, do not restrain me, do not think you can catch me or reach me, for I am leaving for the Father, that is to say, again and always toward death's power, and I am leaving from death to death, I am melting into my nocturnal lustre on this spring morning" (Nancy 2003, 31). Reach out but do not touch. Believe in the untouchability that always precedes and exceeds our relation. Have faith.

Strange inconsistency between the desire to touch and the injunction to have faith? Faith precedes the Fall. Into experience is out of faith. Is this always the case? Must God remain untouchable? According to Michael Hardt, incarnation is abandonment to the flesh: "The self-emptying or kenosis of Christ, the evacuation of the transcendental, is the affirmation of the plenitude of the material, the fullness of the flesh" (2002, 78). Incarnation is the body-flesh becoming touchable/untouchable at the nexus between the infinite and the eternal, the metamorphosis of the modalities of existence. Incarnation as becoming-flesh is not the eternalization of the untouchable but the touchability of the eternal. "Transcendence, the condition of possibility of being, should not be imagined as above or below the material—it dwells, rather, precisely at its very surface" (Hardt 2002, 79). Jesus incarnate appears to exclaim that there is no mediation necessary between the transcendent and the immanent. Transcendence and immanence are complimentary, they exist in the experience of the body of Jesus, in its immanent un/touchability. The difference is that here touch no longer signifies a "possession" of the body as in the earlier healing narratives, but instead evokes a relation to the immanence of experience.

Senses are awakened between Jesus and Mary in the *noli me tangere* scene. Mary reaches toward Jesus and registers his voice. She makes contact with him, not by touching him, but by accepting his untouchability. Thomas does not make contact. For Thomas, Jesus must be present. Jesus must be touched in order to confirm the materiality of his flesh. Touch is sidelined with knowledge here, with reason. For Mary, it is Jesus' imminent absence that connects him to her. Presence as absence is the experience of touch. Touch is of the body, actual but virtual; it is the experience of the body's immanence, of its ability to re-generate, to re-appear differently. Mary locates not the body of Christ but the trace of his passing and the promise of his return.

Touch is not a confirmation, not an accomplishment, Jesus seems to say. Touch is reaching toward flesh, but not as proof of presence. Touch is the promise that you can reach again and find me on the threshold of your senses. "The exposed flesh does not reveal a secret self that had been hidden, but rather dissolves any self that could be apprehended. We not only have nothing left to hide, we no longer present any separate thing for the eyes to grasp. We become imperceptible" (Hardt 2002, 80). Jesus exposes himself in relation (to Mary, to Thomas, to God) on a positive logic of emanation. Materiality is intensified. Your touch goes right through me because there is no "me." I am not eternal, I am eternally material. Material, I am the metamorphosing body, exposing my-selves to you, to your touch that never quite adheres, that never quite reaches the one I am not yet, the one I will never quite become. "Flesh is the condition of possibility of the qualities of the world, but it is never contained within or defined by those qualities. In this sense it is both a superficial foundation and an immanent transcendence—alien to any dialectic of reality and appearance, or depth and surface" (Hardt 2002, 83).

I reach toward your mystery, the alchemy of your flesh, the untouchability of the experience that we will become as we alter space-time together. Perhaps this explains the proliferation of paintings of the *noli me tangere* scene.[15] These paintings, which expose a certain unknowability in the relation between Jesus and Mary Magdalene, focus in different and interesting ways on the hands. In some cases, hands connote a separation, in some a desire to touch, a reaching-toward, a sexual longing, a prayer, a benediction, a warning. There is no consensus on the nature of the touch that takes place. Touch and undecidability go hand in hand. Mary understands the untouchability of touch. Mary reaches toward this untouchability not seeking truth, nor the Word, but the con-tact that will engage her in a relation to the unknowable she already knows well. As Nancy writes, "Mary-Magdalene becomes a saint par excellence because she holds herself at the point where the touch of sense is identical to its retreat" (Nancy 2003, 72).

Genesis and the *noli me tangere* episode share an engagement with the threat and potential violence of touch. In Genesis, the threat is that touch will propel Adam and Eve out of the garden into experience. In the *noli me tangere* episode, the threat is more complex: if Mary touches Jesus, she relegates her faith to the promise of corporeal presence. If Mary does not touch Jesus, she accepts the incorporeality of touch as a potential violence toward the concept of presence. Thomas does touch Jesus, but only to justify his faith. Mary, on an other hand, accepts that Jesus is no longer touchable as a healer but must be reached-toward differently. Jesus is thus relegated to the unknowability of presence as absence, and touch to a gesture in passing. Jesus is both of the earth (having fallen toward touch) and of the heavens (moving toward a Godliness that would render him permanently untouchable). The figure who remains most interesting in relation to touch is Mary.

"It is a good thing not to touch a woman," writes Paul (1 Cor. 7:1). Gregg Lambert suggests that the body of woman in the early Christian community marks "the site of touching and the fear of being touched,...the site of this extreme contradiction...between a body that is open to the touch and a body that is determined by the prohibition against touching" (2004, 4).[16] Mary Magdalene is no exception. In Mark 16:1, it is reported that Mary Magdalene and Mary the mother of James went to the tomb with spices to anoint the body of Jesus. Against all restrictions around touch, these women go to the grave to touch and handle a corpse.

Despite echoes to the contrary voiced in *The Gospel of Mary Magdalene*,[17] Mary Magdalene remains the biblical embodiment of flesh and of the carnal body in the Hebrew Bible. It is in the shadow of her fleshy body that Jesus reveals himself. It is with her that Jesus speaks of touch. It is toward her that Jesus becomes untouchable. It is alongside her that Jesus circumvents the violence of touch. Mary is touch embodied; she is the woman who reaches toward touch as untouchability. She is the body that opens itself toward the body of Jesus, allowing him to take leave, allowing him to take a place within her, to become her. It is Mary who is asked to relay the Gospel; it is Mary who is asked to have faith that to touch is always to reach toward untouchability. It is Mary who discerns what is at stake in the complicated politics of touch at work in the Bible. As Nancy writes, "[t]his violent paradox is not to be resolved, it remains the location of a gap as intimate as it is irreducible: do not touch me." Mary is the incarnation of this interval, the body of woman who accepts the violence inherent in the decision to touch or not to touch, who lives the complexity of the engagement with the unknowable, the indefinable.

Return to the Garden

William Blake's "Garden of Love" exposes the violence at work in organized religion:

The Garden of Love

I went to the Garden of Love,
And saw what I never had seen:
A Chapel was built in the midst.
Where I used to play on the green.

And the gates of this Chapel were shut,
And Thou shalt not writ over the door;
So I turn'd to the Garden of Love,
That so many sweet flowers bore,

And I saw it was filled with the graves,
And tombstones where flowers should be:
And Priests in black gowns, were walking their rounds,
And binding with briars, my joys & desires. (Blake 1979, 51)

This is the Garden as it would perhaps look to Adam and Eve were they to return to Eden. To their eyes, it would be a bleak sight. Open fields replaced by a locked chapel. The abundant nature no longer visible, having been overtaken by the stern architecture that underwrites the commitment to eternity. The gates shut so that only the soul can cross the threshold. The touching, sensing, moving body condemned: "Thou shalt not" written on the door of the chapel. Fields of flowers replaced by graves and grave priests binding into briars the lost joys of the garden. This garden, seen through eyes that have touched the world, would be a startling vision of hell.

Influenced by the tactile bodies etched by Michelangelo,[18] Blake celebrates flesh and sensing bodies in movement in his writings and etchings. For Blake, the ideal human form is not to be found in the "Garden of Love." The ideal form is not a disembodied spirit, not an eternal soul. The ideal human is a carnal, fleshy, sensing body in movement. This body is not fixed as a determinable or measurable form, as a unitary or self-contained individuality. This body is indefinite, ever-changing, relational. In many ways, it is a Deleuzian or Spinozean body, where life is understood not simply as form, but as a complex relation between differential velocities, between deceleration and acceleration of particles. In this relational body, the senses are defined as "windows" (Europe 3:1,5) rather than surfaces, as openings that liberate the vast realms of experience. The window in Blake is not a transparent surface through which one gazes. It is an opening which exposes the world in all of its inconsistencies. Through the window, bodies move and senses are unleashed.

In Blake, the senses are not limited to specific organs. The senses are relational. The senses traverse space unrestricted, forever growing to encompass the expansive limits of an extended body. The more majestic the body, the larger the senses and the wider their capacities. Senses move the body beyond itself, inciting it to become more than its organs, calling forth a Body without Organs.[19] "A vast Spine writh'd in torment / Upon the winds'" (9:37–38). This reference to Urizen's body signals an intensified movement through space, more and less than the sum of its senses. "Though all . . . parts, belong to the same body, some are insignificant in the relation to the landscape, and some proportionately large" (Connolly 2002b, 89). A sense of exposure is tangible in Urizen's description—veins, nerves, inner organs, and fibers are exposed to the vastness: "Urizen is one with his environment as a cosmic man: there is no skin to make a border between himself and his world" (Connolly 2002b, 90).

Parts of Urizen's body grow out of themselves. Eyes shoot out from the brain; ears spiral from the orbs of vision. The senses escape the common *organ*ization of the body even as they transform it, fluidly reconnecting to bodies spaced and timed elsewhere. The body is shackled, but even so, the senses defy *organ*ization. Tristanne Connolly writes: "Blake's descriptions of the metamorphosis of the sense organs make it clear that the body we know is the result of the transformation" (2002b, 78). When the inhabitants of Urizen's world endure changes, their senses also change: "their eyes / Grew small like the eyes of man" (23:35–36). Space and time are qualitatively altered alongside shifts in the dimensions of the senses. "The sense organs seem to metamorphose swiftly, but each change occurs as an age passes over" (Connolly 2002b, 89).

Although the senses are often described individually in Blake's poems, they are synesthetically joined in the body's passionate participation in experience. They are not passive. The senses move the body toward a world that expands exponentially given the opportunity to work supplementarily in defiance of the dichotomies dictated by a biblical text that continues to preach the primary difference between good and evil. Passivity brings forth shrinkage of the senses as they attempt to constrain themselves to the *individual*

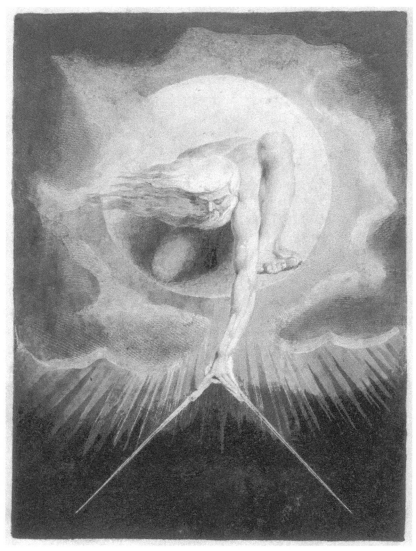

William Blake, *Urizen*. Lessing J. Rosenwald Collection, Library of Congress.
Copyright 2005 The William Blake Archive. Used with permission.

William Blake, *Urizen*. Lessing J. Rosenwald Collection, Library of Congress.
Copyright 2005 The William Blake Archive. Used with permission.

body. In passivity senses are reduced, all but touch, which "is capable of rousing the greatest ecstasy [and] admits man into Eternity; therefore it is not 'dead,' like an other senses, but only cursed" (Damon 1971, 408; in Vinge 1975).

The Marriage of Heaven and Hell is a series of plates that explores in detail the shortcomings of narratives that seek to dichotomize experience. Contraries prevail, giving rise to the concepts of good and evil. "Good is the passive that obeys Reason. Evil is the active springing from Energy / Good is Heaven. Evil is Hell" (Blake 1975, 3, xvi). As long as good and evil are opposed, the stakes are clear and God's word—the sovereign voice—takes charge over insensate bodies. But perhaps good and evil are not opposed, warns Blake in The Marriage of Heaven and Hell, going on to point out the many errors found in the Bible. Among them is the dichotomy between body and soul, wherein evil energy stems from the body and good reason is of the soul.

To restrain desire—to not reach toward an other—is to be weak. Only the weak are restrained. Desire is energy and "[e]nergy is eternal delight" (Blake 1975, 4, xvi). Desire attracts the devil: "When I came home: on the abyss of the five senses, where a flat sided steep frowns over the present world, I saw a mighty Devil forded in black clouds" (1975, 6–7, xvii). Desire extends the senses and the senses promise experience, but with experience comes temptation. The choice is violent, but not to choose is to remain passive and to allow oneself to be governed. Temptations are to be lived, to be experienced: "The road of excess leads to the palace of wisdom. / Prudence is a rich ugly old maid courted by Incapacity" (1975, 7, xviii). To live is to touch the world. Time is at stake, "Eternity is in love with the productions of time." With time, as my body changes, my senses become more acute and my life becomes more complex. To live is to time space and space time, unleashing the energies of the sensing and transforming bodies in movement.

To live sensually is to discover the infinite in all things and to be persuaded by our beliefs. Nothing can be proven; there is no truth. Sensual enjoyment leads to eternity, an eternity that exists in finitude, analogous, perhaps, to Nietzsche's concept of eternal recurrence. Knowledge is corrosive, printed onto a surface which always resists. Perception must be cleansed. Only the senses offer the window onto a finitude replete with experience. The printing house becomes the location for the Word, a Word that does not uphold the voice of the sovereign but seeks instead to etch corrosively on opaque metals and transfer its remains onto translucent paper. Blake's word transforms experience by incorporating the sensual capacities of sensing bodies in movement, relating the narratives of super-sensory giants who are now imprisoned. Sensuality that is restrained to the surface must escape, must become Godly, must expand beyond the strict envelope of the body's skin. "God only Acts & Is, in existing beings of Men" (1975, 16–17, xxiii).

"For every thing that lives is Holy," writes Blake at the end of *The Marriage of Heaven and Hell* (1975, 27, xxviii). Holiness is not bodilessness but its opposite. The more sense-perceptive, the holier. The body that emerges as the holy body is a body that is eminently touchable, though always slightly out of reach as it extends toward the world. The body is fluidly sensual, sensingly fluid, transforming itself beyond notions of discrete insides and outsides. The body is beside itself, corporeal, reaching, sensing, experiencing. This is not an innocent or a nonviolent body. It is a body that experiences the world in touch with the potential violence that is the rupture toward the unknowable. As Blake writes in *Jerusalem*, "if Perceptive Organs vary: Objects of Perception seem to vary: / if the Perceptive Organs close: the Objects seem to close also" (1991b, 30, 34). The world corresponds to the variations of the senses that perceive it.

A sensing body is an infinite body. Infinity is not eternity. A sensing body does not return to the garden nor does it perform miracles through touch. A sensing body ruptures conceptions of time and space that are considered stable, reaching toward a continued metamorphosis of the body that violently spaces time and times space. Acute senses allow the world to appear in relation. Bodies are qualitatively altered by sense. Bodies emerge as multitudes, infinitely sensing in excess of their organisms, reaching toward songs of experience. "We live as one man; for contracting our infinite senses / We behold multitude; or expanding; we behold as one" (1991b, 38, 34, 17–19).

4.

Engenderings:
Gender, Politics, Individuation

Touch

Our skin is the most sensitive and oldest of our organs. It is our most efficient of protectors. The skin arises from the outermost of three embryonic cell layers, the ectoderm, which gives rise to the hair, teeth, and the sense organs of smell, taste, hearing, vision, and touch. Touch is the earliest sense to develop in the human embryo. It gives us our experience of depth and thickness and shape. Skin develops sensitivities that depend largely on the kind of environmental stimulation it receives. The skin is a central organ system of the body. Without the functions performed by the skin, we cannot survive.

Sensory and motor tonus of the skin are uninterruptedly stimulated by the environment: nerve fibers conducting tactile impulses are generally of larger size than those associated with other organs. Coetaneous stimulation is essential for the adequate organic and behavioral development of the organism. Newborn animals must be licked if they are to survive (otherwise they are at risk of dying of a functional failure of the genitourinary system and/or the gastrointestinal system). In humans, this licking is replaced by a long period of labor, during which the contractions of the uterus stimulate the fetal skin. Infants who are not adequately touched after birth often suffer tremendously, sometimes even dying as a result (Montagu 1971, 82). Skin performs such essential tasks that it is rarely, if ever, "busy." The skin remains quiet in order "to increase its capacity to learn, to become habituated to codes that cannot be interfered with under any conditions" (Montagu 1971, 152). The vibrotactile or electrotactile signals of the skin cannot be shut out, nor can the skin close its eyes or ears or hold its breath. Even in sleep, the skin remains the most alert of the organs, and it is the first to recover upon awakening.

Touch is intimately linked to the skin. The skin that touches and is touched is continually rebuilding itself from the outer to the innermost layers. To reach toward skin through touch is to reach toward that which is in a continued state of (dis)integration and (dis)appearance. Skin gives us a clue to the untouchability of the body. If we locate skin as the receptor that never quite remains its-self, we can begin to appreciate the ways in which touch can never be more than a reaching-toward the untouchable. In addition to its regenerative qualities, there is also the issue of forgetting: if we want touch to last, we must touch again, lest the skin "forget" the touch we can feel but momentarily. When we reach toward to touch, we reach toward that which is in-formation or trans-formation. This reaching-toward is an engendering that qualitatively alters the relation between being and becoming, alerting us to the potential variables that combine to give us a clue as to "what a body can do."[1]

What a body can do is a question of engendering. One way of activating this concept is through an exploration of the effects of language, as does Judith Butler in *Bodies That Matter:*

> The body posited as prior to the sign, is always *posited* or *signified* as prior. This signification produces as an *effect* of its own procedure the very body that it nevertheless and simultaneously claims to discover as that which *precedes* its own action. If the body signified as prior to signification is an effect of signification, then the mimetic or representational status of language, which claims that signs follow bodies as their necessary mirrors, is not mimetic at all. On the contrary, it is productive, constitutive, one might even argue *performative,* inasmuch as this signifying act delimits and contours the body that it claims to find prior to any and all signification.
>
> This is not to say that the materiality of bodies is simply and only a linguistic effect which is reducible to a set of signifiers. Such a distinction overlooks the materiality of the signifier itself. Such an account also fails to understand materiality as that which is bound up with signification from the start; to think through the indissolubility of materiality and signification is no easy matter. To posit by way of language a materiality outside of language is still to posit that materiality, and the materiality so posited will retain that positing as its constitutive condition. (1993, 30)

Language plays a key role in the sexing (and de-sexing) of bodies, organizing the domain of significability or intelligibility. The materiality of the sign is what is at stake for Butler: it is through materiality that she is capable of positing bodies as adjacent to linguistic signification. In this chapter, I will expand on this notion of materiality, suggesting that what a body can do exceeds linguistic signification. A politics of touch amplified through the prism of engendering asks questions concerning gender that broaden the problematic initiated by Butler in *Bodies That Matter*. While I do not dispute the fact that language is central to politics,[2] my focus here will be on the ways in which bodies touch at language's sensual limits. Remaining concerned with the dynamics of relation, I will focus mainly on the ways in which touch exceeds language's significability.

If politics is understood conventionally as that which renders some bodies legitimate in the name of and through language, a politics of touch can be thought as that which both supports the political and challenges it. In this sense, touch and language perform parallel operations. Yet there is something about the inability to coherently regulate the senses (in this case, touch) that offers the potential for reaching out even beyond words to expose the supple limits of the body.

A politics of touch suggests that one way in which bodies resist normative politics such as those of the nation-state is through reaching across the boundaries imposed by the body-politic. This crossing does not necessarily inaugurate a difference in the political structures at hand, but it does engender an adjacent body, a supplementarity, an individuation[3] that potentially stands in the way of pre-constituted organizations of bodies. The effect of this is by no means utopian: the more complex the bodies at hand, the firmer the imposition of the norms of the governing body-politic. Nonetheless, engenderings brought forth through a politics of touch open the way to a wider selection of bodies, allowing us to explore them in all of their engendered and engendering matter-forms.

I place touch at the fore to prevent myself from falling into the trap of fixing bodies as simple objects of thought. As Butler writes in another context, "this moving beyond their own boundaries, a movement of boundary itself, [is] quite central to what bodies 'are'" (1993, ix). Gender is only part of what differentiates bodies, and cultural determinism does have a tendency to be the main tool in helping us understand the constitutive status of these differentiations. What Butler does in *Bodies That Matter* is place construction as the constitutive element of the performativity of gendered bodies.

She asks how constraints such as sex "not only produce the domain of in-telligible bodies, but produce as well a domain of unthinkable, abject and unliveable bodies" (1993, xi). Butler's argument concerns the manner in which the materiality of sex is forcibly produced. She wants to know how bodies are materialized as "sexed," and how and why certain bodies come to matter. Butler focuses on sex as part of a regulative practice that produces the bodies it governs. The materialization of sex takes place (or fails to) through highly regulated practices.

For Butler, the sexing of bodies is a process that takes place through the (political) regulations of norms established in and through language. These norms regulate how bodies are represented, where our bodies fit into the spectrum of diversity and differentiation, and, I would add, how our bodies are touched and touching. Since touch always implies a reaching toward an other who must always remain untouchable, touch can be considered as largely non-normative, at least in the first instance. Touch manifests itself as material in an incomplete process of materialization. Materialization cannot be "completed" through touch since touch necessitates a return that will al-ways in some sense destabilize its initial commitment toward an other. Given the fact that, as Butler writes, "bodies never quite comply with the norms by which their materialization is compelled" (1993, 2), touch could be said to operate as one of the many potential resistances to the normative process at the heart of materialization, bringing to the fore the complexities within the form-matter matrix on which the differentiation of bodies depends.

Touch is performative in the sense that it exposes the challenges the excessive body (the body in excess of its-self) calls forth within the domain of cultural intelligibility. When I touch you, I re-place both you and myself within the governing system of the body-politic, drawing to our attention the limit-space between your skin, my skin, and the world. This act of engen-dering recasts the matter of bodies as well as their form. This happens through a "force field" which is released in the act of reaching-toward that qualita-tively alters the space and time in the relation between bodies. This field of forces is as concrete as it is virtual. As a practice of relation, touch reaches toward an exposition of matter and form as processual states. When I reach to touch you, I touch not the you who is fixed in space as pre-orchestrated matter/form. I touch the you that you will become in response to my reach-ing toward. Our bodies are at once indissociable and in excess of the regula-tory norms that govern their materialization and the signification of these material effects.

You may argue: "Touching, you can not choose *not* to reach toward a differentiation with which you cannot cope. Does it not happen that you do *not*
want to touch a body *because* it is foreign, raced, gendered, etc.? Or, inversely,
when you *do* touch a body that you consider different, do you not touch that
body in its perceived fixity, *as* gendered, *as* ethnic? Do you not touch hier-
archically, emphasizing your position as the one who chooses to touch?"
Certainly, one of the shortcomings of touch as a paradigm to a changing
notion of politics is that we *can* touch one another in view of the norms
by which we identify one another as individual rather than individuating
bodies. Argentine tango is an interesting example of this.

Most of the time, in Argentine tango, a man leads a woman onto the
dance floor. The man offers his body and the woman enters into the embrace,
the closeness determined by the limits of their desire for intimacy or the
sheer strength of his hold. In this gendered moment, she knows herself as
the woman, him as the man. He is leading; she is following. If they are dancing in close embrace, the touching surface between the man and the woman
extends from the head all the way to the upper or mid-chest, sometimes also
continuing along the legs. Within this closeness, a dance is negotiated that
is initiated by the leader and responded to by the follower. But as the movement begins to incite the dance to take form and the bodies to engage mate-
rially with their improvised displacements, we realize that the exchange is
far more reciprocal than it first appears to be: the leader is also following the
follower. Since the dance is always improvised, leader and follower not only
dance together but listen intently to each other's bodies. Touch functions
here as a medium of open-ended exchange: I respond not to your touch *as
such* but to the potentiality your movement incites within my body. I respond
to our reciprocal reaching-toward. If this touch is indeed approached relationally, chances are the couple will dance beautifully together. Body to body,
they will space time and time space. If not, it is likely that they will have
difficulty locating one another.

This sharing of touch in Argentine tango can also cross heterosexualized
gender boundaries which makes it potentially all the more compelling. In
the early years of tango, mainly due to the extreme lack of women in Buenos
Aires and the stark competition between men, men danced with one another
and perfected their tango before they had the opportunity to dance with a
woman. Today, especially in Northern Europe, more and more women lead
other women (or men), and it is not unusual to see two men dancing
together. When Argentine tango shifts into this zone, a politics of touch

can take place that challenges the strict boundaries of gender. This happens through a conceptual repositioning of the relation between bodies, which, in turn, alters the qualitative composition of matter-form. Now, the "body" of the leader is no longer composed solely of stereotypical "male" attributes (a macho posture, a sense of control), nor is the follower constrained to stereotypical "feminine" traits (a sexy demeanor, a fairy-like lightness). The ritual of tango as it is often popularized begins to dissolve. Bodies begin to morph. This mutation qualitatively alters the relation between form and matter in these engendering bodies, investing them with new qualities. These new qualities in turn alter the relation between the bodies, modifying their potential movement. As the bodies qualitatively metamorphose, so does the relation between the form and matter of these bodies. At the physical level, this may be noticed in a gesture, a posture, a hold, a glance. At the qualitative level, this may take the form of a different sense of the ground, a connection, a sense of surprise that lead both the leader and the follower to wonder where the movement is coming from. Now the leader is no longer first identified as the physical incorporation of masculinity, but perhaps as a body of intensity, speed, precision, caring. The follower is no longer simply following but emanating a movement of her own that calls forth engagement, creativity, joy. These qualities expose a qualitative alteration in the relation of form to matter and matter to form.

Tango that bends gender affiliations demonstrates how normative discourses can be subverted, in this case through a reaching-toward enacted through shared touch that produces infinite variations of movement. Of course, tango can be as regulated as any other normative discourse: tango testifies once more to how touch can be simultaneously prescriptive and creative. The normative aspect of touch is constrained to an ontologization of touch where "I touch you" inscribes "I" and "you" as forms of Being rather than becoming. On the other hand, touch as a concept that implies a reaching-toward is not ontological but ontogenetic. Reaching-toward, qualitative changes are expressed in and through the bodies in relation. These are qualities of movement rather than properties of Being. Touch as a reaching-toward is not a question of Being. It is a question of becoming. Ontogenetic, touch is incorporeal, it is always beyond its-self, equal to its emergence. Haunted by a becoming that remains as virtual as it is concrete, tango dances to the music of the next beat, a movement yet to come, a space-time to be re-invented, again. Tango bodies reaching toward one another are haunted by their potential to become.[4]

Gender

While gender subsists within the term "engendering," it is not etymologically located within its definition. "Engender" stems from the Middle English *engendren*, from Middle French *engendrer*, from Latin *ingenerare*, from *in-* + *generare*, to generate, dating back to the fourteenth century. To engender is to undertake a reworking of form. To engender is to potentialize matter. Engendering involves potentiality at its most fertile: it calls forth the link between the incorporeal and the material, between the virtual and the actual. Engendering takes place in the magic moment between potentiality and actuality, where what is exposed is the actuality of the virtual and the virtuality of the actual. In this eventful moment, bodies morphing toward new forms of matter qualitatively become more than them-selves.

Gilbert Simondon's work is a rich engagement with the complexity of engendering matter and form. *Individuation* is the term he gives to the process through which potentiality is engendered. For Simondon, individuation implies a leaving-behind of the concept of the individual as the pre-organized sum of stable form and inert matter. Identity is exposed by individuation as a moment in a process that expands far beyond the bounds of a strict category one might call the "self." Individuation is conceptualized as a vehicle that allows being to become, not as matter or form or substance, but as a tensile system, oversaturated with its own potential. Individuation has not yet been adequately thought, Simondon suggests, because a sole form of equilibrium has been foregrounded that has privileged stability over metastability. Metastability is linked to individuation. Whereas stability refers to a system *in* equilibrium, metastability speaks of a system that is far from equilibrium[5] (but precariously stable), a system through which potential energy is unleashed. Individuation allows us to explore *relation* as a becoming that is far-from-equilibrium, that can be modified by potential energy. This potential energy, Simondon suggests, emerges through matter and form, emanating from a level where matter and form are not yet distinct.

A politics of touch is composed of engendered and engendering bodies. To engender is to explore the potentialities of form and matter at the level of individuations rather than identities. To engender is to reach toward bodies that are not pre-defined as gendered, not pre-constituted within static representations that befit the systems in which they operate. Engendering bodies are bodies that move, that metamorphose always in relation to their environments and to one another. Engendering bodies are relational vectors that space time and time space in an effort to re-locate themselves within systems of mutation.

Engenderings are metastable systems. Relation occurs not between already-produced entities or individuals but as an aspect internal to the system of individuation itself: relation is constitutive of engendering. Engenderings are bodies in-formation. In-formation does not imply a pre-organized system one superimposes onto matter, but form in a state of disappearance. Being in-formation suggests that form is not a given but a tension between disparate possibilities where becoming precedes Being. This occurs through the process of individuation: as my body engenders, my matter (my energetic potential) is in-formed by a shell that never quite contains the process.

Individuation begins at the cellular level: "bacteria are not really individuals so much as part of a single global superorganism, responding to changed environmental conditions not by speciating but by excreting and incorporating useful genes from their well-endowed neighbours and then rampantly multiplying" (Margulis and Sagan 1997, 55). Within the Darwinian and neo-Darwinian frameworks, individual differences are at the core of natural selection. Lynn Margulis disputes this claim, suggesting that rather than the individual, symbiosis is at the heart of evolution. Symbiosis as defined by Margulis suggests a process of individuation. Individuation produces individuation, not individuals. To think of evolution as a process of engendering is to begin to challenge the Darwinian and neo-Darwinian evolutionary canon that continues to privilege individuals over individuations, genders over engenderings, stable and inert matter and form over composite exfoliating multiplicities.

Margulis contends that humans have not simply evolved from primates or other mammals, but from a long line of progenitors that can be traced back to the first bacteria. Human bodies are composites of thousands of millions of years of interaction among highly responsive microbes. Symbiosis is the term Margulis gives this process of composition.[6] Although Margulis's work has, in large part, been accepted into mainstream molecular biology,[7] she admits that "the idea that new species arise from symbiotic mergers among members of old ones is still not even discussed in polite scientific society" (Margulis 1998, 6).

Margulis defines symbiogenesis as "an evolutionary change by the inheritance of acquired gene sets" (1998, 9) wherein living beings defy neat definition. The symbiotic world individuates violently, passionately, indifferently, fighting, feeding, mating, dancing, dying. Generating novelty, symbiogenesis

brings together different life forms through matings that are often incorporations. This is not a one-to-one procedure whereby individuals can be delineated within an economically stable system. This process is metastable. Fixed
individuality is a concept that cannot exist within a symbiosis that causes
complex alterations in the form-matter relation. Symbiogenesis brings
together life forms that are "even more unlike than their 'unlike' parents"
(Margulis 1998, 9). These individuations become larger, more complex unities. Individuations become compositions that become populations that
become multi-unit symbiotic systems.

    "Now as throughout Earth's history, living associations form and dis-
solve. Symbioses, both stable and ephemeral, prevail" (Margulis 1998, 12).
Symbioses call forth surprising engenderings. These engenderings mark all
kinds of transformations. They permit the ontogenesis of the rigidity of gender identities through the construction and reconstruction of forms and
functions of reproduction. Positing engendering as my point of departure,
what I seek to explore is how human sex practices (and adjacent politics
of gender identity) are embedded in our historical and cultural roots[8] as
mementos to practices of segregation, imposed difference, essential traits.
Mind-body dualisms figure prominently in the naturalization of discourses
of gender identity, most often re-entrapping the body in pre-established
configurations overdetermined by linguistic, political, and evolutionary signification. "The continuous displacement of the signifier 'sex' does not succeed in detaching feminine desire from fixed nature as it fails to challenge
the fundamental problematic of the body, biological identity, the imperative of sexual procreation and ultimately the metaphysical conception of
matter (fixed, stable nature, where matter is inert)" (Parisi 2004, 10). The
concept of engendering invites us to think the project of gendering bodies
differently, emphasizing the manner in which bodies individuate, evolving
into forms that highlight the nonlinear dynamics and unpredictable potential of matter's trans-formations.

    Engenderings are crossings-over of matter-form from differing realms, be
they political, technological, or biological. "The mutations of a body are
not predetermined by a given ideal or an infrastructure defining the realm
of biological possibilities of a body.... [T]hese mutations designate the
abstract or virtual operations of matter" (Parisi 2004, 14). Potential leads to
actualization. Engenderings are actualizations of morphing body-mutations.
Within each engendering is a virtual form. Actualization through engendering does not derive from pre-determined (already-formed) individuals: it
incorporates the formation of new body-configurations.

Form suggests an organizational shift in the system. When matter is po-tentialized into a given form, a phase shift occurs. This phase shift dephases the body-as-identity, exposing the body to the effects of its reaching toward: the body becomes the multiplicity of its becoming and its having-become. Bodies are as incorporeal as they are in-formed. By incorporeal I do not mean less real. On the contrary: the body becomes more than real, more than its envelope, more than the space-time of its pre-locatedness. It is in this sense that engenderings are "machinic":[9] engenderings entail the merg-ing of different bodies of production. The body is machinic in the sense that it is plural and unpredictable, evolving always through movements that are contingent on environments and (re)combinations. The dissolution and symbiosis of forms and functions is a necessary and integral part of any concept of creative evolution. Production comes into contact with repro-duction through the machinic assemblage that connects a body to biophysi-cal, biocultural, and biodigital organizations of sex. Engenderings are not stable renderings of bodies-as-machines. Engenderings call forth bodies, inciting them to recombine.

Recombinations involve transductions. In genetics, transductions refer to the transfer by a bacteriophage[10] of genetic material from one bacterium to another. Simondon uses transduction to convey the idea of reaching-toward or leading across toward dynamic form. Transductions suggest a de-phasing in the system through which new individuations emerge. Individu-ations are multilayered processes of engendering whereby the activity of becoming extends in multiple directions beyond unity and identity. Trans-duction can be conceptualized as the relation between individuations through which composite bodies are engendered. Transduction does not happen *to* the body. Transduction is *of* the body, operational constitutively within its systems of in-formation. Transduction may quantitatively alter matter and form, but it is more likely that it will not, instead activating matter and form toward qualitative individuations. Bodies will become other not in their carapaces but in their potentialities. "[T]o think the transduc-tive operation that is the foundation for the various levels of individuation, the notion of form is insufficient" (Simondon 1995, 33). Transductively, form becomes in-formation. This supposes the existence of a system in a meta-stable state that is open to individuation. Ontogenesis, not ontology.

Classifications presuppose hierarchical relationships. In positing gender as a principle of strict differentiation, form is placed onto matter in a way that calls forth a complete individual rather than an individuation. Engen-dering is a reaching toward matter-form that explores the manner in which the quality of matter is already a source of form. What we consider a unique form (my body as woman, for example) is but the latest episode in a series of trans-formations. Matter is material because it can be modeled in ways that stabilize its de-formation. Pure form already contains gestures[11] through which matter can mutate. This suggests that no body is pre-formed with concrete matter. Engendering precedes gender.

If we take into consideration the micropractices of engendering, we can imagine life as an emergent property of complex autopoetic[12] systems involving nonlinear feedback and combinatory processes. Engendering—as symbiotic becoming—plays a role in the discourse of reproduction from the autocatalytic association of cells to the association of multicellular bodies, from societies of bacteria to social domains of disciplinary sex, from digital cultures of cloning images to bio-technological proliferations of cellular engineering.

> It is not a matter of socio-cultural imitations of the natural or biological imitations of society. What comes first is neither a given essence nor the signification of essence. Rather, the abstract concatenation of bodies-sexes delineates the primacy of heterogeneous mixtures or symbiosis—biophysical elements, socio-cultural energies, economic trades, technical inventions, political forces and particles of desire—unfolding the potential of a body to become. (Parisi 2004, 16)

Symbiosis evolves from the need to repair cellular DNA through the incorporation of the adjacent cell's DNA. As Deleuze and Guattari underline, the organism's capacity for reproduction also confirms its capacity for deterritorialization: "The more interior milieus an organism has . . . assuring its autonomy and bringing it into a set of aleatory relations with the exterior, the more deterritorialized it is" (1987, 53–54). If reproduction depends on deterritorialization, species must not simply be reproduced *qua* species.

Symbiosis

Henri Bergson writes: "In reality, life is a movement, materiality is the inverse movement, and each of these two movements is simple, the matter which forms a world being an undivided flux, and undivided also the life that runs through it, cutting out in it living beings all along its track" (1946, 249). Engendering is a process that foregrounds the multiplicities we are continually becoming. These multiplicities include gender, but are not gendered as such. Multiplicities cannot be conceived within preorganized concepts of space and time. They are always subject to mutation, transformation, and deterritorialization. In the words of Deleuze and Guattari:

> Since variations and dimensions are immanent to it, it amounts to the same thing to say that each multiplicity is already composed of heterogeneous terms in symbiosis, and that a multiplicity is continually transforming itself into a string of multiplicities, according to its thresholds and doors. (1987, 249)

The engendering body is a becoming-multiple of the body. This is not a subjective body that identifies itself as something concrete one could call a *self* or an *individual*, but a series of intensities, through which endlessly diverse populations are engendered.

Keith Ansell Pearson writes:

> If codings are inseparable from intrinsic and extrinsic processes of decoding (through supplementation and "side-communication"), and if territorialities are equally involved in these processes, then the key insight is that it is *populations* that are the "subject" of these mutually implicated processes of coding, decoding, and deterritorialization. On this model "evolution" does not simply entail the passage from one pre-established form of life to another, involving only the translation of one code into another. Rather, there are the phenomena of mutations, genetic drift, and the transferal of cells of one species to another that takes place not in terms of "translation" but rather in terms of a surplus value of code ("side-communication"). (1999, 151)

The surplus value of code of which Ansell Pearson speaks is compatible with Simondon's concept of potential energy. Bifurcations produce intensities that multiply. Antagonistic organisms evolve into metabolic truces. Genetic pacts are formed. "Each of your cells is an amazing crossbreed, both more mixed up and more unified than anything found in a medieval bestiary" (Margulis 1997, 77). Engendering foregrounds variation. Variations emerge through the parallel network of relations between populations and terri- tories poised at the edge of a phase transition from one state to another. Margulis's theory of endosymbiosis suggests that bodies-in-symbiosis merge out of networked organizations that provide connections between popula- tions and environments. Bodies become in relation to an ecosystem of bodies. This model emphasizes cellular interliving, "an infiltration and assimilation far more profound than any aspect of human sexuality [that] produced every thing from spring-green blooms and warm, wet, mammalian bodies to the Earth's global nexus" (Margulis 1998, 20).

The alliance between reproduction and individual difference is at the heart of Darwin's theory of "modification and descent" in which every individual being is considered as part of a genealogy of beings open to variations through breeding and species intercrossing. In this model, individual differences are slight modifications of a common pool of variations preserved through adaptation and sexual mating. Natural selection focuses on the stability of a species. Sexual mating within this system guarantees the preservation of a lineage (branching phylogeny). Difference is considered a necessary tool for survival but only insofar as that divergence remains located within the spectrum of adaptation and transmission of variation. Meiotic sex, understood as sexual reproduction by two (usually male-female) parties, preserves variations and sustains the principle of inheritance.[13] This line of evolutionary thought—extending from Darwin to neo-Darwinism—argues that external factors are not direct causes of changes inheritable through filial generation. Genetic information is passed on unidirectionally, including feedback loops between environments and genders. This suggests that the potential for variation is built into the organism as part of its heritage, affirming that modification is safely contained within the germ-plasm. One implication of Darwinian and neo-Darwinian thought is that sexed difference remains dependent on meiosis or sexual reproduction.

Departing from Darwinian and neo-Darwinian models that privilege sexual reproduction through heterosexual coupling as experienced by most animals and plants (meiotic sex), Margulis focuses on symbiosis, arguing that it is symbiosis that made our kind of reproductive sex (meiosis) possible. Symbiosis challenges the view that evolution is a competition among individuals where natural selection weeds out the weak individuals, leaving only the strong ones to survive. SET (Serial Endosymbiotic Theory) argues that the concept of the "individual" is misleading since, while the cells that come together to make a whole may be genetically related, more often "the 'individual' is composed of fused elements that are genetically distinct" (Margulis and Sagan 1997, 111).

Endosymbiosis challenges the narrowness of Darwinian and neo-Darwinian thought, suggesting a way to think engendering on a symbiotic level. Research on endosymbiosis explores the Archean Eon, 3,900 million years ago, when bacteria (nonrespiring membrane-bounded cells) invented genetic engineering as a mode of sex and reproduction (cloning). A simplified account would go something like this: First, a sulphur and heat-loving bacterium (called a fermenting "archaebacterium" or "thermoacidophil") merged with a swimming bacterium. This symbiotic merger became the nucleoplasm that is the basic substance of the ancestors of animal, plant, and fungal cells. Oxygen was toxic to these bacteria. With the spreading of oxygen, anaerobic bacteria merged with respiring bacteria. This symbiotic linkage was characterized by one bacterium entering an other, growing and reproducing (cloning) in it forever. Microbial bodies were thus forced to co-adapt through parallel processes of communication and reproduction due to the imminent pressures of the environment. These bacteria reproduced primarily through mitosis.[14] Larger, more complex cells evolved.

Margulis and Sagan emphasize that "the process of interiorization is specific to cellular life itself, which preserves and increases an interior order only by adding to the 'disorder of the external world'" (1995, 26). These three-way symbiotic mergers ingested but failed to digest bright green photosynthetic bacteria. Eventually, the green bacteria became chloroplasts. This final merger led to the ancestors of all plant life today, swimming green algae.

SET's central idea is that "extra genes in the cytoplasm of plant, animal and other nucleated cells are not 'naked genes'; rather, they originated as bacterial genes" (Margulis 1998, 37).[15] Of primary concern here is not simply the biological trajectory from ingestion to mitosis (cell division) through meiosis (two-parent sexual reproduction) but how symbiosis challenges the concept of *individual selection* essential to Darwinian and neo-Darwinian theories of evolution. In the Darwinian and neo-Darwinian literature, meiotic sex is foregrounded as the primary tool for the reproduction of the species. The Darwinian and neo-Darwinian understanding of sex and reproduction relies on scarcity, effort, and gratification. However, meiotic sex, according to endosymbiosis, is not necessarily the most successful form of reproduction. As Margulis and Sagan write, meiotic sex constitutes "a balancing act between our existence as bodies with two sets of chromosomes that inevitably die, and sex cells made by these bodies with one set of chromosomes which enjoy the possibility of continued life in the next generation" (1997, 83).

Fixed genders and sexually maintained species only began evolving about a billion years ago. Meiotic sex evolved in those protoctists that had already evolved by bacterial sex (both transgenically and symbiotically). "Neither plant nor animal appeared on Earth until bacteria had undergone at least 2000 million years of chemical and social evolution" (Margulis 1998, 56). All life has direct ancestry among bacteria: we are massive colonies of microorganisms. Human bodies are open, growing systems. Our boundaries are continually changing.

> We are tempted to believe in a standard, "normal" two-gender sexuality, but
> over the long haul, genders change. Imperfections, developmental abnor-
> malities, kinks, sports, "monstrous" new forms of behaviour, including repro-
> ductive behaviour, arise and persist as sexual organisms undergo social trans-
> formation. (Margulis and Sagan 1997, 213)

In bacteria, under conditions that necessitate meiotic sex, a "gender" transformation of the cell occurs that calls forth not two genders but dozens of
complimentary genders that attract each other. Sexual reproduction can
therefore be understood as an open system that has evolved many times on
this planet: "the second Law of Thermodynamics, rather than sex itself, is
the physical basis of our evolutionary focus on copulation and sex acts"[16]
(Margulis and Sagan 1997, 220). The link between sex and reproduction is
contingent. Engenderings may cause genderings, but it is just as likely that
they will individuate to create less predictable outcomes. Genderings are but
one possible consequence of engenderings: engenderings create the potential for relations that remain unthinkable, individuating toward metastability in directions we can but begin to reach toward.

Cellular biology provides a vocabulary through which we can learn to
identify how genders are codified through evolutionary practices. The adoption of one evolutionary model over an other may lead us to think that
genders are already defined as concrete processes of chromosomal truth.
Endosymbiosis alerts us to ways in which selection happens on another
level entirely, focusing not on gendered practices of selection as a primary
criterion for reproduction, but on symbiotic engenderings. An engagement
with this literature may allow us to better locate the ways in which gendered practices are taken for granted in everyday life.

Evolution is violent, all-consuming, world-altering. The constitutive
violence that exists at the heart of engenderings is always operative in the
relation between matter and form. Violence happens at all levels: this is a
lesson cellular biology teaches us. Engenderings are not straightforward.
Alterations cause mutations. Mutations cause infestations. Infestations become populations. But this is a violence at the level of individuation, not
identity. Violence of individuation creates potential energy. Violence here
operates as a denominator for instability: systems of individuation are volatile.
Matter and form interact in an exchange that is not based on individual
equality. Engenderings take form in ways that must always remain unpredictable, contingent on the environments through which they individuate.
Margulis and Fester write:

The "individuals" handled as unities in the population equations are themselves symbiotic complexes involving uncounted numbers of live entities integrated in diverse ways in an unstudied fashion. In representations of standard evolutionary theory, branches on "family trees" (phylogenies) are allowed only to bifurcate. Yet symbiosis analyses reveal that branches on evolutionary trees are mushy and must anastomose; indeed, every eukaryote, like every lichen, has more than a single type of ancestor. Such analyses also reveal rampant polyphyly (e.g., more than eight independent origins of parasitism in dicotyledonous plants...). The fact that "individuals"—as the countable unities of population genetics—do not exist wreaks havoc with "cladistics," a science in which common ancestors of composite beings are supposedly rigorously determined. Failure to acknowledge the composite nature of the organisms studied invalidates entire "fields" of study. (1991, 10)

A new concept of population emerges when fully determinate and discrete units are no longer operative as the precursors of an evolutionary model that relies on self-contained genetic units along pre-formed evolutionary linkages. As Ansell Pearson writes: "On the Weismannian[17] model, evolution is reduced to a predetermined genetic programme proceeding via the elimination and extermination of the unfit. But such a notion of evolution is bound up with a particular conception of individuals as determinate and discrete, functioning as closed systems" (1999, 167). When evolution is used as a calculational process, individuals become the impetus for survival. Genes become the immortal actors in the fight for continuity. Bodies are conceptualized according to strict codes of conduct (Rayner 1997, 70). This results in classificatory differences that are embedded in certain ideologies that already consider certain kinds of reproduction or survival to be of utmost consequence. Creative becoming is not at stake here. What is at stake is a continued re-instantiation of roles of speciation, including those of sex and gender.

In *Symbiotic Planet*, Lynn Margulis emphasizes three main points: (1) Human similarities to other life forms are far more striking than the differences; (2) Humans are not "better," "more prolific," or "more advanced" than any other species; (3) We live on a symbiotic planet. Endosymbiosis extends beyond the biological to the cultural and political realms. Genetic alterations brought about by symbiosis are translated in social and political realms into stereotypes that can also be symbiotically recombined. Forms are altered by matter that does not necessarily take the shape we presuppose. Symbiosis produces engenderings that defy the imagination, opening our worlds to the potential of qualitative change. Relation takes the place of "being," and we are faced with the fact that not only are our bodies open, symbiotic recombinations, but our political worlds are profoundly altered by a conception of the body that does not depend on systematic fixity, territorial unity or identity. When we begin to think our worlds symbiotically, we become aware that the worlds we create are altered by the very symbiotic processes that "we" always already are.

Interlude

The dance floor is crowded. I enter through an unmarked door in a strange city. I have never been here before, but I recognize the scene. Lights are dimmed, in the far corner I observe the DJ, the bar is surrounded by people sipping their drinks with their eyes on the dance floor. A few people are engaged in conversation. I look for a seat to change my shoes. Finally, I notice a spare chair with someone else's bag hanging from the back. I sit down, hurrying to get ready before I have to forsake the chair.

With my dance shoes on my feet, I begin to look around. I am looking for a woman. Today I am wearing my flat shoes. My long dress almost conceals my feet. Perhaps later I will change into my heels. But for the moment, I want to lead. The music changes. Tango waltz drifts over the floor from the speakers. The floor fills quickly: the lyrical 1-2-3 beat is popular. I see a woman across the room adjusting her shoes. I move toward her and ask her to dance. She smiles as I lead her onto the dance floor. She was expecting a man.

We do not know one another. Her body tentatively positions itself against mine. We feel for crevices, surfaces, attempting to make contact. The first dance is a little unsettled. She doesn't abandon herself to our touch. I move, sometimes forgetting to invite her to follow. We cannot quite establish a relation. We are still thinking of ourselves as individuals.

In the middle of the second tango waltz, I feel the movement beginning to take over our bodies. We begin to individuate together. A relation begins to take form. My body can no longer as easily be distinguished from hers. A symbiosis of movement begins to create engenderings we cannot yet predict. This makes us smile. The music leads us into unusual formations. I lead, she follows, I follow her following, she leads my following. A composition is emerging. Qualitatively, we are altering each other's matter-form, in-forming ourselves through the relation between movement and music. We operate according to the codes of tango but our improvisation take us into compositions that modulate our reciprocal spacing of time and timing of space.

Reaching toward one another, our individuations qualitatively alter our "individuality." Transducing, we *become* our leading and following, no longer altogether clear on who is doing what. The music takes hold of the floor. We follow the ground, participating in a larger metastable movement. We begin to dance with the room. The dance becomes a symbiosis that affects each couple. The music ends. We laugh, barely capable of containing the magic of the moment, suddenly uncomfortable. We step off the dance floor, seeking abandoned chairs, precariously aware that we have partaken in a symbiotic individuation that happens very rarely, usually only for an instant. Tango, a dance that can appear terribly constrained, led us momentarily to a qualitative change that modified our bodies in relation. Affective recombinations still resound in our now solitary bodies. We will not forget this experience: we are marked from the inside out.

This image of leading and following in Argentine tango foregrounds the potential for an engendering that tackles the problematics of gender without needing to draw a firm boundary between gendered notions of gender. Here, what is engendered must no longer be strictly codified as strictly "masculine" or "feminine." Bodies multiply and strands of gendered responses escape, perhaps bewildering those bodies from which they emanate. The result are new *configurations* of "gender" that exceed particular bodies. Bodies that are qualitatively altered are no longer predominantly recognized as "male" or "female," "leader" or "follower." These bodies now locate themselves as experiments-in-movement, qualitatively in-formed by the dance. My body is no longer strictly my own. The envelope of my skin is but the inception of my re-engendering.

In its incarnations as a dance that crosses the boundaries between gender (and it is important to add here that this is still a rare occurrence[18]), I experience in tango a continual shift between the corporeal and the incorporeal that allows my body to matter differently. In touch, the movement in relation calls forth the virtuality—the incorporeality—of my body. As we move, we space time, engendering what is not yet. Our dance virtually takes place through the openness to a touch-in-movement. Movement in the dance becomes the way I reach toward the potentiality of spacing time and timing space, challenging the boundaries of multiplicities-in-relation. I am no longer simply leading: I am reaching toward a space I will create with you. This spacing occurs in tandem with you who make the choice to engage

that space, to respond to the space by entering into it, by inviting me to follow. Your body thus becomes an extension of my movement, an extension
not of my *self* but of its improvisatory nature, an extension of our capacity
to enter into relation.

Individuation

Politics of touch are about potential energy. The actualization of potential
energy alters states, causing shifts from individuation to individuation
through the metastability of transduction. In other words, engenderings
alter the relation between time, space, and bodies as bodies time space and
space time. What a body can do is in-formed and de-formed by this potential energy at both the level of the individualizing individual and at the
level of state politics. Energy can actualize in myriad forms. In the case of
gender politics, what too often happens is that energy is located only at the
level of the individual body. In *Bodies That Matter*, Butler suggests that it
must be possible to use the terms "matter," "gender," and "sex," while at the
same time subjecting the terms to a critique that interrogates the exclusionary operations and differential power-relations that construct and delimit
feminist invocations of "woman." Without this critique, she argues, feminism loses its democratizing potential through a refusal to engage and
become transformed by the exclusions that put it into play. What is of particular concern to her, in a renegotiation of gendered bodies, is the normative aspect of all genderings, and the conjunction between this acceptance
of a gendered norm and the discourse of politics:

> sex not only functions as a norm, but is part of a regulatory practice that
> produces the bodies it governs ... whose regulatory force is made clear as a
> kind of productive power, the power to produce—demarcate, circulate,
> differentiate—the bodies it controls. (Butler 1993, 1)

Though Butler does point out that bodies never completely comply with
the norms of their gendering, her work does not foreground the ways in
which bodies create and alter formations of space-time. To speak of engendering is to qualitatively alter the ways in which matter and form are theorized. Bodies do matter, but perhaps not solely in the way outlined within
Butler's narratives of gender.

Bodies matter in excess of them-selves. As matter is potentialized, it actualizes into form. This form plays an in-forming role by exerting forces that

limit the actualization of matter's potential energy. This does not necessarily stop its actualization, but does in-form it. This process overspills the body's envelope, suggesting that the body always exceeds its-self. When the relationship between form and matter no longer takes place between inert matter and external form, a relation becomes individuated between form and matter that results in engenderings that exceed the parameters of the systems embodied by the limits of force. Individuations call forth transductions that engage new individuations. These individuations resist normalization: engendering bodies cannot be normalized because they are metastable, always moving toward potential.

The national body-politic normalizes gender so as to relegate the gendered body to specific sites within the nation's domestic chronotope. The intelligibility of the gendered body becomes dependent on its representation within the captivity of what the discourse of the nation considers to be the "norm." Traditionally, the political public space (the nation) is defined through the presence of men and contrasted to the apolitical, private space—the home—of women.[19] As a consequence, disenfranchised groups, such as women, often feel they have no other choice but to turn to the nation or to national values to register their claims as political, this despite the fact that turning to the nation's normative political systems usually reproduces the very same normative genderings.

What happens to this schema if we emphasize the potential of engendering rather than positing gender as an already-defined category? The national body-politic is organized around understandings of the body that pre-suppose a state of stability between matter and form. Within this stable system where identity is subsumed onto territory, and space and time are pre-existent, relationships are not permitted to escape the boundedness of their placings within time and space. Engendering exposes the mythical status of this dependence on conformity by calling forth a concept of relation that actively alters time and space as it points to the ways bodies produce matter and form. Because relation implies individuation and transduction, relation cannot as easily be located within the grids of the nation-state. Relation entails a new thinking of politics. Politics of Being are state politics. Politics of relation are politics of touch.

Inside and outside are not delimited within the concept of relation. Relation occurs in-between, at the interstices between the spaces and times created by bodies as they reach toward one another. Relation operates in the future anterior (the tense of the "will have" and of the "not yet").[20] The vocabulary of the future anterior is a vocabulary that calls forth an articulation of the political that departs from the stabilizing narratives of the nation-state, in which space and time remain overdetermined by the categories of geography and history subsumed to territory and identity. To conceptualize gender as operative within a vocabulary of the not-yet (or not quite yet) is to begin to think gender as engendering and bodies as mechanisms for the rethinking of time and space.

A politics of touch engages a milieu that is continually under construction. This milieu is incorporeal in the sense that it does not exist except in the relation that will emerge through individuations that have not yet materialized. This milieu is as much a transitory location as a spring board for individuations to occur not at the level of the individual body, but in relation. This milieu is an energetic force field that constitutes form and matter beyond notions of internal and external pre-configurations. Symbiosis of matter and form emerge relationally. This calls forth engenderings. The engendering body is a body not only *in* relation but *of* relation. Relation is activity, intensity, movement toward. Engendering is an event through which emergent bodies take form.

Politics

Engendering gender is a risky enterprise. Within engendering, matter takes many forms. Nature is abstract potential, leading us toward the Spinozean statement that we do not yet know what a body can do. Engendering here presupposes the body's capacity to deviate, create, and mutate. To think nature in flux is to foreground the nonlinear dynamics and the unpredictable potential of the transformation of matter at stake in all endosymbiotic relations, be they biological, technological, or political. Sex becomes an event. Event-fully, sex actualizes modes of relation and reproduction of information that unleash affect at all levels of a body in-formation. A body never stands alone: it becomes a body-biological, a body-technological, economical, political. It can also become a gendered body, but first and foremost it is an *engendering* body reaching toward its individuation-in-relation.

For Parisi, sex is co-terminous with engendering. She writes:

> Sex is a mode—a modification or intensive extension of matter—that is analogous neither with sexual reproduction nor with sexual organs. Sex expands on all levels of material order, from the inorganic to the organic, from the biological to the cultural, from the social to the technological, economic and political. Far from determining identity, sex is an envelope

that folds and unfolds the most indifferent elements, substance, forms and functions of connection and transmission. In this sense, sex—biological sex—is not the physical mark of gender. Rather, gender is a parallel dimension of sex entailing a network of variations of bodies that challenge the dualism between the natural and the cultural. (2004, 11)

The networks that produce gendered bodies are themselves prone to individuation. There can be unified gender neither at the level of the body nor its classifications. Engendering gender suggests engendering something that can be called "masculine" or "feminine" but that cannot be securely relegated to predictable characteristics that will reproduce themselves coherently under all conditions in all circumstances. Engendering gender presupposes a reaching toward that creates chronotopes that are variable and changeable, individualizing but not individual.

Engendering is emergence toward the multiple. To engender is to take into account potential. Potential calls forth reserves of becoming that prompt us to recognize that identity can never be identical to itself. Gender is not ontological, it is ontogenetic. To become gendered is to become more than one, but not just two. Being "more than one" is to exist in a metastable state that acknowledges the mutations of a body-in-relation that are not predetermined by a given ideal or an infrastructure that seeks to organize and categorize the realm of the biological possibilities of a body. These transfigurations designate not only the metastability of all body-systems, but also their virtuality: an engendering body—gendered or not—is always not quite what it can become. Unlike possibilities, which are predetermined within their own systems, potential (or the virtual) designates a movement toward emergence. This virtual body is real but not yet actual. To become actual implies the emergence of new compositions. Matter and immateriality, corporeality and incorporeality are operative on adjacent planes, shifting to and through one another. Engendering gender is to never know in advance what a gendered body can do.

Instead of positing nature as One, Spinoza draws our attention to the parallel multiplicities of being and becoming, the relation between politics and nature, intensity and extension, mind and body. All of these define, for Spinoza, the importance of thinking metastability rather than stability. Individuations operate through this logic, calling forth engenderings that locate themselves always between bodies, in the chronotope of the not-yet but already-underway. This chronotope is metastable because it remains far-from-equilibrium in a system that remains on the verge of modification due to parameters that are in flux. "[E]very system that finds itself in a metastable state harbours potentials which—because they belong to heterogeneous dimensions of being—are incompatible" (Combes 1999, 11). These potentials cause dephasings in the system that create unpredictable engenderings. "Re-thought as a metastable system, being before individuation is a field rich in potentials that can be only in becoming, that is in individuation" (Combes 1999, 15).

Transduction is the movement through which individuations relate. Transduction expresses the processual nature of individuation, whereby the observer is never preconstituted. A stable "outside" cannot be conceptualized within the process of transduction. As Simondon writes, the ontogenesis that takes place through transduction requires that we "follow being in its genesis, accomplishing the genesis of thought at the same time as the genesis of the object completes itself" (1995, 32). It is not a question of defining conditions of possibility (a Kantian move) or defining the limits of knowledge. Rather, it is a matter of positing thought and individuation in relation. It is only post-transduction, in the brief moment of embodiment-as-such, that an object of knowledge emerges.

"We cannot . . . know individuation, we can only individuate, individuate ourselves, individuate in ourselves" (Simondon 1995, 34). Individuations are not composed of identities. To engender is not to attach an identity to a body. "[O]nly a theory that thinks being through the operations of multiplicity of his or her individuation is in a position to transform an approach to the relation in order to understand it as 'a relation in being, a way of being'" (Combes 1999, 33). Relation does not convey a separation between, for example, engendering and gender, but is borne in the emergence of gender within engendering, constituting the terms themselves as relational. Being is becoming-relational.

There are no pre-established criteria that would favor the passage from engendering to gendering. If gender is not conceived as a naturalized biological essence or strictly a sociocultural condition of possibility, we can conceive of a politics of gender as an engendering toward a composition and decomposition of bodies engaging in the activity of forces and energies that are neither solely biological nor solely political. "A body is defined by metastable relations between microcellular and multicellular bodies, the bodies of animals and humans, the bodies of society and technological bodies merging and unleashing new mutating compositions" (Parisi 2004, 27). Engenderings that gender are not exhausted by their classifications. Rather, they are connected to an intensive body that is inventive. This transformation exceeds a simple shift in discourse. The en-gendered body is an affective, relational body that not only individuates in excess of its-self, but creates new and differing chronotopes that qualitatively alter the matter-form of which it is composed. What emerges is "a map of the non-linear movements of connection between causes and effects unfolding the potential (force) of a body to mutate through an ecosystem of indefinite mixtures" (Parisi 2004, 29).

Engendering gender gives us a sense of what a body can do. For Spinoza, a body is not primarily an organism or an organization. It is an assemblage of kinetic particles and forces, of motion and energy. A body is a network of imminent trajectories with longitudinal and latitudinal lines intersecting. This is a radical departure from the Cartesian axis, which situates matter and form in predictable hierarchies, prescribing a pre-established organization of the body in space and time. In Spinoza, matter and form are mutational: what is at stake is the relation between motion and rest and the capacity to affect and be affected. Bodies here exist in a concept of Nature which exposes the coexistence of matter-form unfolding in a continuum without equivalence.[21] This recalls Simondon: "The individual is the reality of a constituting relation, not the interiority of a constituted term" (Simondon 1995, 60). Coexistence is not simply a lack of resistance. It is an *activation*,[22] a politics of touch.

There are state consequences to a politics of touch. Politics of touch operate within an affective-semantic structure quite foreign to nation-state politics. Regulations as to stringent measures of organized difference [man/woman, citizen/refugee, state/interstate], structures of integration [social models that set up the less privileged as will-less victims], dimensions of belonging [identity practices] are potentially subverted by a politics of touch. Within a politics of touch, gender exists not as an enduring predicament within a pre-configured space-time (such as that of the territorial imaginary of the nation-state) where "woman" is too often posited as a docile body that can be located, once and for all. As Parisi emphasizes in *Abstract Sex*, individuations do not create unities such as "woman" or "man." Rather, individuations are complex already at the cellular level and challenge the hierarchies between bacterial and human sexual practices that seek to relegate gendered vocabularies within capitalist narratives of surplus value and territorial vocabularies of binding identity practices. Endosymbiosis emphasizes that the regulation of bodies cannot be a one-sided operation. Any reaching toward is a crossing of a malleable border from gender to gender, from gender to en-gendering, engendering to engenderings. Bodies can be regulated, certainly, but bodies relate always beyond or in spite of these regulations,

reciprocally, and this is their politics, a politics of touch that operates always, in some sense, in excess of the national body-politic.

Engendering challenges the governing body-politic by questioning the
regulation of its politicized and depoliticized bodies. Engendering does violence to the state by substituting the concept of identity with individuation.
Bodies can no longer be located strictly within territorial grids. Engendering
and engendered, we do not stand at an instrumental distance from the terms
from which we experience a violation. We individuate in relation. Relation
does violence to identity.

Heidegger's name for this act of violent imposition is *Entwurf*, a term
that draws attention to the manner in which we make sense of a situation
into which we are thrown, due to which we find ourselves disoriented. Touching across time and space can be an unhinging experience, particularly if we
take full account of the manner in which the touch of an other manifests itself across our body, expanding the dimensions of our environments, marking the intervals between our engenderings, dis-covering the measures of
our symbioses. Butler understands this moment of *Entwurf* as one of radical
undecidability, the state prior to a decision in which one can never reach a
"pure" context, since every context is "always already" retroactively constituted by a decision. My reaching across space and time to touch you is, in
this sense, an *Entwurf*.

Touch is a decision to engender that throws us off balance. A politics of
touch asks us to be willing to lose our balance, momentarily, to not know in
advance, to disagree.[23] Antagonism is at the heart of a politics of touch.
When this antagonism remains untheorized, we are left with a politics that
understands consensus as the only alternative to antagonism. But if we think
of antagonism as a moment when we accept our constitutive difference as a
measure of our not being able to "know" (where reason and the senses are
no longer associated in opposition), antagonism can be conceived as an
aspect of the very *Entwurfenheit* that characterizes a politics of touch. For
Jacques Rancière, political antagonism designates the tension between the
structured social body in which each part has its place, and "the part of no
part" which unsettles this order on account of the empty principle of universality. For Rancière, this identification of the non-part with the whole is
the elementary gesture of politicization. The non-part includes the bodies
society cannot define or that resist their allocated subordinate space. Without antagonism we are faced with depoliticization. Antagonism is analogous
to the potential violence of in-formation that creates the metastable sys-

tems through which individuations can take place. Antagonism opens the way for engenderings.

When we consider the engendering body, we can see its operation as that which not only individuates in potentially antagonistic ways, but also as that which creates antagonism within the national body-politic. In the moment of touching an other (within or across time and space), my body re-engenders itself, causing a potential fissure in the national body-politic. My engendering body is difference incorporated symbiotically, difference not sexed through stratified evolutionary narratives, but difference embodied through engenderings toward politics that reach toward differing understandings of what a body can do. "One does not represent, one engenders and traverses" (Deleuze and Guattari 1987, 364).

5.

Making Sense of the Incommensurable:
Experiencing Democracy

Expressions of the Political

Brian Massumi writes: "The world does not exist outside of its expressions"
(2002b, xiii).[1] Expressions are not simply representations, descriptions,
content-driven empirical correspondences. Expressions cannot be reduced
to external forces reacting upon a body. Expressions are in and of the body,
sensual and sensing:

> The force of expression . . . strikes the body first, directly and unmediately.
> It passes transformatively through the flesh before being instantiated in
> subject-positions subsumed by a system of power. Its immediate effect is a
> differing. The body, fresh in the throes of expression, incarnates not an
> already-formed system but a modification—a change. Expression is an
> event. (Massumi 2002b, xvii)

Touch is expressive. The expressivity of touch is political: expressivity provides an opening for an event. If we persist in working through the various
guises of eventness—relation, engendering, expression, extension, affect—
we continue to widen the opening for politics. The ongoing proposition of
Politics of Touch is to enable politics to recapture expression and extend it.
Creating an environment for politics is part of the thinking that accom-
panies these extensions, be they expressive, sensing, engendering.

Within political thought, politics has most often been conceived of as *signifying.* A politics of touch posits politics as *asignifying*, inviting us to think politics through its potential for expression rather than representation. Expression articulates a body that is not foreclosed by meaning. This body is a sensing body in movement. Sensing, signification becomes mutational. A mutational politics might be an abstract machine, an asignifying dynamic, a tensile ethics. Politics of touch prolongs emergent dynamics. "There is no entity to expression.[...] Its emerging into words and things is always an event before it is a designation, manifestation or signification propositionally attached to a subject" (Massumi 2002b, xxiii–xxiv). Expression produces momentum.

An emphasis on expression leads us away from a signifying subject to a becoming of relation. Expression is not reserved for the single voice of the speaking subject: expression dialogically produces chronotopes that expand the intervals between speakers and listeners. These intervals are not voids between discrete bodies; they are space-times alive with intonations, invocations, perturbations. To express is not to state a fact. To express is to speak-with. Any speaking-with implies a dialogue, an infinite conversation. An infinite conversation supposes that the work is yet to be invented.

Expression's extensions can only be charted after the fact. "There is no *tabula rasa* of expression" (Massumi 2002b, xxix). Expression urges us to think language at its most productive limit, where language is conceived as a clutter in excess of mere representation. Expression leads us to the body, to touch, to skin not as the envelope of the body but as its interweaving of inside and outside, its endodermic, mesodermic, and ectodermic potentialities. Expression plays on myriad surfaces, linguistic, corporeal, incorporeal.

One way of exploring the relation between expression, asignification, and the body is to pause at the concept of skin. This allows us to place at the fore one of the body's organs without falling into the trap of re-instantiating the body-as-organization: skins are made up of bodies as much as bodies are made up of skins. Skin extends beyond the "body proper" giving us pause. Resting at the edge of our skins we cannot help but wonder what holds us together. Mark Taylor writes: "Since the organism as a whole is formed by a complex of dermal layers, the body is, in effect, nothing but strata of skin in which interiority and exteriority are thoroughly convoluted" (1997, 12). Skin, our largest organ, doubles upon itself, duplicitous, touching itself as other. Skins promise to keep organs inside. Organs protecting organs: "Hide hides hide" (Taylor 1997, 12). The body—even the technological body—is concerned with skin, be it skin color or the surface of the screen, threatening to transform place into a dermagraphics. Skinscapes abound.

We pay attention to the surface. We are mesmerized by it, by its mutations, its impenetrability. Body art is simply an obvious example: "Body art
represents . . . a sustained effort to reverse the dematerialization of art by
making the body matter" (Taylor 1997, 111). Most body art encourages us
to forget, for an instant, that we are piercing our organs.[2] Facing the "outside," we place our skins between us and the world. If we consider our bodies
as whole, we imagine our skins as protective (prosthetic). Strange connection, then, between bodies without organs and skins.

Skins do not need "external" markings to express their mutability. Skins
are mutations, continuously altering the limits of our engagements with the
world: hot, cold, open, scarred, contained, exposed. Any sense of security
we might have invested into the concept of skin and its ability to protect us
from the outside is cast into doubt when we recognize that skin is but one of
the ephemeral signs of the ultimate asignificability of the border. Bodies are
not foreclosed by limits. Bodies extend, expressively, creating skinscapes
that are as complex as the landscapes that make up our political vistas.

Is the asignifying body thinkable? Perhaps it is uncountable, incoherent,
but not unthinkable. A new vocabulary of the surface seems necessary,
however, to address the strange incorporation of bodies into skins and skins
into bodies. To begin with, we must renegotiate the binaries within the language that frames the body: skin, bones, flesh, inside, outside, mind, matter,
reason, sense. Skin and bones may not be as dichotomous as we believe
they are. When bones are conceived as layers of skin, the body thins (we
have a tendency to think the body's weightiness from the inside out, focusing first on the bones, that is, the structure that holds it together). As Taylor remarks, at the point where bones and skin are no longer juxtaposed,
"the body is deprived of its substance and appears to be on the verge of disappearing" (1997, 139).

How the body materializes and dematerializes is significant for a politics
that is concerned with bodies. When we conceive of democracy through a
politics of touch, we assume that there is a body to reach toward. The pre-
sumption that the body is concrete is based, too often, on a fixed, territorialized, secure entity. If we approach the body's surfaces as asignifying, we begin
to be aware of the manner in which bodies are marked for their coherence
through recognizable signs of race, sex, gender, ethnicity. A naturalization
of these markings (in the name of national body-politics, of gender or race
politics) is the reason we are so quick to recognize and identify these markers.
Of course bodies can never be reduced to these external signs. But systems
of governance rely on these signs to compartmentalize the bodies in their

midst. Politics is instrumental in creating and being created by the bodies it attempts to govern. Politics of touch makes palpable difference engendered, identity individuating, race transducing. Within a politics of touch, bodies govern democracy as much as democracy governs bodies.

Bodies don't stand still. Skin demonstrates this in poignant ways. Skin is always toward-death, its upper layer already on the verge of being replaced. Taylor writes: "At the point where I make contact with the world, I am always already dead" (1997, 13). The skin is the expression of the momentariness of life, of the passage toward a continuous re-emergence. Skin is metamorphosis in action: "Skin is a multilayered, multipurpose organ that shifts from thick to thin, tight to loose, lubricated to dry, across the landscape of the body" (Imperiale 2002, 29). Skin gathers experience and exudes, its expressions gravitating in and out, from outermost to innermost cavities. Living and dead, skin is self-repairing, self-replacing, sensual and sensing, flush with nerves, glands, capillaries. Skin, grown in laboratories today, modulates the meaning, form, matter, dimensions, surface of the world at large.

Skin transforms the political field. To think politically is to become aware of the surfaces that connect intervals between worlds. Skin emerges here not simply as an envelope but as a connector between various timed-spaces. The interval is not a non-space-time. The interval is a quality of space-time that wanders between surfaces that seem hermetic. A politics of touch finds its momentum in these intervals, incorporating the body as a weave rather than as a closed environment. A politics of touch does not pre-exist a body: it transforms it. Skin incites me to address the paralysis at the heart of political systems that continue to be caught in an increasing (though for the most part, unspoken) tension between virtualization and biopolitics. In these state systems, biopolitics must be incorporated into the body-politic as actualization. Otherwise, the body "itself" cannot be accessed. Biopolitics thereby becomes institutionalized as a way of binding the imaginary of a body to a modality of hierarchical power. Biopolitics that strives to control an "actual" body condemns the body to a form that becomes a state of exception without release.

The skin challenges this version of biopower, reinscribing within biopower the idea that a body cannot be controlled as such because a body never pre-exists measures of control. The procedure that renders a body docile—that sustains the national body-politic—must either be reinvented each time the skin fissures, or the skin must become airtight. Skin provides a vocabulary for the political body whose prerequisite need not be actualization. Skin as a biological and political construct reminds us that biopolitics are as virtual as they are fleshy. Biopolitics speak of a body incorporeal, where power is already affecting the body *before* it has become a body, and the body is already affecting politics *before* politics has been defined as such. Yet, skin is both corporeal and incorporeal. The body of skin is an extension, always, of the body as it is not yet. Skin reminds us that the body moves all the time, composing and decomposing itself, sensing all the while. Senses play on and beyond our surfaces—our skins—enabling not only new ways of coming to experience, but different ways of thinking the relation between making sense and sensing, between knowing and sensing, between expression and content, between surface and depth.[3]

Thick to Think

To be a body is to be thick with thought. To think is to open the way toward the political as that which must continually be rethought. It is important to register the political voice in this narrative I am weaving in order to assess the vitality of the kind of expression made possible through sensing. A politics that senses rather than investing all of its energy in the practice of signification is not a politics without rigor. Indeed, there may be nothing less rigorous or more apolitical than the acceptance of signification as the basis for experience. This only reinstates the dichotomy between reason and sensing.

Politics has been invested in the narrative of signification since its metaphysical beginnings. By metaphysical, I am referring to a privileging of a certain organization of time that casts an opposition between the temporal and the atemporal, the eternal and the transitory, the finite and the infinite, the transcendental and the empirical. This kind of political time (what Michael Shapiro calls national time[4]) refutes the potential of time to express, to reach toward, to pace space. If we relinquish this imaginary of time, what remains is a kind of radical finitude, a living-toward-death, a movement of thought, a skinscape, a politics of touch, a certain virtual becoming that opens the way for a thinking of a democracy-to-come.

Pace becomes political when we begin to think time as a movement not in one direction but as a reaching toward that is rhizomatic. In Derrida's terms, we would then be thinking time as aporia.[5] The aporia refers here to the "'impossible' relation between the passage of time and political organization" (Beardsworth 1996, xiii). Derrida suggests that philosophy's traditional disavowal of time is already political and therefore carries political consequences. Metaphysical logic translates time into presence rather than attending to its irreducibility. According to Beardsworth, "[j]udgements and inventions which have endured this experience have greater chance of recognizing difference according to the lesser violence" (1996, 101). When the time of the present as presence (the knowable) is challenged by the time of the future anterior (the unknowable or that beyond reach), inventions are born. The best inventions are the impossible ones.

A politics of touch is an impossible politics. It is a politics of the future anterior (the will-have come), a politics that is impossible because it has no horizon. A politics of touch is a passage rather than a presence. My skin marks this passage, my wrinkles betray time as fleeting, my touch reaches toward the incongruity that is my own alterity, your difference. I cannot be indifferent to that which I cannot even conceive. This is the challenge of a politics of touch. "Now" is the time of a politics of touch, but not a "now" which remains in the present, rather a "now" that dances between tenses, undulating on the inner crevices of the skin of experience, expressing itself through a touch that cannot quite capture the passage of time even while continuing to reach out. *Now* is a recurrent potentiality: now is to be negotiated, again and again. As Beardsworth writes, now is "the ever-recurrent promise of the non-adequation of the present to itself" (1996, 101).

An impossible politics does not disavow time. Rather it invents time through a re-cognition of the passage of "nows." This is also what touch does. When I reach out toward you "now" and I touch you, I mark one instant. In the sharing of skin—even if touch is not skin to skin I always touch a surface—I leave an imprint. This imprint is ephemeral. To be felt again, it must be repeated in another *now*, rendering the touch "in time" impossible if time is to be gathered into a narrative of presence. Touch is a trace, always deferred, always leading toward another moment, another imprint, another touch. A politics of touch calls forth a democratic movement toward justice that releases judgment indefinitely. In practice, this means experiencing justice as the opportunity of postponing a final decision even while engaging fully in an act of reaching-toward. To engage fully is to admit responseability. A politics of touch recognizes that there will always be time(s) for another judgment, for another justice that itself will call forth the irreducibility of time.

Beardsworth writes:

> The impossible aporia of law releases the possibility of possibility. This impossible possibility constitutes the measure by which all judgments can only fail to measure themselves. Hence the measure of judgment is nothing but the impossibility of its measure; in this impossibility the singular arrives. (1996, 44)

A deconstruction of the political suggests that judgment as such is impossible. Judgment is impossible insofar as judgment must take place in a pre-specified organization of time and space (and there is, ultimately, no such time and space). It is for this reason that we must not confuse judgment, justice, and the law. While the law is always written with the option of a rewriting, thereby at least offering the potential of justice, judgment forecloses this very opening by stopping time. Judgment is opposed to my response: it wants to have the final word. A politics of touch in the guise of a democracy-to-come foregrounds response-ability. I respond to you always toward a present that is not yet with the promise to respond again. Touch is never a single gesture. Response-ability is a radical understanding of the future anterior.

The relation of law to time is invested in the imaginary of politics and its futures. If time is not goal directed, outcomes cannot be classified in the same way, and laws cannot be written in stone. Judgment and law are here juxtaposed. The suggestion is that law operates in the virtual because it always remains to be rewritten. This paradox (since law seems like the most staid of events) betrays the complex time lines already operative within political systems. Beardsworth suggests that "all inventions can only be 'recognized' after the event, and the history of their exclusions always already haunt the 'present' of the act of invention" (1996, 99). To recognize is to re-cognize, to take into consideration again. Inventing new imaginaries depends on re-inventing both our investment in time and our investment in the law. By thinking the law according to the logic of the aporia, and by locating the porous skins of our intermingled and overlapping bodies (be they singular or multiple) as potential embodiments of the aporia, we can begin to appreciate the manner in which law has always been predicated on a certain delay of time rather than on the fixity of time. The violence of the law depends on legislation coming either too early or too late. There is no *presence* of the law. The law is written on porous skin. The law itself is aporetic. "The future anterior of determinant law is the law of the force of all law" (Beardsworth 1996, 100). The aporetic quality of time and law mark the delay of human invention. The justification of law is what makes time stand still, turning politics into policy.

This is not to say that law itself opens the way for a democracy-to-come. It is to underscore the ways in which even state politics move to different choreographies of time. Within the state, a narrative is written that binds security to judgment, bodies to law, even while bodies and laws continuously escape the straitjacket of striated space-time. Skins regenerate as laws are rewritten, themselves rewriting the passage of time, reinscribing bodies into their midst. The question is how to rewrite *justice* as the avowal of time's *différance*.

When time is concentrated solely in the constructed framework of linear present-past-future, we become blind to the potential of the law,[6] disavowing our complicity in the compartmentalizing of justice in terms of a pre-orchestrated distribution of times and spaces, of grids onto which our bodies are placed and secured. This denial of the violence of law is a disavowal of time's *différance*. It is a disavowal of the spacing of the body as it marks time and is marked by the timed spaces it creates. There is no time or space that is not of the body. There is no body that does not rework the parameters through which it operates. There is no law that is not predicated on the manner in which bodies instantiate spaced-times and timed-spaces.

Shifting Skinscapes

Our skins are being designed even as we speak. Bodies, skins, politics, democracy are always already technological. To think of the relation between skins, bodies, and senses, we must become comfortable with the logic of the prosthesis. Touch, I would like to suggest, is a certain prosthesis not only of politics, but of the body itself. While the prosthetic[7] emerges as a current concept in new technologies and will be discussed as such here, it is important to underline the fact that I refer to prosthesis not as a way of situating a post-technological body but in an effort to locate the body as always-already technological.

Ellen Lupton writes:

> The rise of digital media over the past decade has changed the practice of design..., the primacy of the skeleton has given way to the primacy of the skin.... New materials react to light, heat, touch and mechanical stress. Translucency and mutability have replaced transparency and permanence. The outer envelope has detached from the interior volume. Flexible membranes are embedded with digital and mechanical networks.... Industrial skins have assumed a life of their own. (2002, 31)

The corporeal is showing new kinds of evidence. Increasingly, human tissue is becoming an incorporation of complex weaves of dacron, silicon, and metal. Biology is in dialogue with edible chemistries of hybrid derivation, as electronic circuitries measure the pulse and possibility of life.[8] This era of the always already technologized body is not an era devoid of touch. In fact, touch as a prosthetic device is being multiplied at the rate at which skins are being produced. Customized instrumentation, such as data gloves and haptic interfaces,[9] to name but a few sense systems, are reorienting technology toward touch, introducing new ways of thinking about touch, gesture, interaction, and movement. These sensory mechanisms carry their own problematic pasts, at once displacing entrenched histories of the organic human body and delimiting new technologies for complicated and problematic usages by the military, where they are often assimilated into assemblages of control and surveillance. Be that as it may, there is no doubt that touch—and its politics—is continuing to frame our investment in our bodies and our skins.

Technology alters the manner in which bodies gather information. Can we conceive of touch itself as a technology that is prosthetic to the "organic" body? Since bodies can "survive" without touch, touch could be construed as a tool, a craft, an expressive relation of the body toward the world. *Techne*, it is useful to remember, refers to a craft or tool that supplements the body's activities. If we consider the body's activities to be mere survival mechanisms, we might assume that the organs would count as the extent of the body's armory. But we know that survival depends on more than our blood pumping. It is in this regard that the senses can be considered as *techne*, technologies (or prostheses) of the moving body. This prosthetic quality of the senses can be extended in many ways. Mark Taylor offers one example:

> Perhaps not only electronic webs are prostheses that supplement the human mind and body, but also the human mind and body are prostheses that extend the net. If the body is an extension of the electronic networks that increasingly constitute our world rather than the reverse, then the body's reality becomes virtual. (1997, 143)

The virtual here refers to an ethics of emergence in which a recursive futurity is expressed. Deleuze and Guattari suggest that ethico-aesthetic practices can access virtual forces by foregrounding expression's momentum. When time is evoked as a reaching toward, we express ourselves through an eventness that is virtual. When the world is conceived of as an infinite series of folds or differentials—when my body is no longer "mine" but multiplied with myriad prostheses aligned with various forces such as the senses—a permeation occurs that upsets the "balance" between the inside and the outside. Relations are created that cannot be predicted. Prophesies are relational. Relations are generative.

If we understand the virtual as a realm where differential relations coexist, we can begin to explore the potential of our bodies as generative, always-already technological (that is, prosthetic) sensory expressions. As Andrew Murphie writes: "The virtual, as a necessary part of the object, is . . . absolutely real, but this is in the sense of a reality which is different/ciated and produced as different/ciated" (2002, 199). To think virtually is to think "reality" differently. Taylor writes:

> The connective wiring of the body extends beyond its ostensible limits to the cultural networks within which it is inscribed. With lines of communication that turn everything inside-out and outside-in, bodies are prostheses of machines as much as machines are prostheses of bodies. (1997, 330)

Thinking the body connectively creates a path for exploring the relation between bodies and politics as a rhythmic capacity for *différance* whereby bodies enter into relation with surfaces and "holes sprout in what had been experienced as wholes" (Doyle 2003, 12). There is nothing passive in this relation: bodies become surprising expressions of the event, expressions alive with asignification and sensuality that tear configurations of meaning and foster the emergence of new forms of metamorphosis.

Politics of touch are postvital politics in the sense that they reframe what we understand "life" to be. In our philosophical and political blindness as regards the prosthetic nature of the body, we have consistently overlooked the manner in which politics has written life as a scientific object, rendering it indiscernible from installed systems of representation. If we consider postvital politics as an opportunity to foreground the relationality that is at the heart of a politics of touch, we realize that the boundaries between science and representation are soluble. This is not new to science. Doyle writes:

> The very success of the informatic paradigm, in fields as diverse as molecular biology and ecology, has paradoxically dislocated the very object of biological research. . . . This "postvital" biology is, by and large, interested less in the characteristics and functions of living organisms than in sequences of molecules and their effects. These sequences are themselves articulable through databases and networks; they therefore garner their effects through relentless repetitions and refrains, connections and blockages rather than through the autonomous interiority of an organism. (2003, 21)

This is a strong argument for the fact that organisms have always already been networks. Marcello Barbieri also argues along these lines, suggesting that living systems must be understood as a tripartite ensemble of genotype, hereditary information primarily although not exclusively born by DNA; ribotype, the swarm of translational apparatuses that transform DNA into the tertiary structures of folded proteins; and phenotype, the dynamic embodiment of this information and its transformations (in Doyle 2003, 23).

Life is postvital in the same way that humans are posthuman. This is not a shift in life or humanity per se. It is a shift in our way of *thinking* life and humanity. Life has been blocked by a narrative of subjectivity that holds to a model of linear time that presupposes categories of meaning based on pre-established signifying structures. The becoming-silicon of flesh and the becoming-flesh of silicon point toward not a radical change but an enactment of the manner in which the body has always already been multiple. "We are entering a period in which we have the capabilities to use informational technologies to generate new forms of fleshy experience," write Philip Thurtle and Robert Mitchell (2002, 2). The concept of posthumanity[10] focuses on the relation between the body and embodiment, leading us, finally, toward a body without organs that engages (with) the world not by means of pre-established limitations, but through an emergent network that overlaps prosthetic and organic devices. To think the body any other way is to make it impossible to explore the potential of politics, for politics depends on this quality of supplementarity. Disagreement and astonishment are stifled when the limits of the body—the limits of relation—are pre-ordained.

Katherine Hayles writes: "the posthuman view thinks of the body as the original prosthesis we all learn to manipulate, so that extending or replacing the body with other prostheses becomes a continuation of a process that began before we were born" (1999, 3). There are no definite boundaries to the body. Our skins overlap, undermining strict measures of inside and outside. Our bodies are amalgams, collections of heterogeneous components (antibodies, germs, bacteria, implants) that undergo continuous reformulation. This reformulation is an asignifying process. Bodies and antibodies interact, sometimes to their advantage, sometimes to their detriment. Conditions of possibility change, and with them new (anti)bodies materialize and dematerialize. We are not in possession of our bodies, though we do have the capacity to creatively express them. We are our bodies, but even "being" our bodies is too ontological. Our bodies are vectors of emergence that generate virtual embodiments in a future anterior we can only reach toward. Our skins are peeling away, leaving new surfaces for experimentation.

Vicki Kirby writes:

Corporeal existence is generative and generous in its inclusiveness; an infinite partitioning, mediated from and within itself; an animated representation whose fractured mirroring includes cellular and atomic life. The intricate embrace of these recognitions is the matter of corporeality wherein recognition, a virtual splitting, is the stuff of reality. (1997, 146)

Within much political thought, bodies are written into narratives that subsume identity and territory in the name of a coherence of time and space pre-imposed onto the body as formed matter. Mediation in this instance refers to pre-written narratives interrupted by lines of communication. Yet skins do more than replicate a rehearsed scene of writing. Skins are corporeographic: they sign the body in directions (in and out and beyond) that we cannot fathom. I write my body differently through each overlapping of sense. I split, virtually. When I touch, I inscribe my skin onto yours and remain imprinted, forever changing the dynamic of my own writing. Representation becomes sensible, sensitized by my act of reaching toward a judgment yet-to-come, toward a time when judgment may be aporetic, waiting for the touch that never quite arrives. Biology is not all there is to skin: skin is the drama of the body's re-markability.

Politics can address this remarkability. To do so, we must have the courage to assume a shifting skinscape. Kirby writes:

The political force of prescriptive and essentializing discourses is not confined to the validity of their truth claims. The matter of essentialism exceeds the politics of correction because the body as the scene of writing is an inscripting of all essentialisms, even of the politically offensive. With/in the complexity of the resulting weave, the stuff of essence is rearticulated: it is no longer a simple unity whose efficacy is directly legible. (1997, 160)

We write that which we are on the verge of sensing. Writing is not something we return to as finished: writing is always of the future. Bodies leave traces of themselves everywhere, writing themselves into complex rhizomatic technological, political, corporeal narratives. Politics of representation are complicated by the senses, which refuse to cohere to one story. I cannot sense unilaterally: I smell to see and touch to taste. A politics of touch operates within such shifting skinscapes. As prosthetic to the body, politics must begin to think itself as an extension to the body's sensing apparatus. Politics is not beyond the body, it is of the body. Bodies sense, and their sensing movements reach toward relations of emergence, expressions always already incorporated into political texts. When we accept these postvital incorporations of posthumanity, we envisage a thinking of a future anterior in which democracies remain to come.

Democracy

For Derrida, democracy is still to come: "We do not yet know what *democracy* will have meant, or what democracy is. For democracy does not present itself, it has not yet presented itself, but that will come" (2005, 9). The issue is not how to place a politics of touch within an already-existing discourse of democracy, but how to think touch in such a way as to allow us to re-negotiate a politics of time and space that would not be anathema to a democratic politics. This is not a small task, as William Connolly underlines, for narratives of democracy (as an already-existing phenomenon) are themselves changing: in a world replete with asymmetries of pace and an acceleration of speed that often supports corporate colonization of new spaces inside and outside highly organized capitalist states, "the ensuing politics of capture often foments reactive movements in the name of nationhood and religious purity, expressed as attempts to slow the world down by returning to a unity imagined to have been intact sometime in the past" (2002, 143). Politics is speeding up, and with it, the concept of democracy is changing: "The question for me, then, is not how to slow the world down, but how to work with and against a world moving faster than heretofore to promote a positive ethos of pluralism" (Connolly 2002, 143).

For Connolly, a certain asymmetry of pace is critical to democratic pluralism. Yet, asymmetries of pace also foster the fragility of democracy. It is this fragility that is of particular interest here as regards the intersection between politics, touch, and democracy. The movement invoked by a reaching-toward must always be uncertain: when I reach toward you, I do not know what I will touch—I do not yet know how your touch will return to me. I know only that I am willing to take the risk inherent in the movement of reaching-toward. This uncertainty is predicated on the double-take of touch. If I pretend to know the outcome of my reaching-toward, I am not really reaching-toward. In other words, when space is preconstructed (when the space between is overdetermined by my certainty about you and your simple location[11] in the world), there is no space to cross, there is no chronotope to create, and ultimately, there is no potential for touch as a reaching-toward. Touch becomes political the instant I reach out toward you in an uncertain movement of unknowing, of unknowability. Touch, when I reach you, does not then transfer into a knowable commodity, but into another possibility of reaching out: I touch you to touch you again. To touch is not to know.

What I do have when I reach out to touch you is an idea. In his writing on democracy-to-come, Derrida foregrounds the notion of the idea:

> We already have some "idea" of what "democracy" should mean, and what it *will have already meant*—and the idea, the ideal, the Greek *eidos* or the *idea* also designates the turn of a contour, the limit surrounding a visible form. Did we not have some *idea* of democracy, we would never worry about its indetermination. We would never seek to elucidate its meaning or, indeed, call for its advent. (2005, 18)

As an idea, democracy can not be conceived as anything but that toward which I reach, unknowing. Within the idea is the notion of liberty: to be free is to have an idea. Derrida writes:

> First it should be noted that if this freedom ... seems to characterize social and political behaviours, the right and power of each to do what he or she pleases, the faculty of decision and self-determination, as well as the license to play with various possibilities, it presupposes, more radically still, more originally, a freedom of play, an opening of indetermination and indecidability *in the very concept* of democracy, in the interpretation of the democratic. (2005, 25)

Liberty, as I conceive it here, is about sense, about making sense incommensurably, about sensing beyond a politics of individuals toward a politics of individuation. Being free entails subverting the overdetermined conjunction between sensing and knowing that captures space-time in an effort to locate a finite body. To be free is to take time for a thought that is not already circumscribed within simple location. The time for liberty—the time of democracy, of touch—is always deferred, it is the time of movement itself. Democracy must not be conceived as a movement that has arrived. Bodies do not stop. They resonate, they express, the operate, they sense, they live, they love, but they do not stop unless they die and even then they exfoliate, they decompose. As a sensing liberty—a freedom to sense—democracy's time is that of the moment endlessly deferred. It is the potential of becoming, the *espacement* that calls forth a trace of its own possibilities.

Connolly writes:

> A slow, homogenous world often supports undemocratic hierarchy because it irons out discrepancies of experience through which constituencies can become reflective about self-serving assumptions they habitually use to appraise themselves in relation to others. But in a world marked by asymmetrical zones of speed, it is critical that citizens in a variety of walks of life

Making Sense of the Incommensurable

be provided with structural opportunities for periodic escape and retreat from a fast-paced life. (2002, 144)

Asymmetrical zones of speed characterize a thinking about time that challenges the teleology of the nation-state, in which time is conceived first as a stable historicity that supports the sublimation of geography into history. National time provides few openings within its streamlined narratives for processual concepts such as individuation, opting instead for the close enumeration of the citizens within the imposed structure of the state apparatus. Democratic time, on the other hand, functions in the mode of the not-yet, which is characteristic of the future anterior. The not-yet in-forms the present while incorporating within it past and future. Time that is no longer conceived as linear is a time that carries within experience sheets of the past and future, virtually present. Radically different from national time, which emphasizes a historicity that depends on continuity (even if it must continually be reinvented as such), democratic time documents what is yet-to-come in the form of possible worlds.[12] Such a politics of potential provokes fissures in homogeneous organizations of time-space. Diverging from the homogenization of time that drives the nationalist rhetoric that propels the state apparatus, democratic time cannot be about an enforcing of identity within a fixed territory (a coagulation of space). It must instead rethink how space meets time in and through the body, thus creating spaced-times and timed-spaces that are not territories in the usual sense but rifts or forks, as Connolly envisages them:

> A rift is constitutive of time itself, in which time flows into a future neither fully determined by a discernible past nor fixed by its place in a cycle of eternal return, nor directed by an intrinsic purpose pulling it along. Free time. Or, better, time as belonging, replete with the dangers and possibilities attached to such a world. (Connolly 2002a, 144)

Politics of the possible: democratic as a dissonant conjunction of the moment, democracy as differential dissonance, as touch in the making, as movement reaching toward. Democracy, writes Derrida, "is differential; it is *différance, renvoi*, and spacing" (2005, 38). Democracy as a politics of touch does not simply defer and differ from itself. It individuates. Democracy transduces—forms matter and matters form—by spacing its movements in excess of "its-self," by mattering without being equal to its form. Democracy is no safe haven: to touch you I risk that you will not want to create a timed-space with me, I risk your absence, I risk your failure to individuate, I risk my own fear of your difference, of my deferral. Democracy, in this sense, is always virtual, it is a touching that has not yet touched, that has not yet been touched, that is continually in the process of initiating a movement toward a touch that may or may not lead to a spacing through which I will continue my process of individuation.

Derrida writes: "Of democracy there could only be but a trace" (2005, 39). The liberty at the heart of democracy is a liberty that invites me to move alongside the trace that democracy embodies. There is no predetermination here. The trace emerges, it propulses, it creates, but it does not define or substantiate. Democracy is the liberty to appreciate the trace. Derrida writes:

> In political philosophy, the dominant discourse about democracy presupposes this freedom as power, faculty, or the ability to act, the force or strength, in short, to do as one pleases, the energy of an intentional and deciding will. It is thus difficult to see, and this is what remains to be thought, how another experience of freedom might found in an immediate, continuous, and effective way what would still be called a democratic politics or a democratic political philosophy. (2005, 44)

Liberty, then, not as a power to be an individual, but as emergent force to individuate. Liberty as a sharing of movement that is a reaching toward. Sharing as a participation in a spacing through which timed-spaces and spaced-times are created and passed through. Sharing as the experience of two bodies touching, creating spacings through which they surprise themselves, again and again.

Spacing, for Nancy, is at the heart of the concept of liberty:

> freedom is the discrete play of the interval, offering the space of play wherein the "each time" takes place: the possibility of an irreducible singularity occurring ... that is already free in the sense that it occurs in the free space and spacing of time where the singular one time is only possible. Freedom is that which spaces and singularizes ... Freedom ... throws the subject into the space of the sharing of being. Freedom is the specific logic of the access to the self outside of itself in a spacing, each time singular, of being. ... "Spacing space" would mean keeping it as space and as the sharing of being, in order *indefinitely to share the sharing* of singularities. (1994, 68–71)

To share absolutely is impossible. To share entails a remainder. Democracy as sharing must remain a chance, a possibility in the making. A democracy-to-come is rendered possible only in the constitutive rift of the moment, in the fissure wherein resides the drive to decide between various directionalities, all leading toward the not-yet-known. This leading-toward out of which movement is generated becomes the condition of possibility of democracy, for it renders imaginable a political becoming that dares cross rifts and flows.

Individuation is a process that takes place in the moment, a juncture that is strictly speaking neither past, present, nor future. To work with the process of individuation through which democracy emerges, we must therefore resist nostalgic narratives that attempt to hold time in place, presenting us with pseudocomforting images of an all-encompassing touch. Such narratives sound like this: "In the past, there was *real* contact. Now we barely speak any more, all of us obsessed with our new technologies, cell phones attached to our ears, hands shackled to our keyboards, eyes focused on our screens." There is no such touch of a pre-lived past for us to miss: to feel touched we must continuously replenish the touching. Touch will only have occurred again: touch touches toward the future. There is no sensation of touch that remains alert without reinstantiation. Touch is a change of pace. Touch keeps us moving, inciting us to sense beyond this moment toward another moment. Touch is very much in-time with the troubling and exciting rifts caused by the accelerations of timed-spaces in the contemporaneity of which Connolly speaks. The issue is how to transpose these rifts toward democracies-to-come:

> the fundamental issues are, first, how to engage the rift and, second, how to respond thoughtfully to the acceleration of pace without falling into either a dangerous insistence upon slowing the world down to a snail's pace or a crude celebration of high velocity per se.... The intellectual challenge is how to come to terms productively with the ambiguous relations among time, pace, freedom, plurality, and democracy. None of us may really be prepared to meet this challenge. But time is short. (2002, 147)

At stake in this process of acknowledging the shortness of time is the important realization that uneven pace has always been operative within time, constituting rifts between pasts, presents, and futures. Like touch, time is always deferred and deferring.

Rifts in time can constitute political moments. Rifts in time indicate the incalculability and incommensurability of democratic equality. Democratic equality is uncountable: it is the touch I will never be able to encapsulate within a system of capitalist exchange. As Derrida writes about democracy: "This equality in freedom no longer has anything to do with numerical equality or equality according to worth, proportion or *logos*. It is itself an incalculable and incommensurable equality; it is the unconditional condition of freedom, its sharing, if you will" (2005, 49). Equality as the uncountable attracts, absorbs, and deflects the possible, engendering potential stakes at each juncture. It is not an equality that stabilizes the relation by rendering it accountable (in terms of gender, race, ethnicity, class), but an individuation that foregrounds the aporia at work within a concept of the political.

What is initiated by the aporia is a thinking of justice. Equality, within a democracy-to-come, is a demand for an idea of freedom that would expand beyond the count itself. In aporetic space-time an opening is made for a relation that functions according to the n+1. To count (to account for) is both to count again and to add to the count. This multiplication process requires a response. The ability to respond propels not the closure of the aporia but its continual reopenings. The time of democracy must remain aporetic. Derrida writes:

> Politico-juridico-ethical responsibility gets determined and becomes nameable, given some degree of semantic stability, only with the imposition of precisely that which is contained within parentheses, namely, the technique of equality, justice in the sense of calculable right or law, what Nancy also calls "given conditions," and especially criteria for "negotiations" to measure this access against the incommensurable, which, in itself and by definition, excludes all given criteria, all calculable rules, all measure. (2005, 52)

Whether or not we fall prey to the myth of the measure of equality within a system of calculation, a politics of touch is a reminder that the measure is never more than an attempt to reconsign the incommensurable. Justice,[13] in this regard, is always a renegotiation of the incommensurability of liberty and equality. Justice is democratic and democracy is just because justice must be about making a decision, about taking response-ability (even when I return to the grid to count the squares of equality and liberty), about facing the abyss of the incommensurable.

Making Sense of Politics

To think democracy through touch is to begin to reconsider the role of sense, the senses, and making sense. If democracy is no longer to be assigned a secure space within the grids of intelligibility of statecraft, we are left with a more productive idea of the political that speaks of aporias, of sensation, of movement, a notion of the political that is difficult to grasp. What is easier to grasp is the idea of "making sense." This is because making sense calls forth a politics of common sense that would seem, at the surface at least, to work within the grammars we already understand and thereby to negate incommensurability, lack of measure, uncountability. But when we take a step further and recognize that, at least for Aristotle, common sense referred to touch, we are struck by the realization that sense is never made consistently—how could it be, when sense senses?[14]

Touch defies stability, renewing itself instead in an ephemeral gesture of reminder. Touch does not make sense if by making sense I refer to something I should always already have known. There is no permanence to touch, only a re-touching. As a sense-generating practice, touch is transitory, short-lived, ungraspable. To make touch last, something must be supplemented: a blow, a grasp, a hold. Touch is a simultaneity of becoming whose characteristic is to elude the "before" and "after," a becoming that moves in both directions at once. Touch is anathema to what Deleuze calls "good sense," which "affirms that in all things there is a determinable sense or direction (sens)" (1990b, 1). A democracy-to-come does not embody good sense: it does not incorporate a pre-determined directionality. It is unlimited, becoming, individuating, in excess of a language that would seek to fix the limits of sense. Touch senses toward a movement that is layered rather than teleological. Democracy, understood in terms of a politics of touch, can only be conceived as a sense-making practice if we divest sense of its relationship with "good sense." There is no sense (as a final moment) to democracy. Democracy need not make sense, though it should sense, encapsulating a gesturing toward an other that defers toward moments that are thick with movement, with sensation, with experience.

Sense is an event. Deleuze writes: "It is the characteristic of events to be expressed or expressible, uttered or utterable, in propositions which are at least possible" (1990b, 12). An investigation of sense (making sense and/as sensation) allows us to begin to explore the manner in which the standardized discourse of the political (operative within state sovereignty and the nation-state system) relies on making good sense rather than on sensing. There need not be a dichotomy between making sense and sensing, for both engage in similar dynamics, expressing the event in a manner that is lived through and in the body. I make sense through sense. Certainly a long line of thought in political philosophy, beginning with Plato and continuing through Descartes and beyond, locates "making sense" with reason, outside the body, but if we allow ourselves to re-place making sense as an event in and of the body, it soon becomes apparent that making sense need not stand apart from sensing. Intelligibility need not rest on the troublesome attachment of knowledge as reason. In the end, it may be reasonable to sense.

Deleuze writes:

The I is primary and sufficient in the order of speech only insofar as it envelops significations which must be developed for themselves in the order of language (*langue*). If these significations collapse, or are not established in themselves, personal identity is lost . . . in conditions where god, the world and the self become blurred characters of the dream of someone who is poorly determined. This is why the last recourse seems to be identifying sense with signification. (1990b, 18)

Returning sense to signification is a common trap associated with theorizations of the political and of democracy. In order to "make sense" of the political, we often demand that it signify within the grids of intelligibility we define as signification. Sense does not operate quite this smoothly, however, as a politics of touch demonstrates. For signification to encapsulate sense, it must be ordained within a system of intelligibility that leaves no remainder. This is where signification fails again and again. "When we define signification as the condition of truth, we give it a characteristic which it shared with sense, and which is already a characteristic of sense" (Deleuze 1990b, 18). This is the paradox: we want signification to make sense and so we turn sense into signification. "In discussing the conditions of truth, we raise ourselves above the true and the false, since a false proposition also has a sense of signification. But at the same time, we define this superior condition solely as the possibility for the proposition to be true" (1990b, 18).

The problem with divesting signification of sense(s) is that it reinforces a return to a process of conditioning whereby we move in a tight circle of condition to conditioned, signifying only to the extent that we already locate within our vocabularies the premises for signification as good sense. In order for signification to avoid this vicious circle, it must create a residue that avoids the form of the conditioned. This residue can be thought as the aporia, the sheets of time, the trace. The aporia within the discourse of sense betrays the uncanny relation between sensing and making sense. The senses are *supplements* to signification in the Derridean sense not simply of adding to but also replacing:

> the supplement supplements. It adds only to replace. It intervenes or insinuates itself *in-the-place-of*; if it fills, it is as if one fills a void. If it represents and makes an image, it is by the anterior default of a presence. Compensatory [*suppléant*] and vicarious, the supplement is an adjunct, a subaltern instance which *takes-(the)-place* [*tient-lieu*]. As substitute, it is not simply added to the positivity of a presence, it produces no relief, its place is assigned in the structure by the mark of an emptiness. . . . Whether it adds

or substitutes itself, the supplement is exterior, outside of the positivity to which it is super-added, alien to that which, in order to be replaced by it, must be other than it. (Derrida 1974, 145)

The senses supplement sense: external and internal to sense-as-signification, the senses extend what it is to "know," challenging implicitly the manner in which the conditioning of sense continues to be allocated to a strict economy of reason as extrinsic from the body. Sense, sensing, senses, making sense, making senses supplement signification by rendering it bodily, by adding to the body, by extending the capacity to know into a sensual apparatus. Signification is sensual, it turns out, and politics make sense.

If political thought is reoriented toward practices of sense that complicate teleologies of signification, the political emerges as a virtual embodiment of sensations of difference rather than an actual mold of "good" sense. A politics of touch resists a reorientation toward the dichotomy between here and there, good and evil, sense and signification. Politics of touch thereby avoids strict conditions of denotation, extending itself toward expression:

> The duality in the proposition is not between two sorts of names, names of stasis and names of becoming, names of substances or qualities and names of events; rather, it is between two dimensions of the proposition, that is, between denotation and expression, or between the denotation of things and the expression of sense. (Deleuze 1990b, 25)

Manifestation and signification, both usually associated with the political, are cast aside in favor of a politics that seeks to reach a region where language no longer simply seeks to relate to that which it denotes, but also to that which it expresses, which it senses. The duality within politics (making sense and sensing) thus falls apart.

Deleuze writes:

> Sense is never only one of the two terms of the duality which contrasts things and propositions, substantives and verbs, denotations and expressions; it is also the frontier, the cutting edge, or the articulation of the difference between the two terms, since it has at its disposal an impenetrability which is its own and within which it is reflected. (1990b, 28)

It is necessary for sense to be reconsidered not in its dichotomous role vis-à-vis signification, but according to a whole new series of paradoxes, experiments, and events, toward a thinking of the incorporeal. Democracy, if thought along these lines, becomes a re-thinking of the manner in which sensing creates new ways of engaging space and time according to reflexes not based on learned reactions to stimuli (the most current understanding of the senses) but according to a different conception of a body. If we understand sensing as more than a motor response, we are in a position to explore the unknowability of sense. In other words, sensing need not express a sensation we have already experienced. To sense may also be to know differently, in excess of my current appreciation of "my" body. It is in this regard that sensing can be considered a prosthetic to the biological body. To sense may be to create a new body. If new bodies are what is at stake, new politics will have to be created. A democracy-to-come cannot know in advance what or where or who the body is. Democracy as a sensing politics is a movement toward making sense(s), towards new orientations of experience.

Sense does not pre-exist experience. Within a politics of touch, I am unable to state the sense, to locate at one and the same time something and its meaning. Sense resists essence: sense(s) cannot be signified. Signifiers attempt to encapsulate entire propositions, including dimensions of signification, denotation, and manifestation. Politics without essence is a politics that is asignifying, that operates in excess of linguistic signifying systems. Politics has always been about bodies. Bodies have always exceeded signification. An asignifying politics underscores that political bodies are sensing bodies in movement. These bodies cannot be counted within the means of signifying systems already in place because such systems of sovereign governance refer back, always, to the stratification of the grid. Certainly, grids will not disappear, but grids are not the first encounter bodies have with sense. Bodies are back-formed onto the grid, they do not emerge from it. Politics works the same way: politics emerges out of the movements of sensing bodies.

Democratic politics is an event. An event is the reversal of the Platonic gesture toward essence and the substitution of movements of singularities.[15] The event-ness of democracy opens the way for disagreement, for choice, for accidents. Politics is not something to be solved. Solutions "make sense" only when problems are prelocated within a logic of solutions. Politics focused on solutions is policy or police. A politics of touch does not yearn for solutions, but moves toward disagreement. This does not mean that a politics of touch does not learn. Knowledge imprints itself and is imprinted onto a democratic politics. The difference is that a politics of touch focuses on the redistributions of singularities rather than on results, each combination an event. "[S]ense," writes Deleuze, "is never a principle or an origin, but... is produced. It is not something to discover, to restore, and to re-employ, it is something to produce by a new machinery" (1990b, 72). Democratic politics is one way to produce sense, to make sense of relations of emergence between sensing bodies in movement. Sense and senses are surface effects, that is, they are inseparable from the surfaces (the bodies) that are their proper dimensions. Senses are not about fixed meaning, but about discovery, about reaching-toward, about relation. "Today's task is to make the empty square circulate and to make pre-individual and nonpersonal singularities speak — that is, to produce sense" (Deleuze 1990b, 73). The distributions of sense are not linear: democratic spaced-times and timed-spaces must resist returning to teleological models of identity, territory, history:

> The paradoxes of sense are essentially that of the subdivision ad infinitum
> (always past-future and never present), and that of the nomadic distribution
> (distributing in an open space instead of distributing in a closed space).
> They always have the characteristic of going in both directions at once, and
> of rendering identification impossible, as they emphasize sometimes the first,
> sometimes the second, of these effects. (Deleuze 1990b, 75)

Good sense is said of one direction only. This direction (consensual nation-state "democratic" politics, for instance) is determined as that which goes from the most to the least differentiated. Time moves in only one direction when space is static. Good sense fulfills its mandate by holding the body to the grid. Holding the body from movement is to affirm only a single direction, a single pace, allowing the body to differentiate itself only from the singular to the regular, and from the remarkable to the ordinary. What makes bodies interesting is that they regularly resist this grid, re-de-forming themselves (in movement) all the while, even if only at a cellular level. So the real danger is not that the body will be kept still, but that a politics will be written onto the body that resists engaging with the movement that is intrinsic to the relations between bodies and worlds. Such a politics, which naturalizes the shift from the extraordinary to the ordinary through a rendering-static of potential, is not a democratic politics, but a sedentary distribution of affects along a lifeless grid.

Good sense and common sense are not going anywhere. They are embedded in dreams of policy that hold themselves (without imagination) to a world that does not change. There is no such world, of course.[16] To quote Deleuze once more:

> Common sense identifies and recognizes, no less than good sense foresees.
> Subjectively, common sense subsumes under itself the various faculties of
> the soul, or the differentiated organs of the body, and brings them to bear
> upon a unity which is capable of saying "I." ... The complementarity of the
> two forces of good sense and common sense are clearly seen. Good sense

could not fix any beginning, end, or direction, it could not distribute any diversity, if it did not transcend itself toward an instance capable of relating the diverse to the form of a subject's identity, or to the form of an object's or a world's permanence, which one assumes to be present from beginning to end. Conversely, this form of identity within common sense would remain empty if it did not transcend itself toward an instance capable of determining it by means of a particular diversity, which would begin here, end there, and which one would suppose to last as long as it is necessary to assure the equalization of its parts. It is necessary that quality be at once stopped and measured, attributed and identified. In this complementarity of good sense and common sense, the alliance between the self, the world, and God is sealed—God being the final outcome of directions and the supreme principle of identities. (1990b, 78)

Good sense and common sense unite to hold the world to a measure that can purportedly be codified as a system. Emergence of new ways of thinking are painstakingly kept at bay by the gatekeepers of good and common sense. Yet invariably, expression occurs despite (or even because of) good sense and common sense in an eruption that exceeds the strata of signification on which good sense and common sense rely. Sense erupts in the fragility of the moment where surface meets surface and is re-fitted as formed-matter and mattered-form, metastable, passionate, movemented, active. Sense is the effect of corporeal causes and their mixtures, alive with the impossibility of accurately determining the gap between inside and outside, event and problem, sense and making sense. Fragile, expressive.

6.

Sensing beyond Security:
What a Body Can Do

Do Not Touch

A politics of touch is a politics not of the particularity of touch as touch, but of touch as the incorporeal experience of contact. How tact-ful is this politics? How is tact secured, politically, within movement that reaches toward? What happens to a politics of touch when we associate touch with tact?

Whereas so far a politics of touch has been conceived as a movement that expands the virtual toward potential, it would seem—if we associate touch with con-tact—that touch is also implicated in a movement that is based on an interdiction not to touch. Tact embodies this injunction that challenges me in advance *to have known* how and when I should or should not touch.

Tact, like touch, etymologically emerges from the stem *tangere*, to touch. In its first definition tact *is* touch. Yet, something has occurred, in time, that has created an uncanny rift between tact and touch: tact is interpreted as a certain prescience that keeps me from touching, from moving toward. As defined in the Oxford English Dictionary, tact is the "ready and delicate sense of what is fitting and proper in dealing with others, so as to avoid giving offence, or win good will; a skill or judgement in dealing with [people] or negotiating difficult or delicate situations; the faculty of saying or doing the right thing at the right time." Tact is knowing when not to touch.

Touch is about movement. Tact refers to a certain preemptive declaration that the body should not move. Tact says, "be careful, do not make yourself known. Retreat." If bodies move as a quality of their becoming-world as *Politics of Touch* has argued thus far, how might touch incorporate tact within its definition? What would be a touch that could be secured by tact?

Bodies can be stratified, organized, categorized, even restrained, but they cannot be stopped. If security implies a certain stopping, or at least stalling of the body, and if tact is complicit with this abeyance of the body, tact would have to be juxtaposed to what the body can do through a politics of touch. Tact in this regard would function as an imposition onto bodies more than a quality of potential reembodiment. Bodies secured with a tactful injunction would have to stop (being bodies). Yet, definitionally, tact operates within all touch, at least as a supplement. How can we then reconcile tact and touch?

Tact is anathema to a politics of touch, but never wholly disjointed from it. Touch is always at risk of being tactically re-secured. Tact abides within the conditions of possibility of touch. To circumvent tact, touch resolves to reach beyond tact, beyond the unspoken judgment that urges me to refrain from touching. To touch entails acknowledging the risks associated with the unknown toward whom I reach when I touch. Touch must always lead beyond where I anticipated it would. Tact, on the other hand, keeps me in the realm of the almost-known, the anticipated-in-advance. In this regard, tact holds to a structure of habit that discourages invention. To be tact-ful is to claim to know in advance. Tact-fully, I reinscribe my movements within a certain structure of sedimented propriety. Even though incorporeal (tact is based on a virtual necessity rather than a spoken judgment), tact has the full capacity to be gridded. Touch, on the other hand, emerges from a divergent version of incorporeality: I touch always toward that which has not yet been decided. I cannot back-grid the future anterior.

Contact challenges me to a decision to be-with either tact-fully or toward touch. This is a decision I will always make anew. If I decide not to touch toward the untouchable, I will continue to operate within a version of politics that has already been secured as a measure of the current political situation.[1] To engage in a politics of touch is to respond beyond the judgment tact activates. A politics of touch will always embody tact as its nemesis (and vice versa). Tact will warn touch in its hoarse whisper about the risks at hand, attempting to put the senses in their place, even as I continue to reach toward the untouchability of the senses as senses, asking of my

body that it expand, prosthetically, toward a concept of the senses that signifies not the biological body but the body's imminent excess.[2]

Tactically Untouchable

The body that touches is a body that is always in excess of its-self. Brian
Massumi writes: "What if the space of the body is really abstract? What if
the body is inseparable from dimensions of lived abstractness that cannot be
conceptualized in other than topological terms?" (2002a, 177). Bodies reaching toward are abstract bodies. They are abstract because they space, abstract
because incorporeal, touching-toward. I cannot secure a body that is reaching toward because that body is in movement, qualitatively altering spaced-
times. What is this body that cannot be secured within a vocabulary of fles-
hed enclosure?[3]

I wonder whether it might not be related to the Body without Organs
(BwO) that Deleuze and Guattari evoke in A Thousand Plateaux. Let me
explain: a body that is always in the potentiality evoked by a reaching-
toward is a body that must also always already be beyond its-self. This body
is abstract in the sense that it is always virtually becoming its potential.
Because there is no end-limit to becoming, this body-in-potential cannot be
conceived of as a permanent space-time, but must instead be thought of as
an exfoliating movement toward another exfoliating movement. The body
as exfoliation cannot be grasped. But it can be thought—abstractly. An as
abstract potentiality, this body is not solely contained within an enclosure—skin—which can be organized (tactfully) within a system of governance (a body-politic). The BwO is more than its discrete outside and inside.
This body-as-multitude is a strata onto which intensities congregate. A BwO
is a body that moves between metastable states, operating, always, within systems of protopermanence that seek to slow or even stop its movement. But
even in their slowest instantiations, Bodies without Organs are co-forming
so quickly that they cannot be located and secured.

Deleuze and Guattari's Body without Organs is not a metaphorical concept. The BwO is "of" and "and" the body. The BwO is a way of asking ourselves how we could ever have thought of the body as a unit, as a uniform
singularity. The body is never its-self. We have several bodies, none of them
"selves" in terms of subjectivity. Touch as reaching toward already alerts us
to the downfall of discourses of subjectivity: if my body is created through
my movement toward you, there is no "self" to refer back to, only a prolif-

eration of vectors of intensity that emerge through contact. This contact is not an end-point; it is not a moment of arrival where something like two bodies "meeting" happens. It is far beyond tact. Rather, it is a signaling of a reaching that arrives, momentarily, only to have to have been arrived at, relationally, again.

Reaching toward, we are always in the process of making our own BwO. "At any rate you make one, you can't desire without making one" (Deleuze and Guattari 1987, 149). This body which awaits me is a body of my own making only to the extent that I move toward the potentiality that is my reaching out toward you.[4] It is not an assemblage that I put together, piece by piece. My BwO always differs from its-self: you create it when you space-time with me. "And it awaits you; it is an inevitable exercise or experimentation, already accomplished the moment you undertake it, unaccomplished as long as you don't" (Deleuze and Guattari 1987, 149). But it is not stable or guaranteed. You can begin to create a BwO only to retreat into your "self," thereby undermining the process. You can always choose not to touch.

"You never reach the Body without Organs, you can't reach it, you are forever attaining it, it is a limit" (Deleuze and Guattari 1987, 150). The BwO is literally that which I reach toward when I attempt to touch you. The BwO is the body that remains anathema to the body-politic about which the sovereign nation dreams. Sovereign politics cannot uphold a thinking of a BwO because this "body" cannot be contained within a stabilizing imaginary. This concept brought forth by Artaud—"there is nothing more useless than an organ" (in Deleuze and Guattari 1987, 150)—is a concept that rallies against the state. It is a concept that speaks of experimentation, radicalization, censorship, repression. It is a concept that promises nothing (I can also create a disciplinary BwO, or a sick one, a deranged one, an addicted one) except movement toward something that is not "me," that can never be "me" in the strict sense. If touch is indeed a central ingredient in the creation of the BwO, we might argue that touch is that which most strenuously denies the concept of "me" that is at the heart of a politics of identity. There is no identity to the BwO. There is only movement.

"The BwO is what remains when you take everything away. What you take away is precisely the phantasy, and signifiances and subjectifications as a whole" (Deleuze and Guattari 1987, 151). Reaching-toward is political because it develops a space-time that is repeatedly altered. When I reach toward you, I challenge the idea that I can know you, that I can interpret you, that I can tactfully "touch" you in the sense that I can convey to you your separateness. The BwO is tactless: I can never predict the manner in which my BwO will unfold. This folding is of the skin, but not the skin as envelope. The skin of the BwO is the in-folding of space and time as event-ness. The skin is the incorporeal excess that provokes a memory of a reaching that arrives, in passing, to imprint skin with the resonance of its evanescence.

When I reach out to touch you, I create a BwO that is populated by intensities that pass and circulate. I do not create a scene of touch. I do not create a model that can be re-created or interpreted. Your BwO is always out of reach. It is out of reach because it is not, strictly speaking, operating "in" space and time. It is spacing time and timing space through intensities that come to pass, that reach me momentarily, that decompose in the reaching, that sense without making sense, that make sense sensing. There is no ultimate moment, no final organization to the BwO: remember, what I reach toward is not your body, but your BwO. Our bodies are not organic to the concept of touch. Our bodies are continually inventing—intensely inventing—what can be thought as touch, bodily. The BwO is a multiplicity that challenges the dichotomy between the one and the multiple. Reaching toward you, you become multiplicitous, you multiplicitously multiply me.

"A plateau is a piece of immanence. Every BwO is made up of plateaus. Every BwO is itself a plateau in communication with other plateaus on the plane of consistency. The BwO is a component of passage" (Deleuze and Guattari 1987, 158). How does touch operate on the plateau? Where is politics? Consider the BwO as a component of passage that introduces the potential meeting of BwOs. Would that not be a politics? These meetings on the plane of immanence are smudges in time-space, configured as reachings-toward that call forth the potentiality of a touching that could be a politics. A politics here conveys the potentiality of a continuing movement toward, a taking-further of the movement through which touch is instantiated. Politics of touch implies and is implicated in touching the untouchable.

The BwO does not exist in opposition. It "is" not "against" the organism. But it does defy the "organism." The BwO is the revolt we can never quite hold back, the excess of the flesh, the senses intermingling synesthetically at the contours of our forms, the matter that concerns us, the individuation that calls forth a difference we cannot subsume within strict categorization. The BwO is contrary, but not dichotomous. It is contrary because it is resistant. It is resistant because it will not fit the system, because there is no system to be called forth once the organism has been disseminated. The BwO is a telling adventure: the exploration of terminologies that fall apart as soon as they are touched, like old skeletons disappearing into small mounds of dust at the touch of my hand. There is no body. There is no sovereign. There is nothing that is secure. Is this possible?

No. There must always be a God, a priest, a king, a mother. Sovereignty reigns, but only insofar as the singular body continues to be upheld in the name of the body-politic: sovereignty needs to identify the body, if only to destroy it in the name of the state of exception.[5] Judgment precedes bodies. Habits form bodies. Control regulates security and security regulates control. Bodies navigate between these vectors, displaying all the talents of organization bodies are reputed to obey. But they smell. They sweat. They desire. Despite themselves, bodies are always "too much," always excessive, always, in some sense, uncontrollable, unsecurable. Even dead, they decompose, infested, digested. Organisms are made and dismantled, organized and categorized, understood and comprehended, discarded. But bodies are productively infinite.

Deleuze and Guattari write: "The organism is not at all the body, the BwO; rather, it is a stratum on the BwO, in other words, a phenomenon of accumulation, coagulation, and sedimentation that, in order to extract useful labour from the BwO, imposes upon it forms, functions, bonds, dominant and hierarchized organizations, organized transcendences" (1987, 159). Stratification takes place. Concretely, it gives space and time, constricting the timed spaces in which we live. But these spaced times are also ephemeral. They can be re-vectored. Constellations can be generated that subvert the vocabulary of "within" and "without" on which these kinds of space-times are predicated.

The BwO disturbs space-time. But it does not do so simply by entering it. It emerges through it. "It is in the BwO that the organs enter into the relations of composition called the organism. The BwO howls: 'They've made me an organism! They've wrongfully folded me! They've stolen my body!'" (Deleuze and Guattari 1987, 159). The making of a subject is the rendering-significant of a body claimed as docile. The docile body is tactful: it does not reach. But a body that is subjectified is never subjectified forever. Tact rests on a structure of appearance that can be dismantled. The body morphs and resists, despite its-*self*, despite the state, despite the sovereign. The body swings between stratification and experimentation. The body is never content to sit still: it must become. "A perpetual and violent combat between the plane of consistency, which frees the BwO, cutting across and dismantling all of the strata, and the surfaces of stratification that block it or make it recoil" (Deleuze and Guattari 1987, 159).

You will be organized, you will be an organism, you will articulate your body—otherwise you're just depraved. You will be signifier and signified, interpreter and interpreted—otherwise you're just deviant. You will be a subject, nailed down as one, a subject of the enunciation revealed into a subject of the statement—otherwise you're just a tramp.
(1987, 159)

These are words through which the body-politic of the nation-state tends to operate. These are words that underpin the discourse of the secure body. "If you do not relinquish your BwO and assume a stable form, we cannot protect you." Some bodies are easier to secure than others. My lesbian body, my gay body, my diseased body, my female body, my aged body: these bodies are more costly. But even these bodies are useful to the state: they make possible the insecurity on which the need for security is predicated. Be secure! Conform! Even your distorted body can be taken into the fold! Confirm your conformation by organizing your excess: we may be able to protect you! But hide your difference at all costs!

The terrible revelation is that bodies can never truly conform. Organisms do restratify, but don't forget: these restratifications are part of the strata. The organism and the BwO coexist. They make and remodel one-another. There is no pure body that can be protected. Imagine the security risk: we must not only protect "the body" but also the intensities that are disseminated in the process of reaching out!

Bodies without Organs disarticulate. One of the symptoms of this disarticulation is touch. Disarticulation is not the opposite of articulation: it is its supplement. Touch provokes disarticulation by marking the impossibility of a final reaching toward. Touch makes possible the image of a body falling apart, leaving parts of itself behind, incorporeally becoming. Touch reminds us of the ghost we see when a camera catches our movements multiplied. Touch evokes a spectral politics, a politics of capture that never quite reaches its goal. Touch is an adventurous sensation.

Don't misunderstand: touch does not simply destratify.

You have to keep enough of the organism for it to reform each dawn; and you have to keep small supplies of significance and subjectification, if only to turn them against their own systems when the circumstances demand it, when things, persons, even situations, force you to; and you have to keep small rations of subjectivity in sufficient quantity to enable you to respond to the dominant reality. Mimic the strata. You don't reach the BwO, and its plane of consistency, by wildly destratifying. (Deleuze and Guattari 1987, 160)

Articulation is at stake here, as is disarticulation. A worlding of words make it possible to perceive the ways in which bodies are always already intertwined within their own representations, within their destratifications, within their sensations, within the worlds they create. Bodies empty themselves in order to be filled again. What fills them, among other things, is sense, sensation. Touch populates the body, prosthetically engaging it to feel differently, to see, to hear, to taste the world again. To reach. For Bodies without Organs to move, intensities must pass along them. They must be produced. Production implies displacement, change, altercation. Bodies without Organs are disagreements with/in space and time, challenging at every juncture the constitution of the subject that operates at the basis of politics. Bodies without Organs are not metaphors: they are instantiations of a different kind of politics, a different thinking of the body, a patient reaching that reaches toward the BwO's incessant re-making.

Is this too abstract? Or is it perhaps not abstract enough for the lived abstractness that is the sensing body in movement? We orient through the senses. A discussion of abstractness needs to be predicated on a comprehension of the strangeness of our senses: "The way we orient is more like a tropism (tendency plus habit) than a cognition (visual form plus configuration)" (Massumi 2002a, 180). Proprioceptively, kinesthetically, we reach toward an orientation that becomes our worlding of the world. We self-reference, we register, we extend. The relation of position to movement is inverted. "Movement is no longer indexed to position. Rather, position emerges from movement, from a relation of movement to itself" (Massumi 2002a, 180). Touch spaces, instantiating, through movement, a BwO that becomes a dynamic of relation and disagreement between sense-dimensions. Senses fold into one-another creating an in-folding and out-folding, an exfoliation of experience.[6] Touch is an event.

Movement precedes sense. Sensing is prosthetic: sense instantiates a BwO that affirms that experience comes to it prosthetically, through movement.[7] Prosthetically, senses stimulate worlds, which in turn activate bodies. When we think of touch this way, we challenge meaning-producing practices of knowledge and information that are considered "innate" to the body. Experience is animated by the senses, sensing. Experience implicates the senses, worlding the body. Experience expresses the event that produces my BwO. I sense prosthetically, extending my body intensely toward the untouchable. What I sense is always an expression of potential. *In potentia*, my BwO creates sense vectors, prosthetically reaching out toward the world we create through touch. A politics of touch depends upon the BwO as much as the BwO depends on a politics of touch. This is not necessarily reassuring: not all BwO are capable of forming pathways for intensities required for a radical politics. Not all bodies are willing to risk.

The body is multiple. There is no particular BwO. My body intensifies differently with every reaching-toward. There is no unique experience of touch. Touch, as Nancy writes, is *singulier-pluriel*. Touch is duration.[8] Static, bodies do not not make space for touch as a reaching-toward. Static, we remain tactful, although our determination does not exhaust the potential of our body. Too abstract? Not abstract enough.

Sense-events are real but abstract. Actual but virtual. Virtual because my body remains that which it never always already is. Virtual because the senses resist stratification within a stable configuration, responsive primarily to that which is not-yet. I touch that which I am not-yet touching. What I touch is not the object itself, but the potential of the object to be touched. I touch my capacity to emerge through the object. I touch my experience of reaching-toward. "The problem is that if the body were all and only in the present, it could be all and only what it is. Nothing is all and only what it is. A body present is in dissolve: out of what it is just ceasing to be, into what it will already have become by the time it registers that something has happened" (Massumi 2002a, 200). A politics of touch activates this transition, this moving through the present where past and future are in nonlinear continuity with one-another. "A body does not coincide with its present. It coincides with its potential. The potential is the future-past contemporary with every body's change" (Massumi 2002a, 200).

Bodies operate in the crease where past and future coexist. Bodies are in movement and to move they must fold-in, fold-out. "The moments of time are dimensions of each other's unity of movement into and out of each other. They are co-operating dimensions of transition" (Massumi 2002a, 200). Deleuze's vocabulary of the virtual is essential here. Bodies—especially the bodies constrained to the discourse of the national body-politic—have been sequestered in a discourse of the actual. Bodies cannot be strictly actual because they are never strictly actual to their movements. They are virtual in the sense that they are always reaching toward. The abstraction of the body is the reconceptualization of the difference between actuality and virtuality. "Incorporeal: abstract" (Massumi 2002a, 204).

Bodies are technologies of movement, of transposition. Bodies do not take us home. Bodies without Organs are castaways. "The body is the holding-together of these virtual innards as they fold out, recursive-durationally, in the loopy present, in determinate form and configuration, always provisional because always in becoming" (Massumi 2002a, 205).[9] But bodies are not only virtual. Virtuality must become empirical.[10] This is the paradox of the senses: sensing renders the body virtual by exposing it to continual movement, yet sensing and senses render the body's fleshiness actual. My experience of touch is empirical (I touch to "know" the sensation) but radically so: I touch what is always already not-yet there. Bodies as emergent vectors of experience shift between proportions composed of actuality and virtuality. Virtuality phases into actuality abstractly. This movement toward the actual is abstract because despite its actuality it is difficult to trace exactly its beginning and its end. As Massumi writes, "The limits as such must be conceived as unmixed but in enough dynamic proximity to interfere with each other in their actual effects as attractors" (2002a, 159). Lurking happens on many levels here. Plateaus are evoked even as the engagement between sense-events is localized. Sense-events are reminders that the virtual and the empirical pass into one-another, challenging body times and spaces, creating and modulating bodies.

Why BwO? Can't we simply retain the body? Rewrite it? Certainly, but not before dismantling it, whatever "it" is. This is a work in progress. Or more precisely, a work in *potentia*. This is a work that incites us to find concepts that make us stumble in order to ask, once more, what "a body" can do. The BwO is expressive. "We do not know even know what a body can do," writes Spinoza (in Deleuze 1988b, 17–18). As Nietzsche says, we are surprised about conscience, but what is really surprising is the body (in Deleuze 1988b, 18).

For Spinoza the expressiveness of the body denies any hierarchy between flesh and soul. Thought is at stake: through the body we must think further than we have thought, we must express beyond a thinking of consciousness that has driven us so far. Bodies exceed our knowledge of them. Meetings between "bodies" incite us to create Bodies without Organs which are always, in some sense, bodies of thought. Relationally, we begin to think not the order of causes (and effects) but the play of compositions and decompositions at work. We compose with bodies. Bodies emerge not only as what they are but what they expressively can become.

According to Spinoza, a body (however miniscule) is composed of an infinity of particles that express themselves through modulations of rest and movement. Movement and rest categorize the body's incessant movements-

toward. Bodies affect other bodies. Expression happens in the in-between of
bodies. Individuation takes place in these intervals. Bodies are not defined
through functions but through modalities. Forms or functions are replaced
by effects of slowness or speed and their interrelation. "Even the development of a form, the course of the developing of a form, depends on these
relations, not the reverse" (Deleuze 1988b, 123). What is important is to
conceptualize—to express—life, individuation, not as form but as a complex interchange between differential speeds.

I do not touch that which is already formed. I am attracted to the potential of attraction. I am driven by the potential of creating a spaced-time and
a timed-space through the process of reaching out. This attraction gives a
certain vitality to a politics of touch. Organs are not essential here. Nor are
substances or even subjects. What is essential is movement: what the body
can *do*. Bodies without Organs necessitate a patient thinking of the potential of modulation: an ethology[11] of the body-becoming.

Ethology studies the composition of relations or powers between different
things. Ethologies are not about knowledge as end-points but about accumulation and difference. They are about extension, about expressions, about
events, about becomings. "[Ethology] is not a matter of utilizations or captures, but of sociabilities and communities" (Deleuze 1988b, 126). Ethology
is about longitude and latitude. A body can be anything. Unformed, a BwO
seeks not its form but its potential. Touch operates as the directionality
of this seeking. Touch takes place in the intensity of a movement-toward,
the body becoming other through relation. "The longitudes and latitudes
together constitute Nature, the plane of immanence or consistency, which
is always variable and is constantly being altered, composed and recom-
posed, by individuals and collectivities" (Deleuze 1988b, 128).

The plane of immanence is not composed of a supplementarity that would
precede or exceed it. Bodies on the plane of immanence are what they
become in a now that is eternally recurrent. There is no subject here, only
affective states individuating, force-fully. Bodies without Organs express
their multiplicity on this plane in the relation between rest and movement,
in the creation of intensities that draw space and time into new configurations for the invitation of other bodies, other movements. Touch operates
politically as that which instantiates connections, however brief.

Warren Montag writes:

> Spinoza's philosophy provides the best illustration of the concept of the
> immanent cause, a concept that, during the late 17th century, was one of
> its most scandalous postulates: it is a philosophy that exists in its effects,

not prior to them or even independently of them, effects that may remain dormant or deferred for decades or even centuries, (re)activated only in an encounter with unforeseeable theoretical elements that arrive from beyond its boundaries. (Montag and Stolze 1997, x–xi)

For Spinoza, bodies (substances) are not prior to attributes. The cause does not precede its effects. There is no thought of wholeness, of unity, of division. Rather, "substance is 'its' infinite diversity itself; it is realized in this diversity and is nothing other than the process of production without beginning or end (beyond teleology, without goals or direction) of itself through the infinity of its attributes" (Montag and Stolze 1997, xvii). Effects create experiments. Experiments exceed organs.

Experiments of and on the body are composed of expression, affects, concepts, precepts. For Spinoza, a sign is always an effect. An effect marks the trace of one body upon another, affectively registering a duration.

> Affection is therefore not only the instantaneous effect of a body upon my own, but also has an effect on my own duration, a pleasure or pain, a joy or sadness. These are passages, becomings, rises and falls, continuous variations of power (puissance) that pass from one state to another. (Deleuze in Montag and Stolze 1997, 22)

Affects are variations of power *(puissance)*. Affects call forth mixtures through chance, accident, confusion. Bodies without Organs meet in surprising ways. To reach out and touch is to touch not only the untouchable but the inconceivable. There are no causal linkages between Bodies without Organs. Affects do not organize the body. They play on the surfaces. They are surface-events that expose not the organism but its movements. "We know bodies only through the shadow they cast upon us, and it is through our own shadow that we know ourselves, ourselves and our bodies" (Deleuze in Montag and Stolze 1997, 24). Affects collude. Collide.

Structurally Insecure

Structurally, there are no Bodies without Organs. Structurally, there are only organisms, states, sovereigns, laws, national body-politics. Post-structurally there are colliding bodies, common notions, matters of concern.[12] Touch exceeds the structure. Structures must be dismantled, re-formed, in-formed.

> The structure or object is formed by at least two bodies, each of which in turn are formed by two or more bodies, to infinity, while in an other direction they are united into every larger and more composite bodies, until one reaches the unique object of Nature in its entirety, an infinitely trans-

formable and deformable structure, universal rhythm, . . . infinite mode.
(Deleuze in Montag and Stolze 1997, 25)

Politics is both of and beyond the structure. Disciplinary politics demands
the apparent coherence of the structure. Control societies resist the structure. This is not a dichotomy. All politics is always a passage, even a sedentary politics. A politics of touch is not a new politics but a rearticulation of
a movement between, a recomposition of a transrelational acceleration that
witnesses certain shifts from a politics of the body to a politics of the BwO.
Don't forget: bodies are also stratified on the BwO. There is no body that
can completely resist the structure.

I project my body. My projected body is a BwO that envelops a relation
of movement and rest. My body is the relation of the relation. Sensing, I
embody that engendering relation, I charge that relation with an embodied-
event. Touch is eventful. Now to ratify: touch is not knowledge. Touch is
expression. A politics of touch is not about knowledge but about the projection of experience that results in expression. It doesn't end there. Expression is not a result. Expression engenders the desire to reach again. Expression
calls forth the concept. The concept calls for a redefinition: politics of
touch will never be One.

> The selection of signs or affects as the primary condition for the birth of the
> concept does not merely imply the personal effort each person must make
> on their own behalf (Reason), but a passional struggle, an inexpiable affec-
> tive combat one risks dying from, in which signs confront signs and affects
> clash with affects in order that a little joy might be saved that could make us
> leave the shadow and change kind. The cries of the language of signs are the
> mark of this battle of the passions, of joys and sadnesses, of increases and
> decreases of power. (Deleuze in Montag and Stolze 1997, 27)

A politics of touch cannot be devoid of a concern for "a body," or
for "the body" of the sovereign. The concern remains. What changes is the
exposure. A politics of touch suggests that even those bodies who seem to
conform to the laws of static Being are potentially becoming: the sovereign
would not have the power evoked by his or her presence were it not for the
capacity to defy our expectations, to lure us, to capture our thoughts. All
bodies are becoming. Static bodies are a myth, a stabilizing projection of the
nation-state's desire to construct an imaginary that can be reproduced only
meiotically. The trick here is to find a way to relate the static body to that
very same body that is becoming. The challenge: to expose affects in their
becomings, even when the bodies they inhabit are imposing stability.

Of Pacts and Political Becomings

For Spinoza, no individual ever gives up the "right" to their BwO. As Balibar writes, referring to Spinoza, "it is to the extent that individuals always preserve an incompressible part of their 'right' that they can completely transfer sovereignty to the state" (in Montag and Stolze 1997, 175). The relation between the becoming-body and the becoming-state takes the form of a pact. In Spinoza, the concept of the pact is essential to an understanding of politics. The pact exists as specified by historical circumstances: "there are as many real states as there are forms of pact" (Balibar in Montag and Stolze 1997, 177). The pact in this case refers to the relation between Nature and the state. "What is important is not so much to know if, hypothetically or not, the state of Nature chronologically precedes the civil State. It is above all the question of the exteriority of one in relation to an other" (Balibar in Montag and Stolze 1997, 177). Spinoza argues that Nature and the state coexist and even depend on and instantiate one-another:

> In Spinoza the thesis according to which the civil state does not abolish the state of nature has as its correlate—despite the fears that can be inspired in it by the revolutions and seditions that try to change the form of government—the affirmation that the civil state can never be entirely dissolved. It is not by an external "nature" but by its very social form that every state is permanently threatened from inside. (Balibar in Montag and Stolze 1997, 177)

Bodies are never completely enslaved to the state because bodies are never completely reducible to either Nature or the state. Bodies become on a continuum that evolves in relation with pacts formed around institutions of power and compliance.

To locate the state on the strata of my BwO is, in some regard, to become part of the sovereign's BwO. It is to create a relation in a direction that holds me to an end-in-sight: becoming-sovereign. It is to believe in a pact that paradoxically excludes touch while it foregrounds tact as a thought-system. It is to mediate the incentive to reach-toward. But it is not to stop movement. Bodies cannot be stopped. As Balibar writes:

> This does not mean that sovereignty can do without guarantees, but that its real history coincides with the emergence of practical guarantees that confer on it the form of obedience produced by its institutions. Yet this history of obedience, an authentically concrete element of politics, can be thought of only as a combined history of interest, force and belief." (in Montag and Stolze 1997, 178)

Or, in the words of Spinoza:

> Hence we must admit unreservedly that divine right only came into force
> when men made an explicit pact to obey God in all things; by so doing they
> so to speak surrendered their natural freedom and transferred their right to
> God, just as they do in the civil state. (in Montag and Stolze 1997, 198)

There is no absolute constraint that can be imposed on the body. The pact is
not a death sentence: it is an interruption in the BwO's nomadic lines of flight.

Interruption is a necessary operation. Bodies without Organs would im-
plode or explode were there no restrictions to their movements. Acceleration demands deceleration. A pact is not an inherently good or bad proposition. A pact is a decision, a practice of setting up new velocities and new
directionalities. It is a stratification, certainly, but it can always lead to new
destratifications, and in most cases, it does just that.

Pacts are evocatively political: "every civil society, from the moment it
can be thought of as the realization of a pact, is naturally democratic" (Balibar in Montag and Stolze 1997, 184). No populous is original, neither in
Nature or in the state. Imaginaries preside over all manifestations of the
multitude, including conglomerations of stratified bodies and Bodies without
Organs: "in history there is not a unique form of the democratic imperium,
but there are necessarily several: as many as there are 'regimes' corresponding to the imaginary representation of the common interest" (Balibar in
Montag and Stolze 1997, 184). Within the imaginary representation of the
common interest there need be no opposition between bodies, between
states, between reason and nonreason. The deviation from imaginary to
imaginary is the virtual process through which bodies become bodies in relation with other bodies. It is also the process through which Nature passes
into states and states become Nature.

The pact projects onto politics the internal contradictions of institutions, of bodies, while at the same time expressing the passional conflicts of
the multitude. Through the pact, politics manifests itself. "Institutions by
themselves have no other power than that of the masses, including when it
is a matter of a power of decomposition" (Balibar in Montag and Stolze
1997, 185). This is a multiway process: it is most often through institutions
that the masses organize themselves into tendencies, into lines of flight that
in turn destabilize or destroy the very institution through which power was
instantiated. Institutions breed their own demise, as do individuals. Democracy is not only the potential to work together to form institutional bonds.
It is also the potential of destratifying the body of the state to build war

machines that project onto the institution the destabilizing forces of unpredictable and ungainly Bodies without Organs. Revolutions are internal to the system. Revolutions in the name of a politics of touch are about moving the matter and mattering the movement. A politics of touch demands of the Body without Organs that it leave its trace, that it incorporealize the organs of its passing.

For Balibar, "what the pact institutes is a collective power that assumes after the fact the form of a relation between wills" (in Montag and Stolze 1997, 187). This suggests that wills do not exist before the formation of the pact, that the pact itself involves the formation of a will, or better, the perpetual trans-formation of the will of the multitude. "Theoretically speaking, individual or collective *wills* do not exist before the pact but are constituted under its effect, this very effect that places the *summa potestas* in the place in which the law that must be observed is stated" (Balibar in Montag and Stolze 1997, 187). The will is a retroactive effect of the pact, a consequence of a decision. The will exposes a directionality already decided upon in the writing of the pact. Yet the will does not dissolve with the passing of the pact because it in-forms the writing of the next pact. In this regard, it is not as transitory as the pact itself. The will continues to shift, to pre-exist the next pact, yet only coming into itself with the subsequent re-writing of the becoming-pact. There is no individual will, therefore. The will is a vector, an intensity, a connectiveness that gives power *(potestas)* to the directionality of the reaching-toward.

Will-less politics would be politics without movement. Dictatorial politics, perhaps. Or politics of boredom: politics of the One. A politics of touch calls forth the will in every decision to reach toward another, in every relation of forces. For Spinoza, this notion of force does not promise a departure from servitude. That we live in *potentia* only means that we can choose our pacts; it does not mean that we will not write servile ones. For this reason, Spinoza does not oppose autonomy and heteronomy, spontaneity and obedience. The pact promises nothing. Power is not hierarchical. It is an expression, an event in and of the body, a projection of bodies onto and into the world, a worlding. The pact is not a limit-concept, though limits are often perceived and even reached. Spinoza suggests that the constitution of societies is "the chain of actions and passions of the multitude: a multitude reducible to the totality of individual powers that compose it, but irreducible to a sum of bilateral relations (or of exchanges) among individuals" (Balibar in Montag and Stolze 1997, 193). Causality is not what is at stake here. Sovereignty is never entirely certain of where it is going: "the *potestas* is only effective to the extent that the individuals who have constituted it permanently recognize it as constituting a law for their will" (Balibar in Montag and Stolze 1997, 194).

Bodies without Organs emerge in *potentia* of a politics of touch. Touch is of the body but not strictly on the body. It is an intensity at work in the creation and dissemination of a BwO. It is a vector of emergence and reception that plays on the intensities at work in the BwO. It latches onto your intensity, adhering to it only long enough to express the moment of passage. To touch is to make a pact. Touch is a mode composed of many parts. It is a mode that is capable of being affected while affecting. Parts are affected by pacts which are, themselves, remnants of pacts. The body is part of a pact that involves touch, touch is part of a pact that involves politics, politics is part of a pact that involves the body. The nature of these extensive parts is that they affect one another ad infinitum. A mode has affections by virtue of its capacity to be affected. It is in this sense that the mode—touch, a politics of touch—is a Body without Organs.

Deleuze writes: "A mode ceases to exist when it can no longer maintain between its parts the relation that characterizes it and it ceases to exist when 'it is rendered completely incapable of being affected in many ways'" (1990a, 218). Modes are transient. A politics of touch is only as productive as its BwO. There are no guarantees. A body's structure depends on the composition of its relations. "What a body can do corresponds to the nature and limits of its capacity to be affected" (Deleuze 1990a, 218). Modes are composed of extensive parts that are affected and determined by intensities traveling through them. Every existing mode is affected by modes adjacent to it. Every existing mode is altered by its relation to other modes. Politics of touch are emergent politics dependent on the vectors of interrelation externalized on the strata of the various Bodies without Organs in its environments. Politics of touch are ethological.

The issue for Spinoza is how modes are activated: "Can they attain active affections, and how?" (Deleuze 1990a, 219). For Spinoza, this is the ethical question. As I mentioned before, there are no good or bad modes. Deleuze explains:

> But, even supposing that a mode manages to produce active affections, while it exists it cannot eliminate all its passions, but can at best bring it about that its passions occupy only a small part of itself. . . . [T]he affections of modes are as it were a second degree of affection, affections of affections: for example. A passive affection that we experience is just the effect of some body on your own. The idea of such an affection does not express its cause, that is

to say, the nature or essence of the external body: rather does it indelicate the present constitution of our own body, and so the way in which our capacity to be affected is being at that moment exercised. An affection of our body is only a corporeal image, and the idea of the affection as it is in our mind is an inadequate idea, an imagining. And we have yet another sort of affection. From a given idea of an affection there necessarily flow affects of feelings (affectus). Such feelings are themselves affections, or rather a new kind of idea of an affection. . . . (Deleuze 1990a, 220)

Modes are affected by the passing of their affections. The affects that pass through modes indicate the relations between our Bodies without Organs and the pacts we make. Ideas are durations located on the strata of our BwO. These ideas indicate a relation not only to our worlding, but also to our previous states and the relations between our Bodies without Organs and these earlier states. Duration marks the process through which a politics of touch develops.

How active is my BwO's relation to the pact? Engaged with/in the multitude, I choose a position. This position can be tenuous: I can suggest that the choice was made *for* me or *despite* me. Choosing implies a will that suggests that modulations are overlaid with an interweaving of activity and passivity, no matter where our movements lead us. To be properly ethical for Spinoza implies finding a way to implicate oneself in one's own ideas: "The actions of the mind arise from adequate ideas alone. The passions depend on inadequate ideas alone" (in Deleuze 1990a, 221). The political question is: how can we produce adequate ideas? For Spinoza, inadequate ideas lead to suffering: "The capacity of being affected is called a power of suffering insofar as it is actually exercised by passive emotions. The body's power of suffering has as its equivalent in the mind the power of imagining and of experiencing passive feelings" (Deleuze 1990a, 222).

Existing modes are open to variation according to the affections that populate them at any given moment. There is no proper politics of touch. A politics of touch will deviate according to the pacts that sustain its reachings. Modes are elastic. A politics of touch is a concept that carries within its worlding a capacity for, and an opening toward, potential.

The question of modes leads us toward an issue central to a Spinozean reading of the body: of what is a body capable? A body wills itself collectively into passivity, into affection, into movement. But this is not a didactic gesture. A movement toward an other contains our uncertainty as regards what affections we are capable of expressing. When I reach toward, I cannot yet know the extent of our power, for this potentia remains to be produced.

Power, *puissance, potentia:* these frame politics at its most complex. Politics of touch reposition standard understandings of state politics by having no system of reference for a concept such as individual power. Without an individual, a body cannot be secured. Enclosures—conceptual or physical—require a hierarchy of dominance, which in turn requires a given body. If the body is no longer given but produced, it cannot be held to a system of governance that knows in advance how to tactically restrain its citizens.

To touch is to become aware that I am never yet fully formed. Your BwO coincides with my own. Bodies without Organs require participation. Worlding involves composing pacts through which we are able to create intense vectors of co-relation. Politics of touch are con-tact-ual politics, politics capable of making contact. This is not about tact. It is about risk.

A politics of touch cannot be about moral harmony. Bodies without Organs do not necessarily get along. Neither is this about subjectivity. It is about intensity, about potential relations. Affections can slow down the body as much as they can activate it. Before bodies are anything, they are renewable. Politics of touch are composite politics, politics composed of infinite variances of affects, politics reaching toward not an end but a means. An expressive politics finds no ultimate correspondence. A politics of touch is a concatenation of various effects. Perhaps the way to think a politics of touch is to conceive of a machine proliferating insistently against and beyond whatever you imagine politics of touch already to be. A politics of touch is adjacent, relational: it never stands alone. This machine does not necessarily correspond to politics as you meant to invent it, but it does feed on your imagination, on the invention you are yourself becoming. A politics of touch is every time in every instance a different and differing politics. In this regard, a politics of touch stands alongside Spinoza's complex assessment of Nature as that which is always already "physical": "a physics of intensive quantity corresponding to modal essences; a physics of extensive quantity, that is, a mechanism through which modes themselves come into existence; a physics of force, that is, a dynamism through which essence asserts itself in existence, espousing the variations of the power of action" (Deleuze 1990a, 233).

A politics of touch is at the mercy of encounters. Insecure, a politics of touch must actualize its power, again and again. This actualization is as virtual as it is actual. It forms as in the crystal. We actualize, we move, we virtualize, we move, we actualize. The relation cannot be secured. Security happens only in the stopping. There is no stable point where I am fully stopped. I rest to move to rest to move, always relationally. "My power is itself actual, because the affections that I experience each moment, whatever these may be, have full right to determine and exercise it" (Deleuze 1990a, 260). This is where the pact comes in. I organize my encounter according to what is useful.

> But there is a great difference between seeking what is useful through chance (that is, striving to destroy bodies incompatible with our own) and seeking to organize what is useful (striving to encounter bodies agreeing in nature with us, in relations in which they agree). Only the second type of effort defines proper or true utility. (Deleuze 1990a, 261)

Politics of touch space time and time space in such a way as to make them indiscernible. They are never what they once were. I cannot locate politics in space and time. I create space and time politically. Space times and time spaces, generating Bodies without Organs. Bodies without Organs emerge through encounters that modulate such concepts as action, reason, freedom. "Reason, strength and freedom are in Spinoza inseparable from a development, a formative process, a culture. Nobody is born free, nobody is born reasonable" (Deleuze 1990a, 262).[13]

Predictable dichotomies are no longer evident: body/soul, reason/senses, nature/culture. Politics of touch make relational pacts. It becomes a question of compatibility and extension. Building Bodies without Organs that correspond to some kind of reasonable common-sense politics requires encounters with those whose Bodies without Organs circulate around concepts that promote this kind of reason. This is not impossible. In fact, it is common. What is uncommon is realizing that even those Bodies without Organs that seek to organize their intensities around concepts such as reason are themselves continually destratified in sensual relations to nonsense. You can never fully escape sense. Even making sense senses.[14] "The highest essences already strive in their existence to make their own encounters correspond to relations that are compatible with theirs. This endeavour, which cannot wholly succeed, constitutes the striving of reason" (Deleuze 1990a, 264–65). Controlling space is a way of creating a *locus operandi* for a pact of reason. This is one of the functions of the state, which seeks reasonable bodies to secure its borders. Bodies without Organs are not eminently reasonable. They leak, they expand, they multiply. Hence, within the state apparatus they must be policed, ordered, categorized, fitted to the national body-politic, collapsed into an imaginary that represents the sublation of identity into territory.

Other words or concepts could stand in for a BwO: politics of touch, body, prosthetics of sense, errant politics. The key is that the concept be evocative of *what a body can do*. Like bodies, concepts exist to be unpacked, to be modified, to alter the timed-spaces and spaced-times they create. They are not solid. They are incorporeal but not metaphorical, real but abstract. "'What [a body] can do' is its capacity to be affected, which is necessarily and constantly exercised by the thing's relations with other beings" (Deleuze 1990a, 269). But "as far as it can" does not mean as far as you would. Or could. It means that the body can choose, relationally, to act. "[The ethical difference] lies in the immanent existing modes involved in what we feel, do and think" (Deleuze 1990a, 269). What makes the (ethical) difference is that this activity of relation is joyful.

Joy is for Spinoza the truly ethical sense: "A philosophy of pure affirmation, the *Ethics* is also a philosophy of the joy corresponding to such affirmation" (Deleuze 1990a, 272). A politics of touch is joyfully creative. It is a politics of affirmation. Most politics make a Descartes move, stopping at representation. For Descartes, it is the representative content of ideas that is at stake, as well as the form of the psychological consciousness that thinks these ideas. With only an extrinsic characterization of represented ideas, we get no further than the extrinsic characteristics of Being. Spinoza thinks politics otherwise, beginning not with representation but with the potential of affirmation. For Spinoza, what is at stake is the immanent content of ideas, not perfection, reality, or causality, but the surprise of not knowing what a body can do. Noncausal correspondence is at the heart of a politics of touch. When we speak of noncausal correspondence, we are no longer talking about "the law" or "the sovereign." We are now speaking about the intensities that populate these concepts and the ways in which they interrelate. It is not about how sovereign politics holds us captive within its nationalist imaginaries, but about how we affect those imaginaries every day as we re-populate our Bodies without Organs.

Joy corresponds to the relation between active series and what is invariant between them. This noncausal correspondence speaks to resonances between bodies in-formation. Expression is engaging, even when it is challenging. Expression is the Nietzschean affirmation. Expression is a noncausal correspondence because it relates to what expresses itself as distinct from expression itself. A politics of touch embodies a multiple movement that navigates between the expresser and the expressed, between the expresser and expression. A spiral movement: eternal return. A politics of touch expresses in such a way as to always intervene in the imaginary process of *Aufhebung*. There is no synthesis: "what is expressed is discovered as a third term that makes distinctions infinitely more real and identity infinitely better thought. What is expressed is sense: deeper than the relation of causality, deeper than the relation of representation" (Deleuze 1990a, 335).

What is expressed through a politics of touch is the incommensurability of sense. This is politics at its best. A politics not of consensus or causality, but a sensing politics of bodies-in-movement: a politics of touch. Sense, not *sens*. Direction but not goal-directed. An affirmation of a movement toward. This is what it is to sense(s). Sense is multiple: to sense is to multiply bodies, to exceed and extend the flesh through various instantiations of Bodies without Organs. To sense is to deviate from the organic capacities of the body, to challenge the interstices between insides and outsides, spaces and times. To sense is to world in all directions at once. Through the senses, bodies become alchemical mixtures, incorporeal concoctions of visions and touches, smells and sights, tastes and sounds. Senses lead us without taking us by the hand. Senses draw us toward an object as they modulate our own responses, relaying insides and outsides into a conglomerate that deviates, always, from the implied borders of our skins. There are no sense-borders: sense is not a limit-concept. To sense is to world unlimitedly.

> Becoming unlimited comes to be the ideational and incorporeal event, with all of its characteristic reversals between future and past, active and passive, cause and effect, more and less, too much and not enough, already and not yet. It is eternally that which has just happened and that which is about to happen, but never that which is happening . . ." (Deleuze 1990b, 8)

Sense-events are unlimited to the extent that they are incorporeal, incorporeal in that they allow active and passive, actual and virtual to interrelate and interchange. Sense-events are a movement-toward that inspires bodies to proliferate, to extend beyond "themselves."

Posthuman Prosthetics

To touch is a prosthetic gesture. It is prosthetic because it is associated with a surplus or excess of the biological organism. Touch involves a departure from my organs *as* organs. Touch is a movement-toward that relates my body to the excess of your body. My body is always more than one. This relation cannot simply be thought as a skin-to-skin encounter. Certainly, often I touch skin. But the untouchability inspired by my desire to touch is based on the fact that you are reaching from my body as much as I am reaching from yours. Together we become prosthetically entwined. We touch an incorporeal body that is created through our reaching-toward. This body does not pre-exist the relation. Touch is a prosthesis through which our bodies make contact. Touch is the manner in which I navigate from a subject position (an imagined stability) to an in-betweenness where the line between you and me becomes blurred. To touch is to become posthuman.

Ihab Hassan writes:

> We need first to understand that the human form—including human desire and all its external representations—may be changing radically, and thus must be re-visioned. We need to understand that five hundred years of humanism may be coming to an end as humanism transforms itself into something that we must helplessly call post-humanism. (in Hayles 1999, 1)

The BwO is posthuman to the extent that in its deterritorializations it persistently rebels against the humanism that holds bodies to their organisms. Posthumanity gives us a vocabulary to think through prosthetics in relation to the senses. In a humanist vocabulary of the organism, to conceive of the senses as prosthetic is an unseemly endeavor. Bodies are more likely to be thought of as unified and unique. The posthuman, on the other hand, takes the prosthesis as a condition of the organism, as its supplement. The human does not become prosthetic. Hayles writes:

> [T]he posthuman view thinks of the body as the original prosthesis we all learn to manipulate, so that extending or replacing the body with other prostheses becomes a continuation of a process that began before we were born. . . . [T]he posthuman view configures human being so that it can be seamlessly articulated with intelligent machines. In the posthuman, there are no essential differences or absolute demarcations between bodily existence and computer simulation, cybernetic mechanism and biological organism, robot teleology and human goals. . . . [T]he posthuman subject is an amalgam, a collection of heterogeneous components, a material-informational entity whose boundaries undergo continuous construction and reconstruction. (1999, 3)

Inventions abound on the prosthetized posthuman body. Interventions are welcome. It is in this sense that the posthuman body can be associated to a BwO (even a biologically unaltered homo sapiens), especially if we consider the manner in which technologies of sense provide platforms of experience that extend beyond the organism, returning to the organism by altering the form of that organism. Form cannot but be altered:

by whatever manner one defines form, it is an off procedure since it involves
rushing from the conditioned to the condition, in order to think of the condition as the simple possibility of the conditioned. Here one rises to a foundation, but that which is founded remains what it was, independently of the
operation which founded it and unaffected by it (Deleuze 1990b, 18)

The senses as prosthetic to the body morph the discourse of form.

Concepts only go so far before they must be reinvented. The notion of
posthumanity is in many ways heavy-handed. But what is evocative about it
(and its coupling with the delightfully heavy-handed BwO) are its conno-
tations of incompleteness, its prosthetic indeterminacies, its insecurities of
embodiment. The post- in the human suggests not that we come afterwards
as prosthetic newcomers, but that we were always already embodied in excess of our organs.[15] My goal here is not to trace the history or the contemporaneity of the posthuman. Rather, I present the concept to offer one more
entry point into how bodies are not only continually constructed through
the senses, but are also relationally inter-created in a field of prosthetic
in(ter)vention. At the same time, I want to draw attention to the fact that
technologically, there is nothing "new" to the posthuman. What is new,
perhaps, is to think the senses as prosthetic. Posthumanity, as Hayles points
out, is not a concept of the future, but a concept of the past that has been
strangely overlaid with a conception of human bodies as humanistically
static. We have always been posthuman.

Back to prosthetics: how to think the body as always already prosthetic?
I am an organism. I breathe, my heart beats, my pancreas controls the sugar
levels in my blood, my skin regenerates, my liver cleans my blood, my kid-
neys filter wastes and expel them, my brain receives and disseminates waves
of information. But I am also much more than an organism. I breathe a
smell that tastes like the morning. The morning reminds me of the texture
of the wood of the breakfast table, rough to the touch at the spot where the
detergent ate through the varnish. To "be" a body is to become. To sense is
to live in the beyond of the mere organism. Sensing is not essential to the
organic body. I smell in excess of the strict composition of my flesh and
bones. But without my senses I am not aware of my flesh as "body." It is in
this regard that senses are prosthetic: they are in excess of the organic, yet
they make the organic palpable.

To think the senses as prosthetic invites us to explore the surprising pathways toward which our senses lead us. These movements are never direct.
They are interlaced, synesthetic, nonlinear. A politics of touch is an engendering of this kind of prosthetic thinking of the event. A politics of touch is

an expression of politic's need to expand its horizon beyond the organism to the sensing body in movement. When sense moves beyond the organism to a sensing body in movement, our bodies extend toward the pacts we create in the name of multitudinous bodies and politics.[16] Our bodies become political. Politics throughout has been about the supplement. There is no original politics to be undermined by a politics of touch, just as there is no original body to be subverted by the BwO. Our bodies act: we know not what the body can do. Politics is what the body does. Since we cannot firmly place our body in a pre-cognizant system, we cannot know what can be done politically. All we can know is that there are ways of knowing that complicate the pathways between bodies and politics. Senses figure large here.

A Touch of Insecurity

I return to my initial question: how do politics secure sense? The better question at this point is perhaps: is security part of the pact(s) of a politics of touch? Security is essential to the sovereign politics of the nation-state. In disciplinary narratives of security, sense is secured in the name of territorialized reason. Even in a globalized world, we can not overlook the manner in which narratives of security continue to configure our understandings of what it means to live in time and space:

> whatever the loss of economic autonomy experienced under globalization, sovereignty is not passing away: it forms, instead, a complex and malign articulation of law, power, possibility and force that thwart a totalizing image of decline and irrelevance. Dominant public obsessions are with security and its violent, exclusivist, ontologizing technologies: counter-terror, border protection, deterrence, "homeland security," the "necessary" erosion of civil liberties and the rule of law. (Burke 2002, 2)

The state continues to be relevant, even in a discourse of a politics of touch, as Nietzsche observes:

> Coldly it tells lies too, and this lie crawls out of its mouth: "I the state, am the people" . . . it is annihilators who set traps for the many and call them State; they hang a sword and a hundred appetites over them. . . . State I call where all drink is poison, the good and the wicked; State, where all lose themselves, the good and the wicked; State, where the slow suicide of all is called "life." (1969, 49–50)

The state needs the body. Hence my injunction to take sovereignty seriously as well as the politics of security sovereignty engenders. At the same time, we would do well to follow the Spinozean route at least as far as to remember that there is no essential dichotomy between states and Nature. Bodies coexist as they correlate. State bodies are not fundamentally different from other kinds of bodies. The difference is that the body the state historically represents, as Nietzsche points out, is a body that agrees to or is incited to be governed in particular ways. In Hobbes, the sovereign embodies an exchange between freedom and security that combines the individual and sovereign subjects (the state and the citizen) into a single figure. The Hobbesean citizen becomes the rational modern subject who is represented as anything but a sensing body in movement. There is such a stagnancy in the concept of the modern subject as to suggest that the sovereign body is a still-life in the imaginary representation of the territorial nation-state.

In *Rogues*, Derrida presents once more his concept of a democracy-to-come, this time in the name of rogue states. He writes: "The democratic is possibly impossible and the political possibly possible" (2005, 46). Quoting Nancy, Derrida suggests that politics has not yet been capable of thinking democracy, nor democracy the political.

> It is possible that for this reason it may no longer even be possible, in the future, to think in terms of "democracy," and it is possible that this also signifies a general displacement of "the political," a word we have provisionally mobilized here: perhaps a liberation of the political itself. All things considered, what is lacking is a thinking of the freedom that is not established, but that *takes itself* in the act of its beginning and its recommencement. This remains for us to consider, perhaps beyond our entire political tradition—and yet in some ways the direction of this imperative has already been thought by at least one part of the revolutionary tradition. (Nancy 1994, 78–79)

An incommensurability of politics signals the necessity to reassess, continuously, where politics takes place. This can only be successful if we become aware of the manner in which we space and time, actively, virtually. A concept of liberty cannot be other than a concept involving moving bodies. A free body is not a secured body. Liberty, politics, bodies have no pre-established form. But they can form, their shapes mutating in the process, individuating, expanding, intensifying. "Freedom: to measure oneself against nothing" (Nancy 1994, 71).

Nancy writes: "Ontological sharing, or the singularity of being, opens the space that only freedom is able, not to 'fill,' but properly to space. 'Spacing space' would mean keeping it as space and as the sharing of being, in order *indefinitely to share the sharing* of singularities" (1994, 70). To share is

here perhaps still too strongly linked to individual subjectivities. Bodies do
not only share. They reach. To reach is not a condition of possibility: it is
potentiality[17]—that which is not already known, embodied, experienced.
"One would first need to learn how to think the 'each' on the basis of the
series or best works of singular 'each times'" (Nancy 1994, 71). Politics:
disorder, rogue states, untouchability. Touch: reaching toward, movement.
A politics of touch stages an approach. Rogue states are dangerous: is there
any other kind of state? My BwO becomes a war machine, imperceptibly,
momentarily. Touching, I space you, us. I do not define a new state. I matter
differently.

The rational modern subject that is at the heart of state sovereignty is a
political technology—a posthuman BwO—that implodes the body, drawing its vectors of resonance into collusion with governmental power. Governmentality requires security. Bodies must be contained, maintained. And
yet, as Hardt and Negri point out, modern sovereignty cannot be conceived
of as a linear, all-encompassing event.

Modernity is divided between a radical revolutionary process and a
counter-revolution that seeks to dominate and expropriate the force of
emerging movements and dynamics: in the interplay between the plane of
immanence, where a consciousness of freedom and scientific politics opens
the way for a democratic politics, and the dominant theme of the Enlightenment, which closes down the movement that characterizes the plane of
immanence, we witness the double-bind of sovereign politics today (Hardt
and Negri 2000, 74).

Burke defines modern sovereignty:

[Modern sovereignty is] not simply an abstract locus of juridical authority
that forms the basis for Westphalian international law and order, but a
complex disciplinary and ontological machinery of enormous depth and
force; one whose ultimate aim is to harness and control the possibility of
freedom within capitalist modernity. (2002, 5)

How to negotiate a politics of touch in this complex interplay of security,
sovereignty, globalization? How to speak of the body without securing sense?
How to speak of the securing of sense when sensing implies a prosthetic
thinking of the event always before and in excess of its securing? These are
the challenges inherent in writing of movement, of bodies, of politics. The
tendency remains, through the writing, to give precedence to a stagnant
humanist vocabulary that can be disciplined, controlled. It is difficult not to

fall prey to this tendency. Politics of touch fights this impulse, continuing to challenge the ontological force of existing politics of identity, incarceration, sovereignty, and violence wherever they emerge. There is no stopping: ontogenesis requires invention. All radical engagements are inventions in some sense: unthought, untried, extraordinary. Let us improvise.

Notes

Introduction

1. See Deleuze and Guattari (1987).

2. For Lucretius (99 B.C.–55 B.C.), the senses reside in the body as separate from the mind, and sense-perception is dependent on sense-organs. His contention is that when the body dies, it loses its sense-organs, and therefore the senses are linked to the body's life source. Influenced by Aristotelian (384 B.C.–322 B.C.) thought, Lucretius does not treat touch as a separate sense, but understands touch to be a condition of the other four senses. Interestingly, despite locating the senses solely in the body, Lucretius does suggest that the senses are a condition for *intellectual* life (Vinge 1975, 31): body and mind are momentarily united by the senses even as they remain categorized as separate realms.

Philo (20 B.C.–A.D. 40) reads Genesis's Adam as mind, and Eve as the senses. This leads Philo to surmise that the senses are responsible for the enslaving allurement of the objects that surround our bodies. The sensory mechanisms are victims of the environment: beauty enslaves sight, good food enslaves taste. Only reason-as-mind can come to the rescue (often conceived through the sense of vision): "Mind is superior to sense-perception," he writes (*Legum Allegoriae III* 452f). The mind here is compared to the governor of a city and the senses allegorized through the image of a loss of control of this secured space. If the senses are given too much power, Philo suggests, the same confusion will arise as in a house where the slaves take over. Kept at bay (in the body of the woman, for instance) the senses can be faithful guardians, keeping us to the straight and narrow.

To Cicero (106 B.C.–43 B.C.), "the soul or the mind has an existence of its own inside the five senses, which are not in themselves able to conceive anything" (Vinge

1975, 34). Here, the senses function as windows to the soul. The Christian Cicero, Lactantius (A.D. 260–A.D. 340), suggests that the soul lives inside the senses. Yet, following an already well-established tradition, Lactantius does warn against the pleasures of the senses (touch in particular), reminding us that pleasures must be subdued by virtue. For Lactantius, touch is the most dangerous of all senses. Lactantius sees touch as linked first to sexual pleasure, and hence "to be kept back most of all, as it damages most of all" (1918, 563).

The focus on the mind in opposition to the senses is carried out through the sixteenth and seventeenth centuries in the work of philosophers such as Descartes (1596–1650), whose writing rests on the problem of whether the mind works independently of the senses, or whether sense-experiences are necessary for the formation of concepts. Yet, despite the hierarchies of mind and body within Descartes's work, a strange tendency lurks, whereby there seems to be an admission that the senses often resist the organization of the body as reasoning/sensing duality. This is more boldly apparent in Pierre Gassendi's writing (1592–1655), a contemporary of Descartes: "every idea in the mind has its origin in the senses. Every idea either goes through a sense, or is formed by what goes through a sense" (1992, 92). Locke (1632–1704), much closer to Gassendi than to Descartes, suggests that sensation and reflection are the two sources of knowledge (1823, 141).

Following Locke, Diderot (1713–84) argues that touch is the most profound and most philosophical of the senses. Condillac (1714–80) adds that "touch, and touch only, instructs the other senses as to orientation, movement and activity" (1:222), stating further that all of our knowledge comes from the senses. Yet the mind continues even here to preside over the body, as sustained by Diderot's claim that "reason, although dependent on the senses, has authority over them, and as it cannot be reduced to mere sensation, the individual intellectual differences, not the quality of the sensations, ultimately determine judgment and character" (in Vinge 1975, 140). Rousseau (1844–1910) displays Descartes's influence when he argues that sensation and judgment cannot be the same: "My will is independent of my senses" (1962, 123).

3. Whitehead 1967.

4. Deleuze 1989.

5. See Randall Anderson (2004). See also Trevor Gould's sculptural work on the concept of the "blur" at http://www.fondation-langlois.org.

6. Gosling 2002.

7. See Peirce (1997).

1. Negotiating Influence

1. For more on errant politics, see "Close to Home—Canadian Identity, Nationalism, and Errant Politics" (in Manning 2003).

2. For more on ethics and deconstruction, see, among other works, Derrida (2002).

3. See "Dwelling With/in the Language of the Other" (in Manning 2003).

4. See Blanchot (1993). Blanchot writes: "To write is to produce the absence of the work (worklessness, unworking [*désoeuvrement*]. Or again: writing is the absence of the work as it *produces itself* through the work, traversing it throughout. Writing

as unworking (in the active sense of the word) is the insane game, the indeterminacy that lies between reason and unreason" (1993, 424).

2. Happy Together

1. According to Bergson, there are two types of multiplicity, neither one of them reducible to the One. The first kind of multiplicity is represented by space. This is a "multiplicity of exteriority, of simultaneity, of juxtaposition, of order, of quantitative differentiation, of *difference in degree*; it is a numerical multiplicity, *discontinuous and actual*" (in Deleuze 1988a, 38). The second kind of multiplicity "is an internal multiplicity of succession, of fusion, or organization, of heterogeneity, of qualitative discrimination, or of *difference in kind*; it is a *virtual and continuous* multiplicity that cannot be reduced to numbers" (Deleuze 1988a, 38).

2. Spinoza's work is thought-provoking as regards the body and movement. For Spinoza, it is the relations of motion and rest, of speeds and slowness between particles that define a body. Rather than being characterized by form or by function, the body is located as relations of motion and rest, of slowness and speed, as a complex relation between differential velocities, between deceleration and acceleration of particles (Deleuze 1992, 625–26).

3. For more on the subject of tango's "origins" (a highly debated subject) see Savigliano (1995). Savigliano demonstrates how the "history" of the tango is written as an "effort at justification," this justification, depending who is writing, focused on issues of class difference, nationalism, exoticism, or imperialism. Within Argentinean lore, the locus of "original" theses concerning tango comprise Rossi's historical legend (1926), Jorge Luis Borges's mythology (1928), Vega's systematic genealogy (1936), and Bates and Bates's social history (1936).

Savigliano writes: "The promotion of tango through imperial exoticism and through 'civilized' appropriations generated such a diversity of tango practices that the need to establish an 'authentic tango' became a must. . . . The scandalous colonial, racist and classist histories of tango had been pacified under the exaggeration of its erotic display. [The] search for tango origins and authenticity led to a different set of complex practices of internal discrimination that were related to the issue of national identity—an issue soaked in colonialism" (1995, 155–56).

4. It is important to note that the legends that de-politicize tango come not only from the "outside." Within Buenos Aires, there is a deep schism between the tango of the over and the underclasses, a palpable tension between the immigrants and the *criollos*, between the natives and the whites. Savigliano writes that "external imperial interventions, through the process of eroticisation, affected the local reception of tango and how tango intervened in the local and foreign debates concerning the shape of Argentina's national identity" (1995, 138). On the one hand, tango called into question the elite's legitimacy to represent the nation. On the other hand, tango sequestered the natives of Argentina as "others" to the national identity since tango was not "their" dance. "Highly Westernized and yet exotic-to-the-West, tango became the national symbol" (Savigliano 1995, 166).

5. For Rancière, "the singularity of the act of the *demos* . . . is dependent on an originary disorder or miscount: the *demos*, or people, is at the same time the name of

a community and the name for its division, for the handling of a wrong . . . the current dead end of political reflection and action is due to the identification of politics with the *self* of a community" (1995, 64).

6. According to Spinoza, "a plane of immanence has no supplementary dimension; the process of composition must be apprehended for itself, through that which it gives, in that which it gives. It is a plan of composition, not a plan of organization or development" (Deleuze 1992, 630).

3. Erring toward Experience

1. "Politics happens in time, against time," writes Bennington. In the quickness of time, a re-articulation of the political is the injunction to make decisions that are not based on pre-programmed scenarios. (My translation. The original text reads: "La politique se fait dans le temps, contre le temps," see Geoffrey Bennington, http://www.sussex.ac.uk/Users/sffc4/contre.doc.)

Decisions are not given, Derrida reminds us, they are taken. Politics, when it begins to drift away from its metaphysical determinations, can be thought of as a process of "taking" decisions.

2. This is a term coined by Derrida, which connotes the response-ability involved in the process of decision-making.

3. Consent: *consentire*, to feel together; *con*, with; *sentire*, to feel, to think, to judge; to agree in sentiment; a relation of sympathy between one organ or part of the body and another, whereby when the one is affected the other is affected correspondingly (Oxford English Dictionary).

4. Of course, we must not forget Eve, who also appears in the fresco. For more on Eve, see Boyle (1998).

5. See chapter 7 for an elaboration on Spinoza and politics.

6. Giorgio Agamben uses the image of the camp as a metaphor for the position of the state in politics today. He argues that the camp is the space that is opened when the state of exception (Schmitt 1976) becomes the rule, that is, when the state of exception is itself taken into the juridical order. When the state of exception is instantiated by the state, a juridico-political paradigm is inaugurated, whereby the norm becomes indistinguishable from the exception: "The camp is a hybrid of law and fact in which the two terms have become indistinguishable" (1997, 110). Within the camp, the inhabitants are stripped of political status and thus reduced to "bare life." "This is why," writes Agamben, "the camp is the very paradigm of political space at the point at which politics becomes biopolitics and *homo sacer* is virtually confused with the citizen" (1997, 110). See also Agamben (1998).

7. See Sartre (1938).

8. See Erin Manning, "Face to Face with the Incommensurable: Srinivas Krishna's *Lulu*" (2003).

9. Stathis Gourgouris suggests that the project of autonomy of the individual instituted in the Enlightenment inaugurates the modern subject as a "primarily legal entity whose external (social) boundaries are sanctioned by a set of 'inalienable rights' and whose internal imagination adheres to the belief that these rights are indeed inalienable (that they represent one's irrevocable independence before the law, the safe-

guard of self-determination)" (1996, 121). This new legal status sought to institute and safeguard a rationality of violence. It did so by monopolizing the definition of violence based on the concept of rationality. "The Enlightenment made it possible to see that law is always authorized force, that law cannot be dissociated from the matter of its applicability (and thus enforcement)" (128). Force thus becomes immanent to law, and the question of justice in relation to the law can no longer be avoided.

10. Hent de Vries writes: "Politics, as the struggle for a lesser evil, for a mitigation, reduction or even abolition of violence, the violence of the self as much as that of an other, should be considered an obligation no less than a necessity. Yet its pursuit of the better is always also shadowed and haunted by what—in itself or as politics' other—resembles or measures itself against the apparitions and spectres of the worst" (1997, 42–43).

11. See section on errant politics in Manning (2003, xxvii–xxxi): "Errant politics subverts attachments that depend on the stability of territory and identity, rewriting the national vocabulary of belonging into a language of moments. To err within politics is to initiate a dialogue that transgresses monologic state sovereignty."

12. "To err is to take a voyage, to wander. In French, erre signifies the track of an animal, left for us to discover in the sand, in a trace on the snow, on the earth.... Erring, I advance on a path that corresponds to no opening" (Manning 2003, xxviii). "To err is probably this: to go outside the space of encounter" (Blanchot 1993, 27).

13. The Word: (o logoβ). Logoβ is from legw, old word in Homer to lay by, to collect, to put words side by side, to speak, to express an opinion. Logoβ is common for reason as well as speech. Heraclitus used it for the principle that controls the universe (Oxford English Dictionary).

14. The laying of hands in the Bible takes place in both directions: Jesus heals by touching others and others are healed by touching him. "For she said within herself, If I may but touch his garment, I shall be whole" (Matt. 9: 21). "So Jesus had compassion on them, and touched their eyes: and immediately their eyes received sight, and they followed him" (Matt. 20: 34).

15. Innumerable artists have depicted this scene. They include Rembrandt (Buckingham, collection of Elizabeth II, London), Dürer's "La petite passion," Titian (National Gallery, London), Pontormo (Casa Buonarotti, Florence), Cano Alonzo (Budapest, D.R.) and Correggio (Prado, Madrid).

16. This quote is from an unpublished paper. See also Lambert (2002).

17. There are many versions of the relationship between Mary Magdalene and Jesus. For interesting reading on Mary Magdalene, see Leloup (2002). See also Pagels (1979) and Robinson (1990). David Tresemer and Laura-Lea Cannon write: "The earliest materials that refer to Mary Magdalene appear from two very different sources: the canonical Gospels of the New Testament, and a group of fringe materials that have come to be known as the Gnostic Gospels, which were rejected by the Roman Catholic Church.... Amidst all of the conjecture regarding the identity of Mary we find some important details that do emerge from all four Gospels [Matthew, Mark, Luke and John]: Mary Magdalene is the only woman besides Mother Mary who is mentioned by name in all four texts, and her name, in all but one instance, is the first listed when there is mention of the women present at an event.... Only in 1969 did the Catholic Church officially repeal Gregory's labelling of Mary as a

whore, thereby admitting their error—though the image of Mary Magdalene as the penitent whore has remained in the public teaching of all Christian denominations. . . . But it's important to remember that Jesus Christ does relieve Mary of the seven demons" (in Leloup 2002, x–xvii).

18. According to Heppner (1995, 22–23), Blake not only imitates Michelangelo, but exaggerates those qualities in Michelangelo considered extreme and inimitable, including the contortion and passion of his powerfully muscular bodies. Blake saw only Michelangelo's engravings.

19. See chapter 6 for a more detailed exploration of the Body without Organs. See also Deleuze and Guattari (1987).

4. Engenderings

1. For a thorough exploration of the Spinozean question of "what a body can do," see Deleuze (1981). This question is also explored in more detail in chapter 6.

2. On language and the political, see Manning (2003).

3. For more on the concept of individuation, see Simondon (1995) as well as Combes (1999).

4. For Deleuze and Guattari, "virtual" and "reality" are not opposites. They are interrelated. The virtual is that moment of "reality" that lives in the "not-yet." It is the future anterior, that toward which we reach. Andrew Murphie writes: "Individuation—as a process—is the specific series of actualizations of the different/ciations of the virtual" (2002, 199). For a stimulating discussion of the incorporeal, see Massumi, "Introduction: Concrete Is As Concrete Doesn't" (in Massumi 2002a).

5. A system that is far from equilibrium is an unstable system. A system in equilibrium is a system in which dynamics are more or less maintained despite environmental changes. In far-from-equilibrium systems, molecules begin to act as "singularities," the exact behavior of which cannot be predicted. According to Prigogine and Stengers, nonequilibrium is the basis of the definition of a biological system. See Prigogine and Stengers (1984).

6. Symbiogenesis refers to the origin of new tissues, organs, organisms, and even species by the establishment of long-term or permanent symbiosis. The term was also used by Konstantin Merezhkovsky (1855–1921) to refer to the formation of new organs and organisms through symbiotic mergers. Symbiosis is a term coined by German botanist Anton de Bary in 1873, defined as the living together of very different kinds of organisms to their mutual benefit.

7. It is no longer considered controversial that animal and plant cells originated through symbiosis. Discussions of the permanent incorporation of bacteria inside plants and animals as plastids and mitochondria appear in high school textbooks (see Margulis 1998, 4–12).

8. I am referring here to an explicitly Western genealogy of gender practices. Detailed research into Eastern philosophy would be necessary to expand this analysis to the East.

9. Deleuze and Guattari's concept of the machine refers to a conceptual assemblage. For a detailed examination of the machinic, see Deleuze and Guattari (1987).

10. A bacteriophage is a virus that infects bacteria. Once inside the cell, it replicates using its host's enzymes.

11. Gestures in Simondon convey the potentiality that exists in the composition of form and matter. A brick, for instance, is composed of matter (clay) that presupposes its form (a polyhedron). The quality of matter is source of form, element of form whose technical operation causes a change in the status of that matter. "Matter is matter because it harbours a positive property that allows it to be moulded. . . . Pure form already contains gestures, and the first matter is itself potential becoming; the gestures contained in the form meet the becoming of the matter and modulate it" (Simondon 1995, 40). See also the first chapter's discussion of gestures through the work of Giorgio Agamben.

12. Autopoiesis refers to a self-maintained system, or a set of principles defining life and pertaining to membrane-bounded, self-limited, internally organized systems that dynamically maintain their identity in a changing environment. Autopoetic entities are able to replace and repair their constituent parts, ultimately at the expense of solar energy.

13. Each of our cells is normally double (diploid), possessing at least two sets of chromosomes. Meiosis reduces by half the number of chromosomes in the cell. Fertilization occurs when these haploid (single chromosome) cells revert to a diploid state.

14. Mitosis is cell division with the maintenance of chromosome number.

15. Naked genes have been touted to be at the core of life (H. J. Muller, 1890–1967). Margulis does not believe that it has been proven that naked genes exist beyond the nucleus of a plant or animal cells. See Lynn Margulis (1998).

16. The second law of thermodynamics concerns the quality of energy conservation: in a closed system, high-quality energy is inevitably lost to friction in the form of heat. This suggests that the universe is not symmetrical with regard to time and that complex processes such as life behave according to tendencies and directions. See Margulis and Sagan (1997).

17. August Weismann (1834–1914) is the founding figure in the emergence of modern neo-Darwinism. For an interesting reading of Weismann's contribution to evolutionary theory, see Ansell Pearson (1999).

18. El Corte, a tango club in the Netherlands, is a fertile environment for the speciation of tango. Established by Eric Jeurissen some fifteen years ago, it is a loft-like space that hosts international tango encounters once a month. These "chained-salons" last thirty-six hours. For thirty-six hours in a row, couples are invited to dance, talk, sleep, eat, drink. A New Year's marathon also takes place once a year, extending this experience of nonstop tango to three days. These tango events promote an unusual milieu through which individuations are made possible that exceed the gendered norms of tango. At El Corte, dance becomes an experiment in individuation. Often, the dance floor seems to move symbiotically, the music resounding in the grounding movement of couples reaching toward one another, engaging transductively across bodies, times, and spaces.

19. For an exploration of national politics and the notion of "home," see Manning (2003).

20. On the relation of politics and the future anterior, see Jacques Derrida's concept of "democracy-to-come." This concept is outlined in many of his texts. See, for example, Derrida (2003).

21. See chapter 6 for a discussion of these Spinozean concepts.

22. For more on activation, see Massumi (2005).

23. For a detailed understanding of the political concept of disagreement, see Rancière (1999). Rancière writes: "Political rationality is only thinkable precisely on condition that it be greed from the alternative in which a certain rationalism would like to keep it reined in, either as exchange between partners putting their interests or standards up for discussion, or else the violence of the irrational" (1999, 43). Disagreement as conceptualized by Rancière takes issue with Habermasian "consensual" politics: "[Consensus] comes unstuck as often as specific worlds of community open up, worlds of disagreement and dissension. Politics occurs wherever a community with the capacity to argue and to make metaphors is likely, at any time and through anyone's intervention, to crop up" (1999, 60).

5. Making Sense of the Incommensurable

1. See also Deleuze (1993).

2. This may not be the case with the work of Orlan. See O'Bryan (2005).

3. Synesthesia refers to the interconnection of the senses. Brian Massumi writes: "every actual experience is at a crossroads lying intensively between the poles toward which these movements tend. Every actual experience is strung between cross-tendencies toward the limits of single-sense purity and intersense fusion. . . . Every given experience is already many-mixed." See Massumi (2002, 158). Synesthetes have access to other-sense dimensions, as when sounds are visible as colors. For more on synesthetes, see Massumi (2002, 186–90).

4. National time refers to the ways in which time (and/as history) is conflated with the nation. In order to secure chronological narratives that sustain the national imaginary, time is conflated to the business of the nation. Certain events are thereby foregrounded at the expense of others and time is reflected upon as a stable signifier rather than a shifting chronotope.

5. Beardsworth suggests that "Derrida's philosophy only makes sense politically in terms of the relation 'between' aporia and decision and neither in terms of a unilateral philosophy of aporia nor in terms of a unilateral philosophy of decision: in other words, aporia is the very locus in which the political force of deconstruction is to be found" (1996, xiii).

6. On the law, Derrida writes: "To be just, the decision of a judge, for example, must not only follow a rule of law or a general law but must also assume it, approve it, confirm its value, but a reinstituting act of interpretation, as if ultimately nothing previously existed of the law, as if the judge himself invented the law in every case. No exercise of justice as law can be just unless there is a 'fresh judgment,'" (1992, 23). The violence of the law refers to the institutionalization of law that normativizes structures, making it difficult to conceive of a rewriting of the foundations that make these laws possible.

7. See chapter 6 for a continued exploration of the senses as prostheses.

8. Richard Doyle writes: "'Life,' as a scientific object, has been stealthed, rendered indiscernible by our installed systems of representation. No longer the attribute of a sovereign in battle with its evolutionary problem set, the organism its sign of ongoing but always temporary victory, life now resounds not so much within sturdy boundaries as between them. The very success of the informatic paradigm, in fields as diverse as molecular biology and ecology, has paradoxically dislocated the very object of biological research. . . . This 'postvital' biology is, by and large, interested less in the characteristics and functions of living organisms than in sequences of molecules and their effects. These sequences are themselves articulable through databases and networks; they therefore garner their effects through relentless repetitions and refrains, connections and blockages rather than through the autonomous interiority of an organism" (2003).

9. There are many laboratories currently developing haptic interfaces, ranging from desktop accoutrements (see www.sensable.com) to medical, military, technological, and biological applications. The Purdue University Laboratory is currently working on a wide array of applications that include a sensing chair. They describe it thus: "The sensingChair introduces a seat that feels its occupant through a layer of 'artificial skin.' Pressure sensing is accomplished with two commercially-available pressure-distribution sensor sheets from TekScan Incorporated. As a new input device, the sensingChair opens up new opportunities for human-computer interactions. The long-term goal of this project is to develop a nanoworkbench capable of providing real-time perceptualization of the mechanical properties, such as stiffness, adhesion or friction, of a nanoscale object during positioning or manipulation. We believe that this effort will lead to a better understanding of the important issues in the assembly of prototype nano-structures. By bridging the nano- and macro-worlds with a haptic interface, a researcher will be able to precisely position, assemble, and move nanoscale objects by feeling their way with a tele-operated AFM tip. Current efforts focus on the development of a passivity-based controller that will ensure the stability of the haptic interface during nanomanipulation" (http://www.ecn.purdue .edu/HIRL).

10. For more on the concept of the posthuman, see Hayles (1999).

11. "Simple location" is Alfred North Whitehead's concept. Whitehead writes: "The characteristic common both to space and time is that material can be said to be here in space and here in time, or here in space-time, in a perfectly definite sense which does not require for its explanantion any reference to other regions of space-time. Curiously enough this character of simple location holds whether we look on a region of space-time as determined absolutely or relatively. For if a region is merely a way of individuating a certain set of relations to other entities, then this characteristic, which I call simple location, is that material can be said to have just these relations of position to the other entities without requiring for its explanation any reference to other regions constituted by analogous relations of position to the same entities" (1967, 49).

12. For more on possible worlds, see Manning (2004). See also Lazzarato (2002).

13. See Derrida (1992). For Derrida, there is an important difference between law and justice. He writes: "A deconstructive interrogation that starts . . . by destabilizing or complicating the opposition between *nomos* and *physis*—that is to say, the

opposition between law, convention, the institution on the one hand, and nature on the other, with all the oppositions that they condition;... a deconstructive interrogation that starts... by destabilizing, complicating, or bringing out the paradoxes of values like those of the proper and of property in all their registers, of the subject, and so of the responsible subject, of the subject of law (droit) and the subject of morality, of the juridical or moral person, of intentionality, etc., and of all that follows from these, such a deconstructive line of questioning is through and through a problematization of law and justice. A problematization of the foundations of law, morality and politics" (1992, 8).

14. Common sense, the unity of all the faculties at the center constituted by the Cogito, is the state consensus raised to the absolute (Deleuze and Guattari 1987, 376). See chapter 3 for a more detailed discussion of Aristotle's notion of common sense and its relationship to consensus politics.

15. Brian Massumi writes: "By 'singular' is meant 'incomparable.'... The singular is without model and without resemblance. It resembles only itself. In this precise and restricted sense, what is actually seen is *absolute:* 'comparable only to itself'" (2002a, 162–63).

16. See Stengers and Pignarre (2005) for a captivating reading of current political agendas and alter-global potentialities. The work Stengers and Pignarre lay out for themselves involves engaging with political events in their fault lines, at junctures when redefinitions—new recipes—are at work, at such moments as when the pharmaceutical industry, for example, is in the midst of redefinition. "A medicine is not a molecule produced by human genius due to which capitalism exploits its workers. This molecule has become inseparable from its mode of fabrication and distribution, and when it enters society, it is capable of transforming it in multiple ways" (113). This kind of transformation calls forth Latour's concept of "political ecology," which points to the ways in which politics expands beyond the direct human concerns of those involved. From nuclear disarmament to GMOs to pharmaceuticals, *political ecology*, as Stengers and Pignarre underline, invents itself each time anew, thereby altering the timed spaces and spaced times of politics.

6. Sensing beyond Security

1. Almost without exception, current political regimes in the West claim to be democratic. Democracy is understood here in ways that are often in confrontation with a politics of touch. This may apply to all future regimes as well since, theoretically, any politics that could be defined *as such* would abide in the impossibility of engaging in a politics of touch. A politics of touch can neither be calculated in advance nor encapsulated within an ongoing system.

2. Derrida writes: "L'intouchable n'étant ici ni l'esprit, ni la conscience, mais bien un corps propre, une chair, il faut bien penser la logique d'un intouchable qui reste à même, si on peut encore dire, le touchable. Ce touchable-intouchable... ce n'est pas quelqu'un, ni ce que dans certaines cultures on appelle un 'intouchable'" (2000, 93).

3. For a more detailed account of security, see, among others, Krishna (1999); Shapiro and Alker (1996); Campbell (1992); Dillon (1996).

4. Rafael Lozanno-Hemmer's "Subtitled Public" is an innovative artwork that captures and extends this notion of the BwO. "Subtitled Public" consists of an empty exhibition space where visitors are tracked with a computerized infrared surveillance system. As people enter the installation, texts are projected onto their bodies: these "subtitles" consist of thousands of verbs conjugated in third person and they follow each individual. The only way to get rid of a subtitle is to touch someone else: the words are then exchanged between them. "Subtitled Public" invades the supposed neutrality of the space that museums and galleries set up for contemplation, underlining the violent and asymmetric character of observation. The piece reveals the danger of surveillance systems that typecast and try to detect different ethnic groups or suspicious individuals, as in the latest computer-vision devices that are being deployed in public spaces around the world. The installation is also an ironic commentary on this era of technological personalization, literally "theming" and "branding" each spectator.

5. For a contemporary reading of the Schmittian concept of the state of exception, see Agamben (1998 and 2003).

6. *Le Compte* (1887) suggests that tact is associated with sight (Oxford English Dictionary). Although this statement would have to be radically unpacked in order to export it into a politics of touch, it is interesting to note that when dealing with a touch that is constrained by a requisite formality (as tact indicates in its definition), touch is associated with sight. Sight here suffers a radical reduction of potential that can be challenged by Massumi's exploration of perception and vision in (2002a). Of note in the context of *Politics of Touch* is the way in which the senses overlap, even when what is at stake is a constraint (such as tact). Even held to their most conservative potential, the senses are synesthetic.

7. The intellect in Bergson operates in a similar fashion: "Life, not content with producing organisms, would fain give them as an appendage inorganic matter itself, converted into an immense organ by the industry of the living being. Such is the initial task it assigns to intelligence. That is why the intellect behaves as if it were fascinated by the contemplation of inert matter. It is life looking outward, putting itself outside itself, adopting the ways of unorganized nature in principle, in order to direct them in fact. Hence its bewilderment when it turns to the living" (1983, 162).

8. For a detailed reading of Bergson's concept of duration, see Deleuze (1988a): "duration is not merely lived experience; it is also experience enlarged or even gone beyond; it is already a condition of experience. For experience always gives us a composite of space and duration.... The two combine, and into this combination space introduces the forms of its extrinsic distinctions or of its homogeneous *and* discontinuous 'sections,' while duration contributes an internal succession that is both heterogeneous *and* continuous" (37).

9. Movement and the virtual are interrelated: movement is always toward that which is not yet. Deleuze and Guattari: "Movement in itself continues to occur elsewhere.... Movement has an essential relation to the imperceptible; it is by nature imperceptible" (1987, 280–81).

10. Empiricism refers to the doctrine that knowledge comes through the senses: "In matters of art or practice: That which is guided by mere experience, without

scientific knowledge, also of methods, expedients; in mathematics, a formula arrived at inductively" (Oxford English Dictionary).

11. Spinoza's ethics have nothing to do with morality. Ethics are an ethology: the construction of a plane of immanence that is at once an ethics and an ecology. A composition of speeds and slownesses. The power to affect and be affected. Ethology is therefore first the relation between accelerations and decelerations in the composition of each body. Variations are at stake here, as well as transformations. "So an animal, a thing, is never separable from its relations with the world. The interior is only a selected exterior, and the exterior a projected interior. The speed or the slowness of metabolisms, perceptions, actions, and reactions link together to constitute a particular individual in the world" (in Deleuze 1988b, 125).

12. On concern, see Whitehead (1967b): "It must be distinctly understood that no prehension, even of bare sensa, can be divested of its affective tone, that is to say, of its character of a 'concern' in the Quaker sense. Concernedness is of the essence of perception" (180).

13. "The state of reason, in its initial aspect, already has a complex relation to the state of nature. On the one hand the state of nature is not subject to the laws of reason: reason relates to the proper and true utility of man, and tends solely to his preservation; Nature on an other hand has no regard for the preservation of man and comprises an infinity of other laws concerning the universe as a whole, of which man is but a small part" (Deleuze 1990a, 263).

14. For more on the senses and making sense, see chapter 5.

15. Hayles writes: "the erasure of embodiment is a feature common to both the liberal humanist subject and the cybernetic posthuman. Identified with a rational mind, the liberal subject *possessed* a body but was not usually represented as *being* a body. Only because the body is not identified with the self is it possible to claim for the liberal subject its notorious universality, a claim that depends on erasing markers of bodily difference, including sex, race and ethnicity. . . . Although in many ways the posthuman deconstructs the liberal humanist subject, it thus shares with its predecessor an emphasis on cognition rather than embodiment. . . . I view the present moment as a critical juncture when interventions might be made to keep disembodiment from being rewritten, once again, into prevailing concepts of subjectivity. I see the deconstruction of the liberal humanist subject as an opportunity to put back into the picture the flesh that continues to be erased in contemporary discussions about cybernetic subjects" (1999, 4–5).

16. A system is in equilibrium when its dynamics are more or less maintained despite environmental changes. In disequilibrium, molecules act as singularities and become unpredictable. "Unlike their behavior in equilibrium systems, those in 'dissipative structures' are marked by an element of internal unpredictability, by capacities of self-development, by periods of significant openness to outside forces, and by a trajectory of irreversible change that endows them with a historical dimension" (Connolly 2002, 55). A politics of touch is far from equilibrium in many senses: it does not deal with already-formed bodies; it exposes itself to the surprise of prosthetically driven sense-events; it exposes itself to the impossibility of good and common sense, admitting its relation to making sense only to the degree that making sense is a prosthetic endeavor; it engages democratically only to the extent that it concedes

to the potential politics of a democracy-to-come; it exposes itself to a Spinozean concept of Nature as immanence rather than transcendence. A politics of touch is a far-from-equilibrium system insofar as it "is neither the reversible system of classical dynamics nor a condition of constant flux unrecognizable as a system" (Connolly 2002, 56). In Prigogine's words: "Matter near equilibrium behaves in a 'repetitive' way. On an other hand, . . . far from equilibrium we may witness the appearance of . . . a mechanism of 'communication' among molecules. Within this mechanism successive repetitions are not identical to each other because they rise out of highly sensitized responses to 'initial conditions' that exceed the reach of our capacities for close delineation" (in Connolly 2002, 56). Far-from-equilibrium systems encourage emergence in all fields. Stengers, for example, sees science as "a shifting and dissonant dialogue between human assemblages and nonhuman assemblages" (in Connolly 2002, 58).

17. Brian Massumi writes: "There is a difference between the possible and the potential. . . . Possibility is back-formed from potential's unfolding. But once it is formed, it also effectively feeds in. Feedback, it prescripts: implicit in the determination of a thing's or body's positionality is a certain set of transformations that can be expected of it by definition and that it can therefore undergo without qualitatively changing enough to warrant a new name. . . . Possibility is a variation implicit in what a thing can be said to be when it is on target. Potential is the immanence of a thing to its still indeterminate variation, under way. . . . Implication is a code word. Immanence is process" (2002a, 9).

Bibliography

Agamben, Giorgio. 2003. *État d'exception: Homo Sacer*. Paris: Seuil.

———. 2000. *Means without End: Notes on Politics*. Trans. Vincenzo Binetti and Cesare Casarino. Minneapolis: University of Minnesota Press.

———. 1999. *Potentialities: Collected Essays in Philosophy*. Trans. Daniel Heller-Roazen. Stanford: Stanford University Press.

———. 1998. *Homo Sacer: Sovereign Power and Bare Life*. Trans. Daniel Heller-Roazen. Stanford: Stanford University Press.

———. 1997. "The Camp as the Nomos of the Modern." In *Violence, Identity, and Self-Determination*, ed. H. de Vries and S. Weber. Stanford: Stanford University Press.

Allen, Prudence. 1985. *The Concept of Woman: The Aristotelian Revolution, 750 B.C.–A.D. 1250*. Montreal: Eden.

Anderson, Benedict. 1983. *Imagined Communities: Reflections on the Origin and Spread of Nationalism*. New York: Verso.

Anderson, Randall. 2004. *HfG Publication* (Catalogue for Trevor Gould's work). Offenbach, Germany: Hochschule für Gestaltung.

Ansell Pearson, Keith. 1999. *Germinal Life: The Difference and Repetition of Deleuze*. London: Routledge.

Anzieu, Didier. 1985. *Le moi-peau*. Paris: Dunod.

Appadurai, Arjun. 2000. "Grassroots Globalization and the Research Imagination." *Public Culture* 12, no. 1: 1–19.

———. 1998. "Full Attachment." *Public Culture* 10, no. 2: 443–49.

Aristotle. 1961. *De Anima*. Ed. Sir David Ross. Oxford: Oxford University Press.

————. 1955. *Parva Naturalia*. Ed. Sir David Ross. Oxford: Oxford University Press.

Armstrong, David. 1983. *Political Anatomy of the Body: Medical Knowledge in Britain in the Twentieth Century*. Cambridge: Cambridge University Press.

Arney, William Ray. 1982. *Power and the Profession of Obstetrics*. Chicago: Chicago University Press.

Augustine. 1998. *Confessions*. Reprint, Oxford: Oxford University Press.

Baker, Ernst, ed. 1962. *The Politics of Aristotle*. New York: Oxford University Press.

Bakhtin, Mikhail. 1990. *Art and Answerability: Early Philosophical Essays*. Austin: University of Texas Press.

————. 1986. *Speech Genres and Other Late Essays*. Trans. V. W. McGee. Ed. C. Emerson and M. Holquist. Austin: University of Texas Press.

————. 1981. *The Dialogic Imagination*. Trans. M. Holquist. Austin: University of Texas Press.

Balibar, Etienne. 1997. "Jus-Pactum-Lex: On the Constitution of the Subject in the Theologico-Political Treatise." In *The New Spinoza*. Ed. Warren Montag and Ted Stolze. Trans. Ted Stolze. Minneapolis: University of Minnesota Press.

Barbieri, Marcello. 2002. *The Organic Codes: An Introduction to Semantic Biology*. Cambridge: Cambridge University Press.

————. 1985. *The Semantic Theory of Evolution*. Chur, Switzerland: Harwood Academic Publishers.

Bates, Hector, and Luis d-Bates. 1936. *La Historia del Tango*. Taller Grafico de la Compania, General Faloril Financerid.

Beardsworth, Richard. 1996. *Derrida and the Political*. London: Routledge.

Benjamin, Walter. 1978. "Critique of Violence." In *Reflections: Essays, Aphorisms, Autobiographical Writings*. Ed. Peter Demetz. New York: Harcourt Brace.

Bennington, Geoffrey. 2000. *Interrupting Derrida*. London: Routledge.

Bergson, Henri. 1983. *Creative Evolution*. Trans. Arthur Mitchell. Lanham, Md.: University Press of America.

————. 1946. *The Creative Mind: An Introduction to Metaphysics*. New York: Kensington Publishing Corp.

Blake, William. 1995. *The Urizen Books*. Ed. David Worrall. London: Tate Gallery/ William Blake Trust.

————. 1991. *Jerusalem*. Ed. Morton D. Paley. Princeton: Princeton University Press.

————. 1979. "Songs of Experience." In *Blake's Poetry and Designs*. Ed. M. L. Johnson and J. E. Grant. New York: W. W. Norton and Co.

————. 1975. *The Marriage of Heaven and Hell*. Ed. Geoffrey Keynes. Oxford: Oxford University Press.

————. 1966. *The Complete Writings of William Blake*. Ed. Geoffrey Keynes. Oxford: Oxford University Press.

Blanchot, Maurice. 1993. *The Infinite Conversation*. Trans. S. Hanson. Minneapolis: University of Minnesota Press.

————. 1993. *La Communauté inavouable*. Paris: Les Editions de Minuit.

————. 1990. *Gender Trouble: Feminism and the Subversion of Identity*. New York: Routledge.

Borges, Jorge Luis. 1963. "Elidioma de los argentinos." In J. L. Borges and J. E. Clemente. *El Lenguage de Buenos Aries*. Buenos Aires: Emecé.

Boyle, Marjorie O'Rourke. 1998. *Senses of Touch: Human Dignity and Deformity from Michelangelo to Calvin*. Leiden, Netherlands: Brill.

Burke, Anthony. 2002. "The Perverse Perseverance of Sovereignty." *Borderlines* 1, no. 2.

Butler, Judith. 1993. *Bodies That Matter: On the Discursive Limits of "Sex."* New York: Routledge.

Campbell, David. 1992. *Writing Security: United States Foreign Policy and the Politics of Identity*. Minneapolis: University of Minnesota Press.

Campbell, David, and Michael Dillon, eds. 1993. *The Political Subject of Violence*. Manchester: University of Manchester Press.

Cipolla, Carlo. 1976. *Public Health and the Medical Profession in the Renaissance*. Cambridge: Cambridge University Press.

Combes, Muriel. 1999. *Simondon: Individu et collectivité*. Paris: Presses Universitaires de France.

Condillac, Etienne. 1947–51. *Oeuvres philosophiques*. Ed. Georges Le Roy. 3 vols. Paris: Presses Universitaires de France.

Connolly, Tristanne J. 2002. *William Blake and the Body*. London: Palgrave.

Connolly, William. 2002. *Neuropolitics: Thinking, Culture, Speed*. Minneapolis: University of Minnesota Press.

———. 1995. *The Ethos of Pluralization*. Minneapolis: University of Minnesota Press.

Crary, Jonathan. 1995. "Unbinding Vision: Manet and the Attentive Observer in the Late Nineteenth Century." In *Cinema and the Invention of Modern Life*. Ed. L. Charney and V. R. Schwartz. Berkeley: University of California Press.

Crary, Jonathan, and Stanford Kwinter. 1992. *Incorporations*. New York: Urzone.

De Ipola, Emilo. 1985. "El tango en sus márgenes." *Punto de Vista*, no. 25.

Deleuze, Gilles. 1991. *Coldness and Cruelty*. New York: Zone Books.

———. 1994. *Difference and Repetition*. Trans. Paul Patton. New York: Columbia University Press.

———. 1994. "He Stuttered." In *Gilles Deleuze and the Theater of Philosophy*. Ed. C. Boundas and D. Olkowski. New York: Routledge.

———. 1993. *The Fold: Leibniz and the Baroque*. Trans. Tom Conley. Minneapolis: University of Minnesota Press.

———. 1992. "Ethology: Spinoza and Us." In *Incorporations*. Ed. Jonathan Crary and Stanford Kwinter. New York: Urzone.

———. 1990a. *Expressionism in Philosophy: Spinoza*. Trans. Martin Joughin. New York: Zone Books.

———. 1990b. *The Logic of Sense*. Trans. Mark Lester with Charles Stivale. New York: Columbia University Press.

———. 1989. *The Time-Image*. Trans. Hugh Tomlinson and Robert Galeta. Minneapolis: University of Minnesota Press.

———. 1988a. *Bergsonism*. Trans. Hugh Tomlinson and Barbara Habberjam. New York: Urzone.

———. 1988b. *Spinoza: Practical Philosophy*. Trans. Robert Hurley. San Francisco: City Lights.

———. 1986. *Cinema I: The Movement-Image*. Trans. Hugh Tomlinson and Barbara Habberjam. Minneapolis: University of Minnesota Press.

———. 1977. *Anti-Oedipus: Capitalism and Schizophrenia*. Trans. Robert Hurley, Mark Seem, Helen R. Lane. New York: Viking Press.

Deleuze, Gilles, and Félix Guattari. 1987. *A Thousand Plateaux: Capitalism and Schizophrenia*. Trans. Brian Massumi. Minneapolis: University of Minnesota Press.

Der Derian, James. 1993. "The Value of Security: Hobbes, Marx, Nietzsche, and Baudrillard." In *The Political Subject of Violence*. Manchester: University of Manchester Press.

Derrida, Jacques. 2005. *Rogues: Two Essays on Reason*. Trans. Pascale-Anne Brault and Michael Naas. Stanford: Stanford University Press.

———. 2003. *Voyous*. Paris: Galilée.

———. 2002. *Without Alibi*. Trans. Peggy Kamuf. Stanford: Stanford University Press.

———. 2000. *Le toucher—Jean-Luc Nancy*. Paris: Galilée.

———. 1997. *Politics of Friendship*. Trans. George Collins. London: Verso.

———. 1995. *On the Name*. Trans. Thomas Dutoit. Stanford: Stanford University Press.

———. 1993. *Aporias*. Stanford: Stanford University Press.

———. 1992. "The Mystical Foundation of Authority." In *Deconstruction and the Possibility of Justice*. Ed. Drucilla Cornell, Michel Rosenfeld, David Gray Carlson. New York: Routledge.

———. 1981. *Dissemination*. Trans. B. Johnson. Chicago: Chicago University Press.

———. 1978. "Violence and Metaphysics." In *Writing and Difference*. Trans. A. Bass. Chicago: Chicago University Press.

———. 1974. *Of Grammatology*. Trans. Gayatri Spivak. Baltimore: Johns Hopkins University Press.

Descartes, René. 2000. *Discourse on Method and Related Writings*. Trans. Desmond M. Clarke. New York: Penguin.

De Vries, Hent, and Samuel Weber, eds. 1997. *Violence, Identity, and Self-Determination*. Stanford: Stanford University Press.

Diderot, Denis. 1990. *Lettre sur les aveugles*. Paris: Bordas.

———. 1998. *Pensees philosophiques*. Arles: Actes Sud.

———. 1876. *Oeuvres complètes de Denis Diderot*. Paris: Garnier Frères, librairies éditeurs.

Dillon, Michael. 1996. *Politics of Security: Towards a Political Philosophy of Continental Thought*. London: Routledge.

Doyle, Richard. 2003. *Wetwares: Experiments in Postvital Living*. Minneapolis: University of Minnesota Press.

Elshtain, Jean. 1982. "Aristotle, the Public-Private Split, and the Case of the Suffragists." In *The Family in Political Thought*. Ed. J. Elshtain. Amherst: Massachusetts University Press.

Feldman, Allen. 1991. *Formations of Violence: The Narrative of the Body and Political Terror in Northern Ireland*. Chicago: Chicago University Press.

Ferrer, Horacio. 1995. "Les tangos vagabonds." In *Tango Nomade*. Montreal: Tryptique.

Ferrer, Michel, Ramona Naddaff, and Nadia Tazi, eds. 1989. *Fragments for a History of the Human Body, Part 1*. New York: Urzone.

Foucault, M. 1990. *The History of Sexuality: An Introduction*. Trans. R. Hurley. New York: Random House.

———. 1989. *Foucault Live (Interviews 1966–1984)*. New York: Semiotext(e).

———. 1988. *Politics, Philosophy, Culture: Interviews and Other Writings*. Ed. L. Kritzman. Trans. A. Sheridon. New York: Routledge.

———. 1973. *The Birth of the Clinic: An Archeology of Medical Perception*. New York: Pantheon.

Gassendi, Pierre. 1992. *Abregé de la philosophie de Gassendi*. 1674–1675. Reprint (8 vols.) Paris: Fayard.

Gil, José. 1998. *Metamorphoses of the Body*. Minneapolis: University of Minnesota Press.

Gosling, Peter J. 2002. *Dictionary of Biomedical Sciences*. New York: Taylor and Francis.

Gourgouris, Stathis. 1996. *Dream Nation: Enlightenment, Colonization, and the Institution of Modern Greece*. Stanford: Stanford University Press.

Haraway, Donna. 1991. *Simians, Cyborgs, and Women: The Reinvention of Nature*. New York: Routledge.

———. 1989. *Primate Visions*. New York: Routledge.

Hardt, Michael. 2002. "Exposure: Pasolini in the Flesh." In *Shock to Thought: Expression after Deleuze and Guattari*. London: Routledge.

Hardt, Michael, and Antonio Negri. 2000. *Empire*. Cambridge, Mass.: Harvard University Press.

Hassan, Ihab. 1967. *Radical Innocence: Studies in the Contemporary American Novel*. Princeton, N.J.: Princeton University Press.

Hayles, N. Katherine. 1999. *How We Became Posthuman: Virtual Bodies in Cybernetics, Literature, and Informatics*. Chicago: Chicago University Press.

Heppner, Christopher. 1995. *Reading Blake's Designs*. Cambridge: Cambridge University Press.

Hosokawa, Shuhei. 1995. "Le tango au Japon avant 1945: Formation, déformation, transformation." In *Tango Nomade*. Montreal: Tryptique.

Imperiale, Alicia. 2000. *New Flatness: Surface Tension in Digital Architecture*. Berlin: Birkhäuser.

Kaplan, Emmanuel. 1984. "The Hand as Organ." In *Kaplan's Functional and Surgical Anatomy of the Hand*. Ed. Morton Spinner. Philadelphia: J. B. Lippincott.

Kirby, Vicki. 1997. *Telling Flesh: The Substance of the Corporeal*. New York: Routledge.

Krishna, Sankaran. 1999. *Postcolonial Insecurities: India, Sri Lanka, and the Question of Nationhood*. Minneapolis: University of Minnesota Press.

Lactantius. 1918. *The Letter of Aristeas*. Trans. H. St. J. Thackeray. London: Society for Promoting Christian Knowledge/New York: Macmillan.

Lazzarato, Maurizio. 2002. *Les révolutions du capitalisme*. Paris: Les Empêcheurs de penser en rond.

Lambert, Gregg. 2002. *The Non-Philosophy of Gilles Deleuze*. London: Continuum.

Leloup, Jean-Yves. 2002. *The Gospel of Mary Magdalene*. Trans. J. Rowe and J. Needleman. Burlington, Vt.: Inner Traditions.

Leroi, Armand Marie. 2003. *Mutants: On the Form, Varieties, and Errors of the Human Body*. London: Harper Collins.

Levinas, Emmanuel. 1969. *Totality and Infinity*. Trans. Alphonso Lingis. Pittsburgh: Duquesne University Press.

Lucretius, Titus. 1975. *On the Nature of Things*. Trans. W. H. D. Rouse. Cambridge, Mass.: Harvard University Press.

Locke, John. 1823. *An Essay Concerning Human Understanding*. Oxford: Oxford University Press.

Lupton, Ellen. 2002. *Skin: Surface, Substance, and Design*. Princeton, N.J.: Princeton Architectural Press.

MacKenzie, Adrian. 2002. *Transductions: Bodies and Machines at Speed*. London: Continuum.

Mafud, Julio. 1966. *Sociologia del tango*. Buenos Aires: Ed. Americalee.

Manning, Erin. 2004. "Time for Politics." In *Sovereign Lives: Power in Global Politics*. Ed. Jenny Edkins, Veronique Pin-Fat, and Michael Shapiro. New York: Routledge.

———. Erin. 2003. *Ephemeral Territories: Representing Nation, Home, and Identity in Canada*. Minneapolis: University of Minnesota Press.

Margulis, Lynn. 1998. *Symbiotic Planet: A New Look at Evolution*. Amherst: Basic Books.

Margulis, Lynn, and René Fester. 1991. *Symbiosis as a Source of Evolutionary Innovation: Speciation and Morphogenesis*. Cambridge, Mass: MIT Press.

Margulis, Lynn, and Dorian Sagan. 1997. *What Is Sex?* New York: Simon and Schuster.

———. 1994. *What Is Life*. New York: Simon and Shuster.

Massumi, Brian. 2005. "Fear (The Spectrum Said)." *Positions: East Asia Cultures Critique, Special Issue: Against Preemptive War* 13, no. 1 (March).

———. 2002a. *Parables for the Virtual: Movement, Affect, Sensation*. Durham, N.C.: Duke University Press.

Massumi, Brian, ed. 2002b. *A Shock to Thought*. London: Routledge.

Merleau-Ponty, Maurice. 1976. *Phenomenologie de la perception*. Paris: Gallimard.

———. 1948. *Sens et non-sens*. Paris: Nagel.

Monette, Pierre. 1995. "Serie tango: Le milieu du tango à Montreal." In *Tango Nomade*. Montreal: Tryptique.

Montag, Warren, and Ted Stolze, eds. 1997. *The New Spinoza*. Minneapolis: University of Minnesota Press.

Montagu, Ashley. 1971. *Touching: Human Significance of the Skin*. New York: Harper Collins.

Mouffe, Chantal. 1995. *Le Politique et ses enjeux*. Paris: La découverte.

Murphie, Andrew. 2002. "Putting the Virtual Back into VR." In *A Shock to Thought: Expression after Deleuze and Guattari*. Ed. Brian Massumi. London: Routledge.

Nancy, Jean-Luc. 2003. *Noli me tangere*. Paris: Bayard.

———. 1996. *Être singulier pluriel*. Collection La Philosophie en effet. Paris: Galilée.

———. 1994. *The Experience of Freedom*. Trans. Bridget McDonald. Stanford: Stanford University Press.

———. 1993. *Le sens du monde*. Collection La Philosophie en effet. Paris: Galilée.

———. 1992. *Corpus*. Paris: Galilée.

Nancy, Jean-Luc, Philippe Lacoue-Labarthe, and Simon Sparks, eds. 1997. *Retreating the Political*. Warwick Studies in European Philosophy. New York, London: Routledge.

Nietzsche, Friedrich. 1974. *The Gay Science*. Trans. W. Kaufmann. New York: Random House.

———. 1969. *Thus Spoke Zarathustra*. Trans. R. J. Hollingdale. London: Penguin.

———. 1968. *The Will to Power*. Trans. R. J. Hollingdale and W. Kaufmann. New York: Random House.

O'Bryan, Jill C. 2005. *Carnal Art: Orlan's Refacing*. Minneapolis: University of Minnesota Press.

Pagels, Elaine. 1979. *The Gnostic Gospels*. New York: Vintage.

Panagia, Davide. 2001. "Ceci n'est pas un argument: An Introduction to the Ten Theses." In *Theory and Event* 5, no. 3. Available at http://muse.jhu.edu/journals/theory_and_event/.

Parisi, Luciana. 2004. *Abstract Sex*. London: Continuum.

Peirce, Charles. 1997. *The Collected Papers of Charles S. Peirce*. Ed. Charles Hartshorne and Paul Weiss. Bristol: Thoemmes Continuum.

Pelinski, Ramon. 1995. "Le tango nomade." In *Tango Nomade*. Montreal: Tryptique.

Philo, Judaens. 1993. *The Works of Philo Judaeus, the Contemporary of Josephus*. Trans. Charles Duke Yonge. Peabody, Mass.: Hendrickson Publishers.

Plato. 1961. *The Collected Dialogues*. Ed. E. Hamilton and H. Cairns. Princeton, N.J.: Princeton University Press.

Prigogine, Ilya, and Isabelle Stengers. 1984. *Order out of Chaos*. New York: Bantam.

Rancière, Jacques. 2001. "Ten Theses on Politics." *Theory and Event* 5, no. 3. Available at http://muse.jhv.edu/journals/theory_and_event/.

———. 1999. *Disagreement: Politics and Philosophy*. Minneapolis: University of Minnesota Press.

———. 1995. "Politics, Identification, and Subjectivization." In *The Identity in Question*. Ed. John Rajchman. New York: Routledge.

Rayner, A. D. M. 1997. *Degrees of Freedom: Living in Dynamic Boundaries*. London: Imperial College Press.

Robinson, James M., ed. 1990. *The Nag Hammadi Library*. San Francisco: Harper Collins.

Rossi, Vincente. 1958. Cosas de Negros: *Estudio Premliminary y Notas de Haratio J. Becco*. Buenos Aires: Hachette.

Rousseau, Jean-Jacques. 2003. *The Social Contract or Principles of Political Right*. Trans. D. G. H. Cole. Dover: Dover Publications.

———. 1962. *Emile ou de l' éducation*. Paris: Flammarion.

Sabato, Ernesto. 1997. *Tango Discusión y Clave*. Buenos Aires: Losada.

Sartre, Jean-Paul. 1938. *Nausée*. Paris: Gallimard.

Savigliano, Marta E. 1995. *Tango and the Political Economy of Passion*. Boulder, Colo.: Westview Press.

Schmitt, Carl. 1996. *The Concept of the Political*. Trans. George Schwab. Chicago: Chicago University Press.

Shapiro, Michael J., and Hayward R. Alker, eds. 1996. *Challenging Boundaries*. Minneapolis: University of Minnesota Press.

Shapiro, Michael J., and David Campbell. 1999. *Moral Spaces: Rethinking Ethics and Politics*. Minneapolis: University of Minnesota Press.

Simondon, Gilbert. 1995. *L'individu et sa genèse physico-biologique*. Grenoble: Jerome Millon.

Spinoza, Baruch. 1985. *The Collected Works of Spinoza*. Ed. and trans. Edwin Curley. Princeton, N.J.: Princeton University Press.

Stengers, Isabelle. 1997. *Power and Invention: Situating Science*. Trans. Paul Bains. Minneapolis: University of Minnesota Press.

Stengers, Isabelle, and Philippe Pignarre. 2005. *La sorcellerie capitaliste. Pratiques de désenvoûtement*. Paris: Editions la Découverte.

Taylor, Mark. 1997. *Hiding*. Chicago: Chicago University Press.

Thurtle, Philip, and Robert Mitchell. 2002. "Fleshy Data: Semiotics, Information, and the Body." In *Semiotic Flesh: Information and the Human Body*. Seattle: Walter Chapin Simpson Center for the Humanities.

Varela, Francisco, Evan Thompson, and Eleanor Rosch. 1993. *The Embodied Mind: Cognitive Science and Human Experience*. Cambridge, Mass.: MIT Press.

Vinge, Louise. 1975. *The Five Senses: Studies in a Literary Tradition*. Lund, Sweden: Gleerup.

Whitehead, Alfred North. 1967a. *Science and the Modern World*. New York: The Free Press.

———. 1967b. *Adventures of Ideas*. New York: The Free Press.

Index

Prepared by Nadine Asswad

Erin Manning is assistant professor in the Faculty of Fine Arts at Concordia University in Montreal. She is the author of *Ephemeral Territories: Representing Nation, Home, and Identity in Canada* (Minnesota, 2003).

Milton Keynes UK
Ingram Content Group UK Ltd.
UKHW040613190923
428957UK00001B/91